Luminos is the open-access monograph publishing program from UC Press. Luminos provides a framework for preserving and reinvigorating monograph publishing for the future and increases the reach and visibility of important scholarly work. Titles published in the UC Press Luminos model are published with the same high standards for selection, peer review, production, and marketing as those in our traditional program. www.luminosoa.org

Voices of Labor

Voices of Labor

Creativity, Craft, and Conflict in Global Hollywood

Edited by

Michael Curtin & Kevin Sanson

UNIVERSITY OF CALIFORNIA PRESS

University of California Press, one of the most distinguished university presses in the United States, enriches lives around the world by advancing scholarship in the humanities, social sciences, and natural sciences. Its activities are supported by the UC Press Foundation and by philanthropic contributions from individuals and institutions. For more information, visit www.ucpress.edu.

University of California Press
Oakland, California

© 2017 by Michael Curtin and Kevin Sanson

Suggested citation: Curtin, Michael and Sanson, Kevin (eds.).
Voices of labor: creativity, craft, and conflict in global Hollywood.
Oakland: University of California Press, 2017 DOI: https://doi.org/10.1525/luminos.26

This work is licensed under a Creative Commons CC BY license. To view a copy of the license, visit http://creativecommons.org/licenses.

Library of Congress Cataloging-in-Publication Data
Names: Curtin, Michael, editor. | Sanson, Kevin, editor.
Title: Voices of labor : creativity, craft, and conflict in global Hollywood / Michael Curtin, Kevin Sanson.
Description: Oakland, California : University of California Press, [2017] | Includes index.
Identifiers: LCCN 2016053357 (print) | LCCN 2016056134 (ebook) | ISBN 9780520295438 (pbk. : alk. paper) | ISBN 9780520968196 (ebook)
Subjects: LCSH: Motion picture industry—Employees—Interviews. | Motion picture industry—California—Los Angeles. | Mass media and globalization.
Classification: LCC PN1995.9.L28 C87 2017 (print) | LCC PN1995.9.L28 (ebook) | DDC 384/.80979494—dc23
LC record available at https://lccn.loc.gov/2016053357

CONTENTS

Acknowledgments vii

1. Listening to Labor 1
   by Michael Curtin and Kevin Sanson

COMPANY TOWN 18

2. Editors' Introduction 18
3. Mara Brock Akil, showrunner 22
4. Tom Schulman, screenwriter 33
5. Allison Anders, director 45
6. Lauren Polizzi, art director 56
7. Mary Jane Fort, costume designer 68
8. Anonymous, makeup artist 80
9. Stephen Lighthill, cinematographer 90
10. Calvin Starnes, grip 100
11. Steve Nelson, sound recordist 113
12. Rob Matsuda, musician 126

GLOBAL MACHINE 136

13. Editors' Introduction 136
14. Anonymous, studio production executive 140

15. David Minkowski, service producer ... 146
16. Adam Goodman, service producer ... 158
17. Stephen Burt, production manager ... 169
18. Belle Doyle, location manager ... 179
19. Wesley Hagan, location manager ... 190

FRINGE CITY ... 200

20. Editors' Introduction ... 200
21. Scott Ross, VFX manager ... 204
22. Dave Rand, VFX artist ... 215
23. Mariana Acuña-Acosta, VFX artist ... 226
24. Daniel Lay, VFX artist ... 238
25. Steve Kaplan, union official ... 250
26. Dusty Kelly, union official ... 261

Appendix: Interview Schedule ... 273

ACKNOWLEDGMENTS

Over the past few years, globalization and corporate conglomeration have been signature concerns of the Carsey-Wolf Center and the Mellichamp Global Dynamics Initiative at the University of California, Santa Barbara. Our multifaceted endeavors have been generously supported by the inspiring philanthropy of Marcy Carsey, Dick Wolf, and Duncan and Suzanne Mellichamp. One of them once told us, "It's actually easier to make money than to give it away. You have to find the right people and then give them room to run." Hopefully, we were the right people and ran in the right direction.

We owe a great deal of thanks to friends and colleagues at the Carsey-Wolf Center. David Marshall, Melvin Oliver, John Majewski, Constance Penley, and Ronald E. Rice have provided enthusiastic encouragement throughout this project's life cycle. Sheila Sullivan, Natalie Fawcett, and Alyson Aaris are an incredible trio whose resilient administrative support is matched only by their unwavering friendship.

We especially want to thank some of our closest collaborators at the Media Industries Project. Jennifer Holt and Karen Petruska have been key allies throughout this project, and our ideas are much richer because of them. Likewise, we never conducted an interview without first studying the detailed research dossiers prepared by John Vanderhoef and Juan Llamas-Rodriguez. Thank you for keeping us from embarrassing ourselves. And thank you too, John, for a range of editorial contributions to the final product.

We also want to recognize our collaborators at the University of California Press and the Luminos open-access platform: Raina Polivka, Mary Francis, Aimée Goggins, Paige MacKay and Francisco Reinking. Thanks to Erin Lennon, Rebecca

Epstein, and Lindsey Westbrook for copyediting support, and to Lorena Thompkins for transcription services.

Most of all, we are grateful to the screen media workers who took time from their very busy schedules to lend their voices to this endeavor. We learned a great deal about their creativity, craftsmanship, and professionalism. They also helped us understand the very significant changes that have taken place in the media industries over the last thirty years. Hopefully, readers will follow their accounts carefully and take seriously the complexities they reveal about conglomeration and globalization in the entertainment industry.

We dedicate this book to the labor, creativity, and craft behind these voices in motion picture industries around the world.

1

Listening to Labor

Michael Curtin and Kevin Sanson

At a time when anyone can be a producer, creator, or YouTube performer, we nevertheless spend more hours watching professionally produced feature films and television programs than ever before. We are also awash in media coverage of movie premieres, television finales, celebrity gossip, box office data, TV ratings, and social media metrics. Although some critics contend that we are currently experiencing a dramatic democratization of media forms, audiences remain enamored with "traditional" mass media and the seemingly creative and enchanting environs of Hollywood. Indeed, peeking behind the screen is a foundational component of entertainment news and variety shows, featuring interviews with marquee talent who offer insights about the artistic choices and backstage antics that have shaped some of our favorite entertainments. We may live in an era increasingly dominated by do-it-yourself media, but our fascination with top-line talent endures.

Behind the glitz and glamour, however, offscreen workers invest untold hours crafting scripts, designing costumes, and rigging sets. They also conjure up mesmerizing special effects and manage the mind-boggling logistics of production. Much of their work is organized according to industrial principles that economize at every step in a sprawling creative process, constantly seeking efficiencies and accelerating workflows. Although strategic decisions are made on studio lots in Southern California, the labor process now extends across a vast network of production hubs in the United States, Canada, and Europe, among other locales. Indeed, Hollywood now employs a global mode of production run by massive media conglomerates that mobilize hundreds, sometimes thousands, of workers for each feature film or television series. Yet these workers and their labor remain largely invisible to the general audience. In fact, this has been a signal characteristic of Hollywood style for more than a hundred years: everything that matters happens on-screen, not off. Consequently, when it comes to movies and television, the voices heard most often are those belonging to talent and corporate executives. Those we hear least are the voices of labor, and it's that silence that we aim to redress in the following collection of interviews.

Of course this void isn't unique to Hollywood or to the United States. In most parts of the world and in most industries, expressions of pride, aspiration, or frustration from laborers about their working lives are rarely the subject of much attention. It was therefore striking that WCFL, a pioneer of early radio, sought to overcome this deficit when it took to the airwaves in 1926 as the "Voice of Labor." Inspired and funded by a federation of Chicago labor unions, the station thrived in the face of intense adversity before succumbing to commercial pressures and a right-wing political backlash during the late 1940s.[1] Interestingly, Studs Terkel—an activist actor, author, and raconteur who was blacklisted during the "red scare"— embraced this legacy when he joined another Chicago radio station and launched one of the most legendary careers in American broadcasting. He did so by listening, and listening intently, to everyday stories about jobs, lifestyles, and entertainment but also about racism, housing, and migration. His radio interlocutors proved so eloquent that during the late 1950s a national publisher encouraged him to edit and publish transcripts of his conversations, which led to a string of books, some of them best-sellers, one of them a Pulitzer Prize winner.

Most beguiling was a 1974 book with a simple title, *Working*, and a deceptively mundane subtitle, *People Talk About What They Do All Day and How They Feel About What They Do*.[2] In dozens of interviews the book offers a broad cross section of voices that include a miner, a secretary, a farmworker; a banker, a waitress, a cabbie; a pianist, a welder, and a washroom attendant. Probing gently but persistently, Terkel reveals their respective desires to make meaning out of everyday toil, to turn even an ordinary task into a craft that reveals something about them, their workplace, and the social order. Over the course of Terkel's career, he developed an interview style that mixed journalistic and ethnographic research techniques. Yet rather than focusing on celebrities, elites, or exotics, Terkel spent most of his time systematically exploring the lives and imaginations of everyday Americans. He also probed the memories of his subjects, allowing their quotidian recollections of major events like Pearl Harbor and the civil rights movement to enter the pages of written history. In the process Terkel became a pioneer in the emerging field of oral history.

Inspired by such earlier efforts to document the voices of labor, we set out to listen to the craft secrets and "war stories" of the Hollywood workforce.[3] Our interview sessions unfolded organically, each beginning with an account of professional duties as well as the daily challenges and satisfactions of working on a sprawling creative endeavor. As we heard time and again, success in such ventures is measured as much by what goes unnoticed as by what is. Each frame of a feature film or television show is filled with eloquent but inconspicuous traces of craft. For example, costumes convey a range of character traits and relationships, and are fashioned to harmonize with sets, props, and cinematography. Likewise, a seemingly simple shaft of illumination that backlights a sea of parishioners shines down from a complex lighting rig erected outside a church window, requiring the nimble and collaborative efforts of electricians, grips, and lighting technicians.

Unlike an integrated assembly line, motion picture production is a large-scale industrial enterprise that is distinguished by the collaborative production of prototypes, each one the outcome of thousands of creative choices.[4] Movies are *made*, not mass produced. They are the product of seemingly endless tinkering and deliberation that begins each morning at sunrise and often extends late into the night. Microphones, cameras, and props are positioned and repositioned, angles are tweaked, sound levels are mixed and monitored. A remarkable collection of skills are brought to bear throughout the workday, requiring self-discipline and sociality that are, we found, a source of enormous pride among craft workers and crew, and a baseline requirement for future employment.

This social dimension of labor operates at other levels as well. A costume designer not only visualizes character traits and color composition but also invests hours of affective labor, helping marquee talent to model and approve outfits that will satisfy their on-screen roles and offscreen personae. A makeup artist—the very first person to work with an actor each day—must also manage each performer's professional concerns and personal sensitivities, sometimes playing the role of confidante and therapist while also crafting a countenance that will be projected across millions of screens, large and small, often in unsparing close-up.

But even before the camera is uncapped, thousands of collaborative calculations are made as well in writers' rooms and production meetings. Sets are designed, materials marshaled, and seemingly inconsequential items are flown in from afar. Location permits and government approvals are secured, making it possible to shoot a chase scene through a sleepy suburb or down a crowded city street. Even more daunting, many feature films and television shows that are conceived in Hollywood are executed in locations around the world, requiring a mammoth amount of organizing to pull together the people and equipment necessary for each project. Again, sociality and professionalism are at a premium. Production managers fashion flexible networks, routines, and protocols that allow them to accommodate the disparate demands of each production while also maintaining a reputation for consistency and cost management.

As each project moves into the postproduction phase, sound effects and music tracks are insinuated into the footage, providing yet another subtle layer of craft labor. And perhaps the most remarkable trend in postproduction since the 1990s is the growing prominence of visual effects, which may involve eye-popping flights of visual fantasy or the delicate refashioning of recorded images. In the most extreme cases, actors perform in front of a studio green screen, which is then replaced by computer-generated imagery, a painstaking endeavor that involves months of labor by hundreds of visual artists and technicians working in shops around the world. In other cases the visual effects are less spectacular but still pervasive: hairlines are reshaped, pimples removed, complexions recolored. This postproduction labor is broken down into thousands of specialties and assignments. And although staff members gather regularly to critique footage and coordinate tasks, most of the work is quite solitary, requiring protracted and meticulous toil over the delicate contours of a whisker or a snowflake.

One of the most striking aspects of these interviews is the recurring commentary on the pleasures of craft, the opportunity to recount a creative solution or to describe a project that succeeded against all odds. We took these as both expressions of satisfaction and as performances of expertise. Working from project to project, which is now common in the motion picture industry, requires a cultivated capacity for self-promotion that spills beyond the workplace, even into the context of an interview session where one is invited to reflect deeply about a job that is fraught with harried deadlines and demands. Still, it would be cynical to suggest that self-promotion is the only or even the primary motivation for this pattern of responses. Aesthetic pleasures, sociality, and creative theorizing resonate throughout these interviews because they seem to represent the baseline satisfactions that motivate workers to accept the taxing demands of motion picture production.[5]

Yet despite this passion and resilience, our interlocutors also expressed exasperation with a system that increasingly undermines their ability to do what they are hired to do. With each passing year, they see more obstacles, hurdles, and hindrances standing in the way of a job well done. Unlike the halcyon days of the Hollywood studios, the "genius of the system" seems to be taking a turn toward madness.[6] The movie business today is producing bigger and more spectacular amusements but at the same price point as last year's model, and in less time. Foot to the pedal, the industry is careening along under conditions that many deem unsustainable, with significant implications for the future sustainability of its global production apparatus, and even more dire consequences for the personal and professional lives of media workers.

THE MUTABLE MATRIX OF MEDIA LABOR

In 2010, the Media Industries Project at the University of California commenced a round of meetings and interviews with industry personnel at all levels of the Hollywood hierarchy.[7] Conversations ranged broadly, but time and again, they spontaneously drifted toward two controversial trends that have profoundly transformed the motion picture business over the past thirty years: corporate conglomeration and globalization. Eventually these issues became the focus of a multifaceted research project and the subject of a collection of scholarly essays entitled *Precarious Creativity: Global Media, Local Labor* (2016).[8] Working with colleagues from around the world, we developed a critical framework for recasting debates about media labor around the concepts of precarity and creativity under a globalized regime of industrial production. This companion volume, *Voices of Labor: Creativity, Craft, and Conflict in Global Hollywood*, builds on the critical insights of its predecessor but also plies fresh terrain by encouraging readers to think more specifically about the nature of craft labor as it is refigured in the context of a highly mobilized mode of media production.

Drawing from the detailed and personal accounts in this collection, we offer three interrelated propositions about the current state and future prospects of craftwork and screen media labor:

1. *Craftwork exists within an intricate and intimate matrix of social relations.*
   Historically, craftwork in the film and television industries has been characterized by a detailed division of skilled labor designed to improve workflow efficiencies and productivity.[9] Although instigated by studio managers, many labor organizations and craft workers embraced this system of distinctions because it allowed them to hone their skills and establish a sense of creative identity, pleasure, and pride while nevertheless working in an industrial setting. Craft identities fostered standards of excellence and achievement within each job category, and they provided a context for workers to pursue recognition from managers and colleagues.

   Even writers, directors, and actors have adopted craft identities despite the fact that many of them enjoy profit participation and outsize creative influence. In industry parlance, they are considered above-the-line talent, versus the craft and services employees who are paid only wages and benefits.[10] Creative elites adopted craft identities partly because of the privileges and protections that unionization afforded them. But it also was a consequence of the American legal system, which has allocated authorial prerogatives to the corporate studios, relegating top-line talent—like their below-the-line counterparts—to the status of "work for hire."[11]

   On the other end of the spectrum, service workers are not technically considered creative employees, but many have come to perceive and represent their work as craft-like, since it has become the marker of status and value throughout the industry. Craft also served as the most pervasive principle for labor organizing during the 1930s when actors, set dressers, and carpenters each aligned themselves with unions or locals that were identified with particular job categories. Moreover, craft has served the interests of the major studios, since it elevated the status of a commodity art form by fostering an aura of innovation throughout the workplace.

   This structured sociality of screen media production has fostered a rich history of solidarity and collective identity among the workforce, and distinguishes craftwork from its corollary on the factory assembly line. And yet, most scholarly accounts fail to capture the sheer intricacy and intimacy of relationships among motion picture workers. Remarkably, this aspect bubbles to the surface throughout the following interviews: screen media labor operates within a complex matrix of social relations that are iterative, mutable, and contingent. Static conceptions of class relations between management and labor—or even between producer, talent, and crew—simply fail to appreciate these elaborate social ties or the ways in which they are changing in the current era of corporate conglomeration and globalization.

Film and television production today requires the logistical coordination of a colossal but capricious roster of people, places, and institutions. Workflow schedules and productivity pressures emanate from distant corporate and financial headquarters, while the actual labor of moviemaking now unfolds across expansive spatial terrains, sometimes taking place in multiple locations at once. In the midst of this spiraling complexity, every single person we interviewed talked about the extended web of relationships they must sustain with producers, colleagues, and assistants but also, in some cases, with local residents, business owners, public servants, and even national security officials.

2. *Hollywood craftwork today constitutes a regime of excessive labor.*
We furthermore learned that this highly socialized mode of production has engendered forms of labor rarely associated with craft and crew: soothing an actor's ego; sharing childcare duties; appeasing a disgruntled resident; lobbying disinterested politicians; supervising safety concerns; coordinating logistics in multiple languages; moving to a new location (again and again) to find work. These stories are the largely undocumented social realities of media labor today—the hidden, voluntary, unrecognized, and often unwaged aspects of craftwork.

Many of our interlocutors are now accountable for a range of affective, logistical, and legal duties that stretch well beyond the parameters of the studio or the conventional time clock. Productions are bigger, responsibilities are burgeoning, and workdays are longer, yet budgets are tighter and deadlines are shorter. Time away from home is growing longer, as are supply lines, so that quality resources are often difficult to secure. At the same time, workplace protections are weaker, jobs are scarcer, and frustrations are more visible. And still, pride in a job well done remains an enduring source of pleasure for craft workers, perhaps an even more powerful point of satisfaction because it has been realized under such trying circumstances.

In this context, the notion of excess indexes the persistent pressure for "more" in the workplace, which is a consequence of equally excessive structural change that stems from the concentration of corporate power, the financialization of creativity, the proliferation of far-flung production hubs, and the escalating impact of production subsidies. Many of our interlocutors, especially the more experienced and senior ones, conveyed a sense of resignation about these developments, saying they simply "check out" when the pressures grow too intense. If they need a respite from many months on the road, they simply pass on job offers while they take time to recharge. Some veterans have pulled back more dramatically, restricting themselves to employment opportunities that pay less but keep them closer to home. Others have left the industry entirely because of health and wellness concerns. Overall, veterans sense a pattern of decline, not just in workplace conditions and compensation, but also in the ineffable satisfactions of the job. In an off-the-record conversation, one person confided, "I get the sense that no one seems to be having *fun* anymore."

Although most of our interlocutors grudgingly accept this regime of excessive labor as somehow inevitable, they seem well aware that the escalating demands and general conditions of craftwork have become increasingly pernicious and potentially ruinous, affecting both their personal welfare and their creative capacities. Everyone in some fashion questioned the relentless grind, and acknowledged that it favors a particular kind of worker: young, single, and mobile. Even the most junior employees spoke with some nostalgia for a bygone era when work was consistent, mentorship was an ingrained aspect of the job, and the respect for the craft seemed more palpable. Rather than seeing themselves as career employees with a growing wealth of experience, most worry about how much longer they can stay in the game and stay creative, given the current trends.

3. *Screen media production is a protean entity.*
The factory assembly line is a residual concept of an earlier era of industrialization when capital was understood as a fixed cost that was anchored in place. The productivity and dynamism of the assembly line was derived from the relentless adaptation of processes within the factory that involved swapping out inputs, recalibrating machinery, or redeploying the workforce. The signature feature of fin-de-siècle globalization was for manufacturers to extend these principles beyond the bounds of the factory and the nation-state, creating a global assembly line.

Yet the regime of excessive labor outlined above represents what we consider a distinctive phase of flexible capitalism in the screen media industries, since it is characterized by a mobile regime of socio-spatial relations that entails a more protean mode of production, one that involves a constant refashioning of relations and resources across locations, all the while sustaining a fiction of functional continuity. This is not to say that the motion picture business has entirely turned the page. Remnants of the studio system's integrated and detailed division of labor remain, providing templates for adaptations that now take place at multiple junctures. But these templates are largely symbolic, given new corporate strategies that are increasingly untethered from the exigencies of place.

Today, the persistent resocialization and respatialization of production makes for a much more nimble structure, one that can accommodate incidents anywhere in the system, like a policy change or a tragic accident, by rapidly redeploying resources and personnel. It is like an organism capable of interacting with and responding to changes in its environment: suppressing potential threats, seeking new resources, expunging waste material in its wake, and constantly adapting its configuration to suit the circumstances. The system functions not because it grows the value of its existing human capital but because it constantly harvests an influx of eager aspirants, replenishing its labor ranks with those amenable to a mobile and excessive regime of production.

Critically, this protean apparatus both shapes and is shaped by the diverse and expansive relations that constitute it—it is therefore rife with contradictions and potential ruptures. So, while these interviews offer perceptive commentaries on structural changes that are affecting the everyday lives of media workers around the world, they raise equally important questions about the creative and financial limits of this mode of production. As our interlocutors speak eloquently about the pleasures of craft, we can't help but notice their reservations about the trajectories of change. Yet this tension between creativity and concern may ultimately prove productive. For the commitment to craftwork and collaboration not only provides solace for trying times, but may also provide the means to imagine and instigate alternatives in the future.

LOCATING LABOR IN A GLOBAL CONTEXT

The commentary above and the interviews that follow build on a substantial body of existing research in labor studies, cultural studies, and political economy. It is therefore essential to situate the propositions above in a broader historical and analytical context in order to appreciate the distinctive characteristics of screen media labor as well as continuities with other forms of industrial labor.

Historically, researchers point to the Reagan-Thatcher era as a tipping point in labor relations, as neoliberal principles of deregulation and privatization provided the intellectual foundation for a political movement that opened the door to corporate mergers and a foreign policy agenda premised on free trade. Seizing the opportunity, many companies shifted their manufacturing operations to low-wage nonunionized countries, creating a new international division of labor (NIDL) that allowed them to realize cost economies and counter the strength of unionized labor in the industrial societies of the West.[12]

As major manufacturers departed for distant locales, it tore apart the social and political fabric of working-class communities. It also created a transnational labor market that severely diminished the bargaining power of organized labor and attenuated the ability of governments to act as intermediaries. Countries that resisted this neoliberal agenda were abandoned in favor of more receptive locales where governments either acquiesced or actively colluded with transnational corporate interests.[13] These changing structural conditions profoundly affected the everyday lives of workers everywhere. Societies in the Global North experienced a dramatic loss of manufacturing jobs, and union membership declined precipitously. Meanwhile, in developing societies, millions of new jobs appeared, but working conditions were grim. Lacking union representation, workers toiled long hours in often dangerous conditions for very low wages.

In the media industries, deregulation allowed companies to bulk up into vast conglomerates that expanded their reach to the far corners of the globe. Trade journals and the popular press exuberantly extolled the virtues of these developments and anticipated a future of robust growth.¹⁴ Other high-skill industries were booming as well, including software, biotech, and finance. In response to growing public concern about the loss of blue-collar jobs in the Global North, policymakers responded by pointing to the burgeoning "information economy" or "creative economy" as the logical trajectory for postindustrial societies, conjuring a future of high-wage jobs for urban dwellers and low-cost goods shipped in from manufacturers abroad.¹⁵

In Britain, which had been ravaged by deindustrialization, policymakers proved to be especially keen proponents of the creative economy, seeing it as a sector that could foster economic and social renewal. By offering subsidies and training programs within the context of a larger campaign to rebrand the nation as "Cool Britannia," the government sought to harness new sources of innovation and entrepreneurialism. Growth in the creative sector would arguably replace jobs and regenerate regions devastated by the loss of traditional industry. Soon, other countries and cities joined the game with their own creative industries policies, often seeking to attract screen media productions from foreign sources.¹⁶

Responding to these new enticements, Hollywood—which had been shooting feature films in distant locales since its inception—began to scale up its investment in mobile production. Producers sought out localities across North America and Europe, attracted by favorable exchange rates, lower labor costs, untapped infrastructure, and, most significantly, government subsidies and tax rebates. For instance, in the 1990s, Canadian exchange rates made it possible to trim production costs by almost 10 percent, while exchange rates in Prague (alongside the generally lower costs for goods and services) allowed producers to cut production budgets by a third. As the competition escalated, Louisiana, New York, and Georgia offered subsidies so generous that industry insiders impishly began to describe them as "big bags of cash." In addition to subsidies and incentives, Britain trumpeted its rich pools of talent in theater, advertising, and television; countries like Australia, the Czech Republic, Germany, Hungary, and Italy invested heavily in new or refurbished production facilities; and New Zealand and parts of Asia ramped up their postproduction services. Moreover, the Pinewood Group—a major facilities provider—branched out from its flagship studio complex in London to open soundstages in Wales, Atlanta, Toronto, Malaysia, and the Dominican Republic. Hollywood producers consequently found themselves coveted and courted around the world.

In their landmark volume *Global Hollywood 2* (2005), Toby Miller et al. offer the most stringent critique of these transformations, arguing that compliant governments and labor organizations facilitated the extension of studio operations across a vast terrain of regions and locations.¹⁷ Seeking the "most favorable conditions," producers leveraged the competition to undermine labor protections and secure cost advantages, both at home and abroad. This dynamic gave rise to what the authors call a new international division of cultural labor (NICL), which has had deleterious effects on screen media wages and working conditions worldwide.

While this analysis provided timely insights regarding the broad structural transformations taking place, it too easily conflated film and television work with assembly-line labor and treated creative artifacts as industrial commodities. In doing so, it lost sight of the highly socialized nature of screen media production and tended to gloss over the more localized, everyday experiences of the craft workers themselves. As a political economy operating at a high level of abstraction, it failed to account for the diverse ways that employees—individually or collectively—negotiate, contest, or even understand the structural changes affecting their workday practices. In other words, if screen media work has really become that bad, why do highly motivated, exceptionally skilled, and relatively advantaged workers subject themselves to such severe exploitation?

In fact, policy deliberations about cultivating creative economies have generally revolved around labor practices that are difficult to routinize. It therefore has been argued that creativity flourishes in flexible and informal working environments, allowing workers to pursue their passions, free from the monotony of the factory floor. This often involves short-term contract labor, but policymakers suggested that this form of casualization was a natural fit for the bohemian lifestyles of highly skilled workers aiming to control their professional destinies.

Yet the line separating autonomy from precarity proved to be a tenuous one, as contingent and irregular employment patterns started to define the general working conditions in many industries around the world.[18] Unlike media makers or designers, laid-off factory workers and underemployed youth found it difficult to take solace in the liberty of bouncing from job to job. Consequently, organized resistance to corporate abuses began to mount, punctuated by dramatic mass demonstrations at the 1999 meeting of the World Trade Organization. Around this time, labor studies began to shift attention from broad structural issues such as hypermobility and globalization (the NIDL) to more specific investigations into the ways that informality and precarity have upended workers' lives and workplaces.[19] British academics—often working across the fields of cultural studies, critical sociology, and policy studies—have generated insightful critiques of the normative conditions of creative labor, examining how workers in a range of creative sectors balance their aspirations for creative autonomy with the pressures and uncertainties of casualized labor.[20]

Moreover, media studies research began to show that workers in the creative economy were not doing as well as imagined, especially in digital media, where the start-up culture of Silicon Valley had become a model for the sector as a whole. According to legend, dot-com employees endure long hours and modest wages in return for stock options that promise lavish returns if the company develops a product that catches the attention of investors and consumers. In fact, however, few workers hit the jackpot. Instead, most contract programmers and software developers migrate from project to project and from firm to firm. But given the booming demand for their services, many find it easy to land jobs, allowing them to work for a stretch and then take an unpaid break for personal projects or travel adventures. Researchers found that they prize this flexibility, but that the imagined material rewards have often proven elusive.

For their part, companies value the youthful passion of these employees and their willingness to put in long hours. By tricking out the workplace with trendy furniture, foosball tables, and other supposed diversions, employers have been able to command intense and extended bouts of labor during periods leading up to a product launch or upgrade. Inspired by industry leaders like Yahoo! and Google, tech companies have tried to obscure the boundaries between work and play, both to attract the very best creative talent and to make it unnecessary for them to leave the work/play-ce.[21] This ethos of bohemianism and entrepreneurialism in the tech industry has rippled out into other sectors of the economy. Workers now sustain themselves on reputational capital and professional networks of trusted colleagues.[22]

Although these transformations seemed responsive to workers' desires to escape the drudgery of industrial routine, they fostered new forms of exploitation that allowed employers to evade responsibilities—for health care, retirement, paid vacation, and childcare—that industrial unions had struggled to put in place.[23] Informality takes an even more distinctive toll on female workers, who are often excluded from the homosocial rituals of the workplace. It furthermore poses a challenge to those with domestic duties and care responsibilities, roles that disproportionately fall on the shoulders of women.[24] Moreover, subtle forms of racial and gender discrimination tend to grow more troublesome in environments that lack formal institutions and protocols for representing worker grievances. Since unions are considered antithetical to flexible labor relations, workers have discovered that informality can prove to be a breeding ground for new forms of inequity and laddish behavior.

Consequently, the promise of the creative economy has proven to be a mixed blessing.[25] And the trend toward informalization in the workplace has paradoxically been twinned with the formalization of media institutions around the world via marketization and conglomeration. Another paradox involves the hyperconcentration of corporate power during an era when media production became more decentralized via outsourcing, subcontracting, and the exploitation of amateur talent.[26] Digital technologies have further eroded job categories and work routines, as traditional responsibilities have been delegated to "multimedia specialists" in various parts of the world who perform similar tasks but do so outside the jurisdiction of unions and regulations.[27]

Today, conceptions of creative labor often extol the virtues of individual enterprise and entrepreneurialism in the casual environs of the "gig economy," an increasingly common employment relationship in which the risks of both labor and capital are displaced onto individual workers.[28] The current zeitgeist embraces the image of the autonomous professional who works from his or her own home, furnishes his or her own assets, and leverages new technology and mobile devices to facilitate more flexible and "unfettered" work arrangements. And yet the presumptions don't easily translate to screen media production, where workers try to reconcile contradictory ambitions for flexibility with enduring desires for structural benefits and representation. Craft laborers express frank concerns about the impact of these new management regimes on the creative components of film and television production.[29]

All of this puts tremendous pressure on screen media workers, both at home and abroad. Power remains in the hands of global conglomerates, and risk has been displaced onto vulnerable rank-and-file workers who are subject to tensions between formality and flexibility, both of which are endemic to a hypermobile mode of production.[30] Similar forces have taken a toll on unions, whose ranks have been diminishing precipitously as a consequence of deregulation and antilabor legislation. Wisconsin Governor Scott Walker's high-profile attacks on unions and collective bargaining are nightmarish examples of much broader historical developments. Laws and policies that used to protect workers have been twisted, if not abolished, in many parts of the world.[31] Moreover, informality and entrepreneurialism in the creative sector have been embraced more generally by policymakers, much to the detriment of workers and unions. Contracts, competition, and scarcity furthermore undermine the value of collective consciousness, especially among young aspirants who are willing to work for minimal pay and benefits in exchange for autonomy and self-development.[32]

Historically, the film and television industries have been a stronghold for organized labor.[33] Yet our interviews bear witness to the various ways that employers are undoing many of the benefits of unionization: workdays have been extended, pensions have been reduced, wages have been slashed. Moreover, the dispersal of workers across an expanded geographic terrain threatens the very sociality of motion picture labor. And yet we were heartened to hear many of our interviewees say they are committed to turning back the tide, either through traditional labor organizations or grassroots efforts of their own.

We find resonances with this sentiment in "production studies" research that richly highlights the reflexive and meaning-making activities of screen media workers.[34] This strand of research empirically engages with the working lives of below-the-line labor, grappling with the impact that technological change, productivity pressures, and financial scarcity have on traditional structures of craftwork and unionized labor. Many of these researchers offer nuanced assessments of the transformations taking place, but with few exceptions,[35] they steer clear of linking their conclusions to the larger logics of global capital. Instead, they opt for more localized assessments of creative identities and workplace dynamics. Expressing reservations about causal arguments and reductive instrumentalism, these researchers tend to focus on capillary operations of power and complex terrains of struggle, rather than the larger structural forces reshaping media labor around the world.

Yet many of our interlocutors express an escalating concern about structural issues, often framing them with respect to abstract calculations made in distant corporate headquarters. At one level, this is an outcome of the growing physical and cultural distance between those who actually craft motion pictures and "the suits" who make life harder for workers on the set. On another level it's about the rising prominence of shareholder value as the preeminent principle of corporate governance, a process that some researchers refer to as financialization. These scholars contend that since the 1980s, public policy has fostered a "Copernican revolution" that has elevated the influence of the financial sector in almost every aspect of commercial enterprise.[36] Not only has this shift encouraged corporate conglomeration, but it also has emphasized short-term profitability over foundational investments in research, development, and human capital.

Consequently, today's corporate managers find themselves responding to the relentless and mercurial demands of financial analysts, hedge funds, and institutional investors. Media workers often experience this trend in their dealings with studio executives and producers who privilege market logic over creative risk and novelty. Others say they confront incessant pressures to do more with less, showing little regard for the creative sacrifices or safety risks those directives entail. Time and again, our interview subjects provide evidence of escalating demands that seem insensitive to the realities of the workplace. These stories provide specific evidence of the human toll taken by conglomeration and mobile production, and they raise serious questions about the financial legerdemain that keeps the entire system in motion.

These voices of labor thus reveal the underlying complexities and contradictions of media production in the age of Global Hollywood. They furthermore demonstrate that many of these issues echo concerns expressed by a larger creative workforce that extends well beyond Southern California. Film and television workers around the world are now caught up, however unequally, in the mobile production apparatus of the major studios. Rather than publicity-friendly anecdotes by marquee celebrities, this collection of interviews offers nuanced observations from a range of perspectives, including a showrunner, a scriptwriter, a location scout; a grip, a musician, a makeup artist; an effects artist, a set designer, and a production manager. And although these stories are anchored in Los Angeles, they resonate with interviews in Atlanta, Dublin, Prague, and Vancouver.

In the end, we found a community of workers, from different locations and at different stages in their careers, equally vexed by globalization and conglomeration.

Everyone who spoke with us pointed to the dramatic changes that have taken place in screen media over the last thirty years, connecting broad structural transformations to their more immediate concerns about workplace safety, teamwork, and creative practice, as well as family life, finances, and well-being. We were at the same time heartened by their affirmations that even in the face of adversity, they still have a sense of pride and fulfillment that is unmatched by most other industries. Yet these satisfactions exist in relation to unresolved tensions that permeate the conversations that follow.

ABOUT THE ORGANIZATION OF *VOICES OF LABOR*

We organized the collection into three sections: Company Town, Global Machine, and Fringe City. The first section refers to Hollywood's historic roots as a core component of the motion picture business. This section digs deep into the granular realities of everyday labor across a broad cross section of job categories, uncovering as well the tactics that workers employ to manage the seemingly incompatible pressures to innovate and economize.

The second section engages more directly with the spatial dynamics of film and television production to underscore the economic and political structures that are integrating distant locations into the studios' mode of production. Here the conversations highlight how globalization actually happens, focusing especially on the ways in which "mobility" becomes an embedded experience for many workers and workplaces around the world.

We close with a section on the visual effects sector. The stories shared by VFX artists, advocates, and organizers specifically illustrate how the industry today relies on marginal institutions to sustain its power and profitability. Grim working conditions at the "fringe" are the industry's canary in the coal mine, a powerful portent of what might happen if we allow the economic and political logics of the world's most powerful motion picture studios to run amok.

Collectively, we hope the interviews show how seemingly abstract concepts such as conglomeration, financialization, and globalization are useful tools for thinking critically about changes that are occurring in the motion picture business, but also more generally in our workplaces and culture at large.

NOTES

1. Robert W. McChesney, *Telecommunications, Mass Media, and Democracy: The Battle for the Control of U.S. Broadcasting, 1928–1935* (New York: OUP, 1993); Nathan Godfried, *WCFL, Chicago's Voice of Labor, 1928–70* (Chicago: University of Illinois Press, 1997).

2. Studs Terkel, ed., *Working: People Talk About What They Do All Day and How They Feel About What They Do* (New York: New Press, 1974).

3. See John Thornton Caldwell's comments about the "war story" genre among media workers in his book *Production Culture: Industrial Reflexivity and Critical Practice in Film and Television* (Durham, NC: Duke University Press, 2008), but also in his preface to *Production Studies, the Sequel!: Cultural Studies of Global Media Industries*, ed. Miranda Banks, Bridget Conor, and Vicki Mayer (New York: Routledge, 2016), where he talks about his painting for the cover of the book.

4. David Bordwell, Janet Staiger, and Kristin Thompson, eds., *The Classical Hollywood Cinema: Film Style and Mode of Production to 1960* (New York: Columbia University Press, 1985).

5. John Thornton Caldwell comments on self-theorizing and self-promotion in *Production Culture*.

6. Adopting André Bazin's observation about the prolific creativity of the integrated studio system of production, Thomas Schatz's acclaimed history is titled *The Genius of the System: Hollywood Filmmaking in the Studio Era* (New York: Pantheon, 1988).

7. Our interview strategy relied on snowball sampling to recruit a broad cross-section of screen media labor. We identified individuals through our own personal research networks and through the professional networks of the Media Industries Project at the University of California. Some individuals had no previous affiliation with us but we recruited them based on their reputations in the industry and relevance to the project. We aimed for diversity in medium, job category, seniority, and geographic location, but specifically targeted individuals whose work we perceived as most affected by the spatial operations and cost-cutting strategies of the major studios.

8. Michael Curtin and Kevin Sanson, eds., *Precarious Creativity: Global Media, Local Labor* (Oakland: University of California Press, 2016), DOI: https://doi.org/10.1525/luminos.10.

9. Henry Braverman, *Labor and Monopoly Capital: The Degradation of Work in the Twentieth Century* (New York: Monthly Review Press, 1974); Janet Staiger, "Dividing Labor for Production Control: Thomas Ince and the Rise of the Studio System," *Cinema Journal* 18, no. 2 (1979): 16–25; Frederick Taylor, *Scientific Management* (New York: Routledge, 2003); Max Weber, *Economy and Society: An Outline of Interpretive Sociology* (Berkeley: University of California Press, 1978).

10. Producers assemble above-the-line labor, usually directors, writers, and actors, as part of the development process to help secure financing for a film or television show. These costs are attributed to each individual "talent" identified by name in the budget. Below-the-line labor is calculated at the departmental, rather than individual, level as part of the technical costs of production. The terms "above-the-line" and "below-the-line" are derived from a line on budget sheets that distinguishes the production's development costs from its technical costs.

11. Matt Stahl, "Privilege and Distinction in Production Worlds: Copyright, Collective Bargaining, and Working Conditions in Media Making," in *Production Studies: Cultural Studies of Media Industries*, ed. Vicki Mayer, Miranda J. Banks, and John Thornton Caldwell (New York: Routledge, 2009), 54–67.

12. David Harvey, *The Condition of Postmodernity: An Enquiry into the Origins of Cultural Change* (New York: Blackwell, 1989); David Harvey, *A Brief History of Neoliberalism* (New York: OUP, 2005); Folker Frobel et al., *The New International Division of Labour: Structural Employment and Industrialisation in Developing Countries* (Cambridge, England: Cambridge University Press, 1980); Barry Bluestone and Bennett Harrison, *The Deindustrialization of America: Plant Closings, Community Abandonment, and the Dismantling of Basic Industry* (New York: Basic, 1982); Saskia Sassen, *The Mobility of Labor and Capital* (Cambridge, England: Cambridge University Press, 1988); Peter Dicken, *Global Shift: Transforming the World Economy* (New York: Guilford Press, 1998); Beverly J. Silver, *Forces of Labor: Workers' Movements and Globalization since 1870* (Cambridge, England: Cambridge University Press, 2003).

13. Charles Tilly, "Globalization Threatens Labor's Rights," *International Labor and Working-Class History* 47 (1995): 1–23; Manuel Castells, *The Information Age*, vol. 7, *The Power of Identity* (Oxford: Blackwell, 1997); Fred L. Block, *Postindustrial Possibilities: A Critique of Economic Discourse* (Berkeley: University of California Press, 1990); Saskia Sassen, *Globalization and Its Discontents: Essays on the New Mobility of People and Money*, vol. 9 (New York: New Press, 1999).

14. Less enthusiastic commentators, however, criticized the growing power of media conglomerates and the "Disneyfication" of cultures around the world. Ben H. Bagdikian, "The Lords of the Global Village," *The Nation*, June 12, 1989, 805–20; Edward S. Herman and Robert W. McChesney, *The Global Media: The New Missionaries of Corporate Capitalism* (London: Cassell, 1997).

15. John Howkins, *The Creative Economy: How People Make Money from Ideas* (New York: Penguin, 2001); Richard Florida, *Cities and the Creative Class* (New York: Routledge, 2005).

16. Toby Miller and Nitin Govil, *Global Hollywood* (London: BFI, 2001); Mike Gasher, *Hollywood North: The Feature Film Industry in British Columbia* (Vancouver: UBC Press, 2002); Serra Tinic, *On Location: Canada's Television Industry in a Global Market* (Toronto: University of Toronto Press, 2005); Ben Goldsmith and Tom O'Regan, *The Film Studio: Film Production in the Global Economy* (Lanham, MD: Rowman and Littlefield, 2005); Ben Goldsmith, Tom O'Regan, and Susan Ward, *Local Hollywood: Global Film Production and the Gold Coast* (St. Lucia, Australia: University of Queensland Press, 2010).

17. Toby Miller et al., *Global Hollywood 2* (London: BFI, 2005). See also Susan Christopherson, "Behind the Scenes: How Transnational Firms Are Constructing a New International Division of Labor in Media Work," *Geoforum* 37 (2006): 739–51.

18. Andrew Ross, *Nice Work if You Can Get It: Life and Labor in Precarious Times* (New York: New York University Press, 2009).

19. Guy Standing, *The Precariat: The New Dangerous Class* (London: Bloomsbury Academic, 2011); Massimiliano Mollona, *Made in Sheffield: An Ethnography of Industrial Work and Politics*, vol. 5 (New York: Berghahn Books, 2009); Sian Lazar, "A Desire to Formalize Work? Comparing Trade Union Strategies in Bolivia and Argentina," *Anthropology of Work Review* 33, no. 1 (2012): 15–24; Patricia Fernandez-Kelly and Jon Shefner, *Out of the Shadows: Political Action and the Informal Economy in Latin America* (University Park: Pennsylvania State Press, 2006).

20. Mark Banks, *The Politics of Cultural Work* (Basingstoke, England: Palgrave Macmillan, 2007); David Hesmondhalgh and Sarah Baker, *Creative Labour: Media Work in Three Cultural Industries* (New York: Routledge, 2011).

21. Andrew Ross, *No-Collar: The Humane Workplace and Its Hidden Costs* (Philadelphia: Temple University Press, 2003).

22. For more on professional networks and reputational capital in the film industry, see Helen Blair, "'You're Only as Good as Your Last Job': The Labour Process and Labour Market in the British Film Industry," *Work, Employment and Society* 15, no. 1 (2001): 149–69; Candace Jones, "Careers in Project Networks: The Case of the Film Industry," in *The Boundaryless Career: A New Employment Principle for a New Organized Era*, ed. Michael B. Arthur and Denise M. Rousseau (New York: Oxford University Press, 1996), 58–75. For more on the critical role trust plays in the creative industries, see Mark Banks et al., "Risk and Trust in Cultural Industries," *Geoforum* 31, no. 4 (2000): 453–64.

23. Andy C. Pratt and Rosalind C. Gill, "In the Social Factory? Immaterial Labour, Precariousness, and Cultural Work," *Theory, Culture, and Society* 25, nos. 7–8 (2008): 1–30; David Hesmondhalgh and Sarah Baker, *Creative Labour*; Gina Neff, *Venture Labor: Work and the Burden of Risk in Innovation Industries* (Cambridge, MA: MIT Press, 2012).

24. Angela McRobbie, "Reflections on Feminism, Immaterial Labour and the Post-Fordist Regime," *New Formations* 70, no. 1 (2011): 60–76; Rosalind Gill, "Cool, Creative, and Egalitarian? Exploring Gender in Project-Based New Media Work in Europe," *Information, Communication, and Society* 5, no. 1 (2002): 70–89; Rosalind Gill, "Inequalities in Media Work," in *Behind the Screen: Inside European Production Cultures*, ed. Petr Szczepanik and Patrick Vonderau (New York: Palgrave, 2013): 189–205.

25. Mark Banks and David Hesmondhalgh, "Looking for Work in the Creative Industries Policy," *International Journal of Cultural Policy* 15, no. 4 (2009): 415–30.

26. Ramon Labato and Julian Thomas, *The Informal Media Economy* (Cambridge, England: Polity, 2015); Tiziana Terranova, "Free Labor: Production Culture for the Digital Economy," *Social Text*

63 (2000): 33–50; Vicki Mayer, *Below the Line: Producers and Production Studies in the New Television Economy* (Durham, NC: Duke University Press, 2011), especially pp. 66–100.

27. John T. Caldwell, "Breaking Ranks: Backdoor Workforces, Messy Workflows, and Craft Disaggregation," *Popular Communication* 8, no. 3 (2010): 221–26.

28. Sarah Kaine and Emmanual Josserand, "Workers Are Taking on More Risk in the Gig Economy," *The Conversation*, July 6, 2016, https://theconversation.com/workers-are-taking-on-more-risk-in-the-gig-economy-61797.

29. Mark Banks, "Craft Labour and Creative Industries," *International Journal of Cultural Policy* 16, no. 3 (2010): 305–21.

30. Susan Christopherson, "Beyond the Self-Expressive Creative Worker: An Industry Perspective on Entertainment Media," *Theory, Culture, and Society* 25, nos. 7–8 (2008): 73–95; Susan Christopherson, "Behind the Scenes"; Michael Storper and Susan Christopherson, "The Effects of Flexible Specialization on Industrial Politics and the Labor Market: The Motion Picture Industry," *Industrial and Labor Relations Review* 42, no. 3 (1989): 331–47.

31. Vincent Mosco and Catherine McKercher, *The Laboring of Communication: Will Knowledge Workers of the World Unite?* (Lanham, MD: Rowman and Littlefield, 2009).

32. For a general overview, see David Hesmondhalgh and Sarah Baker, *Creative Labour*, 222–26.

33. See for example David F. Prindle, *The Politics of Glamour: Ideology and Democracy in the Screen Actors Guild* (Madison: University of Wisconsin Press, 1988); Gerald Horne, *Class Struggle in Hollywood: Moguls, Mobsters, Stars, Reds, and Trade Unionists, 1930–1950* (Austin: University of Texas Press, 2001); Denise Hartsough, "Film Union Meets Television: IA Organizing Efforts, 1947–1952," *Labor History* 33, no. 3 (1992): 357–71.

34. John Thornton Caldwell, *Production Culture*; Vicki Mayer, Miranda J. Banks, and John Caldwell, *Production Studies: Cultural Studies of Media Industries*; Miranda Banks, Bridget Conor, and Vicki Mayer, *Production Studies, the Sequel!*.

35. Vicki Mayer, *Below the Line*.

36. Gerald Davis, *Managed by the Markets: How Finance Re-Shaped America* (New York: OUP, 2009).

2

Company Town

Editors' Introduction

The historic core of Hollywood was anchored by a small cohort of major studios premised on a model of industrialized creativity that unleashed a torrent of films and television programs around the world. This prolific system of production bolstered the power of a few employers whose influence extended beyond the studio gates and into the community, leading many to observe that Los Angeles—like its counterparts in Detroit and Pittsburgh—was a company town. Indeed, even today, the *Los Angeles Times* brands its website coverage of the entertainment industry under the title "Company Town."[1] Moreover, the studios' influence extended even further, shaping the operating procedures and work routines of media producers around the world. That's why the opening section of this book focuses on the practices and principles of this quintessential company town, and does so from the bottom up.

Each production employs hundreds of workers in dozens of job categories, so what follows is a sampling of perspectives that offer specific details about the duties and challenges that workers confront, while also demonstrating the passion, commitment, and skills that are sometimes absent from discussions about film and television craftwork. For instance, sound recording is a highly intricate process that requires technical virtuosity to mix multiple inputs into a master recording as well as unsparing vigilance to determine and eliminate potential sources of "noise." The subtle scuff of shoes on a wooden floor or the soft hum of an oscillating fan—these sounds are trivial, if audible at all, to the untrained ear, but to a sound recordist, such minor background noises can be fatal to the film's final audio track.

Our interlocutors take conspicuous pride in both their creativity and their professionalism, the latter defined by one's ability to contribute to complex collaborative ventures under demanding and constantly shifting circumstances. Consider as an example the elaborate motion picture sets built for *The Hunger Games* series (2012–15). Each set was the outcome of extended deliberations among directors, production designers, art directors, illustrators, builders, and set decorators. Drawings were done, models were made, budgets were negotiated. Materials, colors, and lighting setups were debated, sometimes up to the very last minute. Each set was therefore the product of consensus and consultation—a single, collective outcome of numerous individual creative flourishes. Thus, many of our interviewees, regardless of their particular job titles, emphasize teamwork, communication, and problem-solving skills as fundamental aspects of their everyday labor, all of which underscores the high degree of sociality that characterizes production work.

And yet we also heard workers contrast these attributes with what they see as managerial practices that are illogical and inefficient. Bureaucratic layers separate decision makers from frontline practitioners, a distance that has grown significantly with the rise of global media conglomerates that are beholden to Wall Street financial markets. Conglomeration has many deleterious effects, but perhaps the most significant impact on workers is the way it prioritizes cost containment strategies that gnaw away at employee compensation and extract novel forms of unpaid labor. This tendency is exacerbated by relentless comparisons that corporate officials make between production costs in Hollywood versus other places. Los Angeles–based workers are especially sensitive to these comparisons, having watched countless projects flee to distant locales—what they refer to as "runaway productions."

Studio executives exploit these sensitivities by telegraphing their budgetary concerns to workers at every level, often via disingenuous suggestions that corporate cost equations are derived from nothing less than natural law. Unlike the glory days of the 1930s, when most workers were full-time employees with union representation, today only a fraction of the workforce is actually employed by the major studios. The vast majority work for small companies that service the studios on a contractual basis, providing cinematography, set design, and makeup services. Moreover, these contractors mostly hire freelancers who sign on for particular projects. To managers in distant offices, these enterprises and their workers are treated as interchangeable parts, but as our interviews reveal, this perspective glaringly contrasts with the essential sociality of film and television production.

For example, a costume designer or a cinematographer who is making hiring decisions crucially relies on his or her personal knowledge of the skills and capacities of prospective crew members. If they have to look outside their immediate circle of tried-and-true freelancers, they rely on trusted colleagues to recommend alternatives. One's personal work ethic and creative skills are therefore distinguishing attributes that are communicated within a tightly integrated network of professionals.

But by treating workers as interchangeable parts and keeping them on edge about future employment prospects, corporate executives exert leverage in their negotiations. They not only demand more for the same amount of compensation, they turn up the temperature in the workplace so that it's common to hear veteran employees confide that folks aren't having fun anymore, that the job has become a grind. That's not to say that every workplace is beleaguered by hardball management tactics and that the magic of motion pictures has simply vanished. But in those cases where workers do express satisfaction, it's often attributable to the power of an exceptional producer or director who can push back against corporate demands and set a positive tone for the crew.

As jobs vanish and workplace pressures increase, it furthermore affects hiring practices and workplace diversity. Hollywood has become a closed circuit of diminishing job opportunities that is dominated by managerial imperatives and crew bosses who simply hire those they know. We often see headline stories about leading female actors being paid less than their male counterparts or about the lack of racial diversity among top-line talent. Many of our interviewees acknowledged how both employers and unions act as gatekeepers, making it difficult for outsiders to secure work. Freelancers find it hard to get a foot in the door, let alone to land a string of gigs that will qualify them for union benefits. Those who have union status are often scrambling to maintain it.

The situation is especially challenging for women and minorities who confront both personal biases and structural obstacles. Consider the fact that "boy wonders" are indulged and rapidly promoted, while female workers are overlooked or even disparaged. Such personal biases are complemented by institutional preferences that favor big-budget star vehicles and action-adventure stories over productions that specifically address black or Latino audiences. The hyper-commercialism of the industry undervalues these audiences, which in turn sets off a chain of decision making that affects the conception and staffing of shows. Other structural factors discourage diversity as well. Long hours and a lack of family support services make it difficult for women to hold certain jobs.

Systemic issues like these evolve out of institutional choices that are rationalized by common-sense explanations rather than clear-eyed analysis. "We simply can't afford childcare" is a common excuse for failing to support a diverse workforce. And giving audiences "what they want" deflects attention from the fact that market research values audiences in prejudicial ways. Moreover, time pressures and cost consciousness leave little room to experiment with structural reforms that could address these concerns. As the following interviews show, workers make tactical efforts to nurture one another, protect benefits, and open up the hiring process, but we see little evidence that major studios are willing to take on the deep structural obstacles to diversity.

Lest we seem nostalgic for the good old days, it's important to remember that struggles between labor and management have been waged throughout the history of Hollywood. During the glory days of the 1930s and 1940s, studios were integrated factories that offered long-term contracts to workers in almost every aspect of production. Working side by side and often living in the same neighborhoods, screen media laborers embraced unionization during the New Deal era of industrial organizing. In the midst of Hollywood's prosperity they battled and bargained for lucrative wages and benefits, and they gained limited authority within their respective artistic, craft, and service categories. Their geographic proximity and continuity of employment helped to swell their influence.

Today, the situation is far different. Unions have a difficult time organizing freelance employees who work for hundreds of small-scale employers, each servicing discrete productions. The challenges facing unions have grown even more complex due to the mobility that producers now enjoy. Given these circumstances, most of the workers we spoke with seem to understand that unions—with all their shortcomings—remain a necessary and vital force in Hollywood.

Despite the corporate and globalizing pressures outlined above, we also see reasons why this company town remains a central hub of the motion picture business. For it is a place where reputations are built and professional networks are anchored. It's where contractors score their next project and assemble their core workforce even if production duties are distributed to distant locales that offer tax subsidies and other cost economies. Although many workers today realize that they must be mobile to remain employable, their home base and their personal lives remain in Hollywood. Yet this takes a toll on creativity and on family life. It also raises safety issues. In light of these concerns, some have rescaled their ambitions while others have left the business altogether. Nevertheless, Los Angeles is still one of the largest and most productive creative communities in the world. For all its globe-trotting ways, Hollywood remains a company town, a point made abundantly clear by those who spoke with us.

NOTE

1. "Company Town," *Los Angeles Times*, http://www.latimes.com/business/hollywood/.

3

Mara Brock Akil, showrunner

Mara Brock Akil, a twenty-year veteran of the television industry, has worked as a writer, producer, and showrunner on series such as *Moesha* (1996–2001) and *Being Mary Jane* (2013–ongoing). Here Akil delineates the challenges of overseeing an Atlanta-based show from Los Angeles, and touches on issues of diversity in the contemporary writers' room and the industry at large.

Describe your work. What do you do? What does a regular workweek look like?

Both are very difficult questions for me. I am a show creator, showrunner, and executive producer. All three of those things are woven together but require different skill sets. As a show creator, I come up with television show ideas. It mostly involves working through the development of ideas with executives at networks and studios. As a showrunner, I am the CEO of that show. I manage the execution of the idea. I hire a crew of about 100 to 150 people, who work for a particular television project. I work closely with the writers and with the producer. I often say I speak many languages—though I only speak English—because I make sure everyone shares the vision that I have for the show. I make sure that the network that bought the show and the studio that helps me make it are on the same page, and that I'm getting the best from both of them to execute my idea. Typically that's working through big line items, like the budget, and making sure the show is properly supported in the marketplace with adequate marketing, advertising, and press.

Part of my showrunner hat is selling the show. This includes doing TV appearances and magazine interviews. It also includes talking to the actors, writers, directors, and all of the artisans—the production designers, costume designers, hair and makeup, all of them. Do they understand my vision of the show? It requires different conversations with different people who speak different [creative and professional] languages. You need to know what is meaningful to them to effectively communicate your vision. Learning that skill set has been an ongoing experience. If you hire well, that certainly helps the job. If you don't, you can imagine the job becomes tougher. That's in line with my role as executive producer: keeping your eye on the story we are telling but with clear respect for the realities of producing a television show. I make sure we stay creative but don't go over budget. I am the morale booster. I am the cheerleader. In addition to my work roles, I am a mother and a wife. Those things I have to manage as well. I'm constantly thinking about the show, but I also have to think about my children, my husband, my life—and that's what sometimes makes the job harder to do, because I am always running out of time.

When I wake up every morning, I am a mother first. I make lunches and drive my kids to school. I work out, not just for my physical endurance but also because it's where I spend most of my time being creative. When I'm alone, I don't have to hear anybody. I don't have to manage anybody. My first stop after that is at Akil Productions. I talk with my head of development, my producing partner, who is my husband, and our assistants—we're a really small team—about what's needed for the management business of the day. Then I walk into the writers' room between ten o'clock and noon to dump all these ideas I had on my hike or while cycling. I talk about the things I thought about at three in the morning or in the car. I make sure the stories are progressing as they should. If they're not, I can spend all day in the writers' room making sure we get it right. If you don't get the script right, it just snowballs into larger problems throughout the day.

Then, I am often pulled away to answer questions for production. I can be pulled away to do press to promote the show, or to take a call with the network because they have notes or problems. Then I may go into editing. My favorite part of what I do is the writing and the editing. I love editing because it's like putting together a puzzle. If I have another show, I do all of this twice. I do enjoy production, but lately I've been physically away from the site of production. My shows are being produced in Atlanta while I'm here in L.A. Right now, my days end somewhere around seven o'clock. If it's a school night, I try to get home in time to spend some time with my kids and put them in bed. After I put them to bed, if [my husband] Salim is not in town, I go right back to work to keep on top of it all. Sometimes, to be honest, I am so exhausted that I just fall asleep. If my husband is in town, we take a moment to connect, so that our marriage doesn't fall by the wayside.

Working with my husband, it's important that we compartmentalize our lives so that work doesn't take over. If I'm on a work call on the way home, I'll sit in the driveway and finish that call. I won't enter the house on my phone doing business. When I cross the threshold of my home, I'm no longer the showrunner. I'm mommy. It has been important learning how to let go, to trust that the people I hired have my back so I can replenish my real life. Disconnecting also helps me replenish creatively.

That's a very intensive schedule. Do you keep it up all year long, or do you have periods of downtime?

It's most intense during production, because that's when you have to deal with all departments. At that point, every department is fully staffed. You're managing 150 crew members. You're managing the managers [the department heads]. You're managing the network's involvement. Production weeks, from prep until we wrap, were almost year-round this year [2014–15] because I have two shows, ten episodes apiece. We were on production for *Being Mary Jane* from mid-February until June 6 [2015]. However, right before, I was working on *The Game* (2006–15), which wrapped up December 6 [2014], but the writers' room started in June of that year. From June until December, we were working intensely. Because it was the series finale [of *The Game*], it just required more work. I was working that schedule year-round. Now that *Being Mary Jane* has wrapped, I'm currently editing and mixing the show. When it becomes lighter, of course, you don't relax. You add more to your plate. You start thinking, what's next? What else are we developing?

When you became a showrunner, what was the most remarkable difference from your work as a writer? How did your creative life change?

The biggest difference people don't talk much about is how, in the world of television, you enter showrunning through the writing. You have made your mark writing as part of this fantastic team. They're your posse. Once you transition to showrunning, it becomes a little odd. You're still technically one of the pack but you're not. You can laugh with your writers, but you're no longer part of the group. Now, you're the manager. You have to tell people what to do. You're the employer who decides whether they eat or not and when. It changes the chemistry even though you're basically peers. It was one of the first things I had to negotiate and manage right away. For instance, there are times when me being in a room is disruptive, not beneficial. It's like parenting. You tell your kid, this is the lesson, and you walk through it a couple of times. Then they're at a play date at someone else's house and the parent tells you, "Your kid does this and that great thing." You're like, my god, they never do that when *I'm* around! But when they're away from me, they're perfect at it. Sometimes this happens in the writers' room. I can't be part of the minutiae of the script. I created the overall world and the environment, but they have to go build it. I've got to let them do that and keep my eye on the entire thing.

The second difference between being a writer and being a showrunner is realizing that there are many people—not just the writers—whom I've got to manage to keep this ship moving. And it involves a very intentional approach. You have to be a bit of a politician. Like I mentioned earlier, you have to figure out how to communicate to different constituencies in a way that's meaningful to them even if your objective is always the same. I've discovered that my secret weapon is the script. The one thing that keeps people excited and motivated on all levels is a good script, a good story. Down to the audience who keeps watching, it has to be a good story with compelling characters. And it can't be just the one script; they *all* have to be great.

As a showrunner, what is the ideal environment in your writers' room? What do you strive for?

Honest communication. I think that's why I prefer comedy over drama. I was raised in a comedy room. What I love about it is that nothing is forbidden, even if it never makes it into the script. The vulnerability of comedy allows you access to some of the darkest parts of our humanity. It's about putting your stuff out there, making yourself vulnerable, and being honest. You can't be PC [politically correct] because we're not PC people. I want to get to the truth, even if it's uncomfortable. Ideally I want my writers' room to be a space where people can feel confident and safe to get at that truth, so we can get it onto the page and hold onto it until the show reaches the audience.

Do you think that some writers see the environment as more open than others? For example, are race and gender ever factors in the room that affect how the writers interact?

Great questions. In my writers' room, you will typically find an even split between male and female writers. You will find various religious beliefs. You will find diversity in sexual orientation. You will find writers from different class backgrounds. Some have come from affluence. Some have come from poor backgrounds. Honestly, we're all living in this world together, so how can only one of those experiences come to dominate the writers' room? It's that diversity that makes up the core truth about what it is to be American. There can be specificity, like telling stories from the perspective of a black female American. Yet there are still universal elements if you tell the story right. Getting to that truth requires input from a lot of different people with different experiences with regard to whatever subject we're discussing. So how do you get there? That's part of my job as showrunner: to provide a genuine, safe environment to get people to give you the truth. You have to create that environment. It's also part of my job to know that if I can't do it, I need to hire somebody who's good at doing it, to help put together a great team of diverse people.

You actually set out to achieve diversity on your staff? When you set out to hire your team, you aim to establish a diverse room? That's at odds with what we've heard elsewhere. We've heard folks at the Writers Guild and Directors Guild say that they regularly struggle with producers who say, "I only want to hire the best. I only want to hire people I trust. I don't want to take a risk on an unknown just because it's good for diversity. There's too much at stake."

Right. I'm running for the board of the WGA, and increasing diversity is a key issue for me. The WGA has the power to change this within its own ranks. We don't need networks or studios to help us make a difference. I want to say to my peers, "You better catch up because soon you're not going connect with any audience." The audience does not care only about the world of white men. They're just not buying it anymore. In fact, I think there's waning interest in a solely American worldview. We live in a global society, and we are dependent on those global connections for financial solvency. So I would love for people to be more inclusive just for the kumbaya of it, but if you take a closer look at what's happening right now, it's simply good business, too.

Let's say you have a show with an all-white, all-male cast. How do you make five white male lead characters different and interesting? Maybe you give one of them a different class background. Maybe he's from a poor family and the other characters are rich. Why is he living in this world? Now, he's more interesting. Audiences want to know more about him. But we can make it even more interesting. Why don't you write a black woman into the show for one of the white male characters to bump heads with, for them to have conflict, for them—through that conflict—to find some deeper social truth. One of the core relationships in *The Game* is between Tasha Mack and Kelly Pitts, a black woman and a white woman, who initially didn't like each other. We built their relationship around racial stereotypes. They were always flinging disparaging remarks at each other. We got comedy from that. But it was intentional. I knew the conflict would allow them to go through that experience, develop as characters, and emerge on the other side as friends. And that is far more interesting. I've shown you how you can be friends, how you can get past differences and discover what you have in common.

These are complicated issues. On the one hand, some folks talk about "color-blind" hiring practices, where producers say they want only the best writers who are at the top of their game regardless of what they look like. We all recognize this aspiration for excellence. Yet we also know that some writers are given opportunities to train and develop and prove their excellence more than others; it's not an innocent meritocracy.

On the other hand, we argue that diversity makes both social and economic sense. That we have a social responsibility to improve diversity in front of and behind the camera, and market calculations support that goal. Do you think those things are incompatible?

The point I'm making here is that the problem is an institutional one. We're fighting against an institutionalized form of racism that champions excellence but implicitly defines that excellence as white and male. This excludes a large number of writers from ever getting an opportunity to work in the first place, and that puts an entire community of writers at a severe disadvantage. This is the world we live and work in. I know excellent writers who are women, who are minorities. So, I start with them. Once I hire them, I bring in other writers, some of them white and male. I try to mix it up, and then I say to all of them: "The first thing we all have to do is get over this assumption that you are 'less than' if you're not white or male." My room does not endorse that brand of excellence.

They may disagree with me. They may fully embrace the limited ways in which excellence has been branded in this industry, but what they can't deny is that the audience doesn't buy it anymore. They are changing. They don't give a shit about your [white, male] world all the time. In fact, there's already such a large library of content about that world, audiences can simply go seek it out if that's all they want to watch. What we are missing are the other stories. If you see yourself once, you only want more. So we—the storytellers, the creatives, the executives—do need to be more inclusive. If we don't act soon, audiences will find it somewhere else. You can already see it happening on social media. Audiences that have been on the periphery are saying, "Hey, I'll go somewhere else and see myself, even if that means me taking a selfie and putting it on Instagram. I am going to see myself. And I won't watch what you're serving me anymore. It's far better for me to sit up in my room and YouTube how funny and interesting I am before I am going to go watch your show."

People are no longer interested in seeing themselves excluded. They want to be included. If you include them, they will come to the party. I think we're starting to see that through the shows that are becoming successful. If you look at the core of why they're successful, it's that they're telling different stories. And there are audiences out there to sustain them. If you don't start recognizing that, you'll weed yourself out of this business.

So you feel that studio executives or showrunners are feeling more pressure to diversify writing staffs in part because of the new viewing options that audiences have?

Technology has made it possible for people who don't find themselves on any of the traditional media to just make up or seek out their own stories on newer platforms. You can create your own world if no one else is including you in theirs. It's becoming easy to make movies on an iPhone. I'm not saying that it's going to wipe out television, but it does encourage television to better consider how it's going to draw a massive audience to its expensive platform. You can't just assume that it will happen. You have to be more inclusive and tell more interesting stories. And that requires different points of view and voices.

A 2012 story in the Hollywood Reporter about you and your husband [producer Salim Akil] opens with a paragraph that says, "They're black, Muslim, and gorgeous in an industry not known for its diverse embrace."[1] It seems curious that they mention your religion in the header and never talk about it again in the article. And we don't see many references to your faith in other media reports. Do you think your faith plays a key role in your worldview as a showrunner and writer?

Of course it does! It's a part of who I am and how I treat people. You can call me a Muslim. I also live the life of "do unto others as you would have them do unto you." Knowledge, beauty, excellence: all these things are also part of my religion. Islam is inclusive. Right now, it's not depicted that way. But you're not Muslim if you're killing people. And you're not Christian if you're killing people. Interestingly, though, I have yet to bring any of these issues into any of my characters.

Is there a reason for that? Of the episodes we've seen, we didn't notice any particularly significant religious threads. Or are they there, and we are missing something?

I do think about it. You'll see most of my characters have been depicted as Christians of some sort. While we don't talk about religion, we do talk about faith if you look closely. It's more about faith and spirituality. We bring it up because those issues are very true to so many of us. I find that our culture is secular. Religion is secondary. So, I'm trying to use themes of faith or religion within more secular storytelling. When I do decide to address my religion more explicitly, I want it to be very special because it's special to me. And you have to be careful with it.

Faith is such a central part of many people's lives, yet by and large religion is emptied out of our entertainment media. Do you think that will change?

Yes, I do. I think it's already changing. As storytelling has become more niche and more specific, those details matter. One of the reasons why I personally have not done it yet is because it's 2015, but I open my window and it still looks like it's 1964. Authorities are killing black people. They're hosing them down in the streets. So, right now, I am focused on painting the humanity of a black person. I want to create that image so audiences understand what it looks like. It's been a struggle to really, fully take that on, and we have a lot of work to do. But we're doing it. I have to take my time and allow the audience to catch up to ensure a productive dialogue. I'm not quite ready to take on being black and Muslim.

You have written or run shows for both broadcast and cable networks. Do you see differences between them?

There is tremendous excitement in cable because there is so much creativity in that space right now. Cable channels want to make some noise and put themselves on the map. There is opportunity for bold ideas. But not so great in cable are the budgets. There are lots of cost-saving mechanisms to confront. For instance, you may find your production happening in one city and your writers' room in another. One of my fears in this model is that the writers and the show's creator are getting further and further away from the content. You need to be close to the work so you can tweak it as the process unfolds. You can control the quality.

Stacking scripts [writing multiple scripts to film at once] is another mechanism I've encountered. It just makes the process that much more difficult to manage. It's harder to ensure quality execution when you're no longer shooting one but three episodes in a week. It also takes a toll on personal lives. If you go with the production, you're going to miss your family. You can only keep it up so long and still get the best out of people. And overall, writers are getting paid less because the episode orders are becoming smaller. When writers are more worried about being broke than about creating the story, then the project is going to suffer. Those are the downsides.

Broadcast has a much more finely tuned process with the benefit of quality control: the writers come in six or seven weeks before production, and they continue to work while the production is going. You're in much closer physical proximity to the work because so much broadcast content is filmed in a studio. That allows showrunners or producers to keep an eye on it and make sure everything is working well. Maybe the creativity suffers a little because you're focused on appealing to a much larger audience. Are we watering down the story so much that nobody watches?

You just mentioned the dispersal of production to other cities as a growing concern. We wanted to ask you about it. For example, when you started producing **The Game** *for the CW, it was based in Los Angeles. When you switched to BET, the series went to Atlanta. Tell us about that change.*

It was an interesting process. We did five seasons. Each season was a different episode order. We were cancelled in 2009. We premiered again in 2011. Being off air for two years meant that all of the sets and other assets had been destroyed. Our budget was lower, so we couldn't bring any of the writers with us to Atlanta. Comedy needs comedy writers nearby. You need the constant punch up. It's easy to do in Los Angeles when the writers are on set. But we lost that asset in Atlanta. We prepared for it. We knew we couldn't afford to bring them so we decided early on to change the tone of the show in order to better manage quality. We wanted it to be a little more dramatic and a little less funny. It's just easier to control.

Another reason we moved away from the comedy elements was because my husband and our producing partner Kenny Smith decided to cross-board all thirteen episodes. It was completely crazy, and likely unprecedented. But we needed to do it as a cost-savings measure. We needed to do it to get the show on the air. Ultimately it means your actors may film a scene from episode one the same day they film a scene from episode thirteen. You can imagine how difficult it is to keep the story straight when you film in that way. It's not fair. It's not right. And it's certainly not conducive to comedy when you need to see how the jokes land within an episode so you can punch up what needs it.

It was barely manageable, but we knew we had to do it for the show. What we lacked in money we made up for in our labor and creativity. And I could not have asked for a better cast. They were stellar. They took the heat because they're veterans. They loved the show, and they were committed to it. It was absolutely crazy, though. I want to tip my hat to both Salim and Kenny, who managed that on the ground. I helped manage it from afar.

That's an amazing story. Did the scale of resources differ between the CW and BET? What was the difference in cost per episode between the two?

To be very candid with you: I don't know. When I worked in broadcast television, I always knew my budget and how to manage it. When I started to deal with BET—and maybe it was a learning curve for them—they gave me an ideal number within which they wanted me to work, but there always was this idea that we were over budget. I'm like, well, where is the budget? It never appeared. In fact, I told them it was better to shut down the show and get the numbers right because we were hemorrhaging money. I knew we were spending more than what was needed. I'm not trying to throw BET under the bus. I'm only saying that the cost savings you get from the tax incentive in Georgia and cross-boarding episodes doesn't negate the way in which you make a television series. There's a way to do it: you put in more money up front so you can manage your budget once the train starts rolling. Without knowing what you have to spend, you can't prioritize. You end up spending more money because you can't make strategic decisions.

So, I can't accurately answer your question because I never saw a final budget from BET. What I can tell you is that whereas we had about $1.2 million for each episode at the CW, BET wanted us to do it for about $800,000 an episode. It was an impossible number.

Being Mary Jane *started its first year in Georgia. Did you encounter different challenges? Was it easier to produce at a distance because it's a drama?*

I think we learned from the experience on *The Game*. We also benefited from building the series from the ground up in Atlanta. And, yes, I think it's a bit easier to hold onto the creative aspects from a distance when you're not doing comedy. We ended up doing something I don't recommend: we cross-boarded the first season to get it on the air. Because there was this idea that if you stacked eight scripts and then shot them out of order like scenes for a movie, it would save money. But having done it, I don't think that's the case. Now, we just cross-board two episodes. It's more manageable. Ideally you should do one episode a week but no more than two: one director cross-boards two scripts.

My battle was always getting enough money to do the show, but that's not unique to me or to this show. Every producer across every genre and every outlet is going to fight for more money while the studio will always fight to give you less.

But the advantage will always be to do it in Los Angeles. It just gives you more quality control. If you want a great show, you need to have the showrunner and the writers close to production.

So the center of the industry in your mind is still Los Angeles?

You see some locations establishing a crew base there, but we're still flying our department heads from L.A. into Atlanta. Top talent is still based here. And the best of the best in Atlanta or New Orleans are hired quickly. If your production isn't first in line, you miss out. It's challenging.

There's so much talk about motion picture production being dispersed around the country and even the world, but you're suggesting that the critical element—talent and your connection to it—is still rooted in Southern California.

Yes. I want to end by saying this. We're people. We're creative people. We're not robots. There's so much said about runaway production from a cost-savings perspective that we tend to forget that it's actually hurting people. It's tough to manage your relationship with your husband and children when you're in Atlanta and they are in Los Angeles. People do it because they have to work. But I don't know that we're getting the best out of people when they're distracted by these other stressors from shooting out of state.

I get it, some things have to be shot out of state, but you've got to provide a situation whereby people can stay replenished. Replenishment will be different for everybody. For some of us, it may have to do with our family time. That won't be it for everyone. But the idea of replenishing people is about making sure you're doing what you can to get the best out of them. I worry we are losing the ability to get the best out of people. If I'm worried about my kids because I'm so far away from them, I am a distracted employee. Or someone says, "I can do one season. I cannot do two, three, or four." You spend all that time building up a crew and generating chemistry only to have it ruptured every time someone leaves. Of course, people think that you can just replace that person. But finding talent is hard. It's not like replacing parts in a machine.

NOTE

1. Kim Masters, "Hollywood's Undercover Hitmakers," *Hollywood Reporter*, August 9, 2012, http://www.hollywoodreporter.com/news/sparkle-whitney-houston-salim-mara-brock-akil-359947.

4

Tom Schulman, screenwriter

In 1990, Tom Schulman won the Oscar for Best Screenplay for *Dead Poets Society* (1989). He has been a member of the Writers Guild of America, West, since 1986, and served as its vice president from 2009 to 2011. In this conversation, he discusses many of the issues that affect film and television writers, such as licensing, digital disruption, and media conglomeration.

How have things changed for writers over the past thirty years? Do the same issues keep coming back, or do you face new ones? Let's focus on film.

We were looking at a struggling movie industry until the mid-1980s, when suddenly home video cassettes started to provide a lot more revenue to the studios. DVDs came along, and by the late 1990s the studios were much more profitable. But then the DVD market started declining in the early 2000s because of the growing availability of online content. No one has figured out how to monetize the Internet and replace that income stream.

At the same time as we were experiencing these technological changes, the industry was undergoing significant regulatory changes. It was the end of "fin-syn" [the financial interest and syndication rules], and companies were able to buy up assets with which they had previously had to compete. So the same corporation suddenly owned a TV network, multiple movie studios, several cable channels, a distribution arm for DVDs, et cetera. For writers, our relationship with the studios has fundamentally changed as a consequence. Our opportunities have diminished. Studios just don't develop as many projects anymore. In the late 1980s and early

1990s, when I started, the studios developed ten projects for every one they made. Now it's more like two or three to one.

I also noticed another significant consequence: the studio executive mindset has shifted from a "creative" to a marketing-driven perspective. When I started, executives would make a movie, then turn to the marketing people and say, "Go sell it," and the marketing people would snap to attention and do it. Starting in the mid-1990s many of the creative studio heads were replaced by marketing executives or at least by executives with a marketing mindset. The mandate changed from making good movies, to making movies that were marketable across multiple platforms or distribution outlets, to making movies that could be exploited by all of the conglomerate's subdivisions. They wanted to green-light movies that could then go on to be TV series, video games, toys, and theme park rides.

Because of new production technologies, studios also turned away from character-driven, story-driven movies to movies that emphasize special effects. But the cost was astronomical! When I started in the mid-1980s, the average feature cost $17 to $20 million; now it's maybe $150 million. And marketing costs on the average movie went from about $12 million to somewhere between $35 and $70 million. Those costs motivate studios to green-light projects with presold audiences. They prefer movies adapted from successful comic books, young adult novels, plays, or TV series because they know, or think they know, an audience for their movie is out there. They are less interested in original screenplays because they have no proven audience.

We've also moved away from a market that was mostly American. When I started working, about 60 percent of the worldwide box office revenues came from the United States and Canada. Now it's 30 percent domestic, 70 percent foreign. Catering to the imagined tastes of a global audience changes the content of movies. Action and special effects are considered an international language and do better at the foreign box office than comedies and character-driven dramas with lots of cultural specificity. Speaking from a writer's perspective, where character and dialogue are of more interest, it creates a challenge. The reality today is that movies based on original screenplays are an endangered species.

So how do you survive?

Some screenwriters aren't surviving. I'm sixty-two. It's shocking how many of my contemporaries aren't working or haven't worked in a while. The number of working screenwriters has been decreasing by about 17 percent a year since the writers' strike [in 2007–8]. I don't see those jobs coming back. Studios are making 175 movies a year now. Seven years ago they were making 320. When I started they were making 400 to 600 movies a year. It's been a slow but steady decline. Screenwriter earnings also have declined precipitously. Many are now struggling to find independent financing because we can't count on the studios anymore.

I know WGA screenwriters who are trying to get projects going on the Internet. But they are competing with filmmakers who are fresh out of graduate school, using their parents' money or credit cards to make movies for $75,000, $50,000, or less. On the creative side, it's spurred a lot of people to buy or rent a digital camera and start making a low-budget feature and direct it themselves. But it's hard to support a family that way.

Are studios still entertaining original pitches?

The last meeting I had at Fox was with an executive who said, "You know, I'm hoping that within a year or two we'll start taking pitches of originals again. We're running out of stuff to remake."

The studios want a movie that is franchise-able. And now that word means more than just a property with the potential for sequels, prequels, and spin-offs. The studios want to integrate franchises into franchises. Take *Pirates of the Caribbean*. Among other companies, Disney partnered with Maybelline to advertise a line of cosmetics using the actresses in the movie. So Maybelline builds a *Pirates* line of cosmetics and they do a $5 million or $10 million print ad campaign simultaneous with the release of the film. The movie advertising helps Maybelline, Maybelline's print advertising helps Disney. That's the kind of movie the studios are looking to make.

Dead Poets Society and similar originals are not going to be on the studio wish list because that kind of synergistic marketing isn't possible or appropriate. A lot of people think, "Fine, I'll write a movie that can have five sequels," but they don't ask, "Can McDonald's find a hook, can Maybelline find a hook, can a car company find a hook?" The studios are looking for that kind of multi-market exploitability in every concept.

Do you feel like notions of creative authority have changed during the growth of conglomerate media?

Yes. They've added layers of middle management. I first saw it at Disney. When I started writing for them, Jeffrey Katzenberg and Michael Eisner made all decisions, period. Once those two decided something, that was it. I would write a script, turn it in in the afternoon, and at six o'clock the next morning, I'd get a phone call from Jeffrey and we'd talk about it. The lines of authority were clear.

Then Disney decided to expand the company so that Jeffery became an über-boss over Touchstone Pictures, Hollywood Pictures, Buena Vista, Marvel Studios, Lucasfilm, the animated films—all the subdivisions. He turned over all the day-to-day decision making at each of those divisions to other executives and became much less accessible, though he was still the boss. That added layers of management—often it's really good management, mind you—but it made the creative process more team-oriented and it denied writers access to the real decision makers.

At all the studios, you've got middle-level executives who say to a writer, "I know what my boss is going to like. You've got to make these script changes because if you don't, he'll reject this." So you revise and possibly butcher your own work before it even gets to the boss, at which point the boss often passes anyway. The writer has no choice but to comply because he or she's being overseen by a middle-level executive who is saying, "I won't show my boss your script unless you make the changes I suggest."

Most producers are not under contract at a studio anymore. Every studio used to have fifteen or twenty producers with deals there—not anymore. And those producers served an important function. They were the writers' partners; they were the first people who read the writers' drafts and gave them notes. Writers often have no advocacy now and are lost in layers of middle management. It hurts the creative process.

Because movies cost so much, studios are looking to reduce their risk. So they look to equity partners and other outside investors to defray the astronomical costs of production and marketing. Foreign presales—money raised in advance of production by selling off territories based, usually, on the prior box office performance of certain stars or directors—have become a necessity at most of the studios. That biases the studios against new talent who have no proven value in foreign markets.

It's all understandable. You're looking at something that's going to cost $200 million to make and distribute. Investors want as much protection as they can get. But it narrows the scope of what can get made.

Do you think there's a greater willingness to look outside Hollywood for ideas, or do you need to be here to be in the game?

In the last few years there have been some successful movies and quite a few successful TV series imported from the UK. As with the movie studios, it's safer for the networks to take a shot on a TV series with proven commercial success elsewhere than betting on something original from here.

What about other parts of the United States?

You don't have to live in Hollywood, but it helps. It helps to network, find an agent, and meet producers. Once you've established yourself, you can live anywhere.

So runaway production, as it's called, doesn't affect writers much?

It does, but not as much as it hurts cast and crew. Runaway production is a bigger deal for TV writers than for movie writers. I think there are only a few series that are still shooting in Los Angeles. For a TV writer, that could mean relocating outside of Los Angeles, perhaps to Canada. The executive producer / showrunner / show creator often runs the writers' room and helps supervise the production of the show. If the production is in Vancouver, he or she has to be in Vancouver, and if he or she has to be in Vancouver, the writing staff has to be in Vancouver. So runaway production can require writers to relocate.

Are these writers still represented by the WGA?

Yes. It's almost always an American company—a Writers Guild signatory—that produces the show.

Let's talk more about television. What are the big issues facing TV writers?

Network TV shows don't rerun nearly as often as they used to. Instead, the networks run a show once on TV then almost immediately make it available on the Internet. A TV writer used to get a very large residual check when his or her show was rerun. The residual or royalty from the Internet is a fraction of the rerun payment. For example, TV writers typically write an episode of a TV series for scale (union minimum). That might be $30,000 for a half-hour comedy. Upon the first rerun they would get paid close to that amount again. If there was a second rerun they might get 80 percent of that fee again. But now most shows don't rerun. Shows go immediately to Hulu or Netflix where instead of, say, $28,000 for the first rerun, the writer will get about $400. For people who have mortgages and families, it's tough to figure out how you can earn a living when your income is suddenly cut by that much. Union minimums haven't increased enough to compensate for the loss in revenue.

There's a big influx of writers and directors into cable. But cable writers generally get paid about two thirds of what network writers make, so that's a big financial hit. Plus there are no reruns to speak of for cable, certainly not at the pay scales writers get for network reruns. If you're a cable writer, you're making two thirds the money you made as a network writer. In the next contract negotiations with the companies, the WGA will need to bring cable minimums up to the level of the network minimums. But that won't be easy. The companies would rather bring the network minimums down to the level of cable!

Are writers starting to see more compensation from digital platforms like Netflix?

Yes. We will get a piece of streaming, but there is a trade-off. What does a TV show or movie lose in DVD sales, syndication, or even network TV sales when everyone knows they can wait to see it on Netflix? Once a show has been exploited on

Netflix streaming, and Netflix is available worldwide, how do you get your foreign syndication money out of it? Maybe you don't. Someone who knows more than I do can tell you what's happening to those monies. In the old days even a middle-level television series could cash in for hundreds of millions of dollars when it sold to syndication. Sadly, those days are over.

So it's not categorical that Netflix or iTunes is the friend or enemy of writers?

I think it's too soon to know. Because we don't know to what extent these new markets will cannibalize traditional markets. Five years ago someone told me that every episode of *The Simpsons* (1989–ongoing) made $23 million for Fox. That's because in addition to their initial network broadcast they had network reruns, domestic and foreign TV syndication, DVD sales—a whole string of sources of income. I'm betting, partly because of the slowdown in DVD sales, partly because no one's figured out how to monetize the Internet, that *Simpsons* episodes aren't making that much money anymore.

What's the daily working experience like for a rank-and-file TV writer?

I was going to do a series for HBO and we worked 110-hour weeks for eight months just to produce the pilot. During that time, HBO asked us to write a couple more episodes. Writing and producing at the same time was incredibly taxing. I remember remarking during the 2007 strike that TV showrunners seemed quite willing to go on strike even in the middle of the TV season. Somebody joked that that was because they were so overworked and so desperate to get a good night's sleep!

I think this is why so many TV showrunners are in their late twenties, early thirties. I have some friends my age who are running shows and they are just zombies. They look gaunt and hollow eyed. They don't have time to shave. It's a hard job, but it can be extremely creatively and financially rewarding, particularly if your show goes into a third, fourth, or fifth season.

It sounds like at a certain point, showrunners in their twenties or thirties are going to say, "Okay, I'm done." Then what do they do?

If you're successful enough, you'll get a shot at features. Or retire.

Can you talk about Writers Guild qualifications? How are they determined?

You get points for a certain amount of work: say, for example, two points for a feature polish, six points for a rewrite, and twelve points for writing a full feature script. Twelve points qualify you to get into the guild. I started getting work doing rewrites and finally got enough points to get into the guild. Once you're in, you are in for seven years. If during that time you get another job, it gets you five more years. At a certain point—I think it's twenty years of semicontinuous work—you're a member for life. I think the average stay for a member of the guild is seven years. About 20 percent are "one and done"—they get one job and don't work again.

How big is the Writers Guild of America, West?

It has about eight thousand members. Our membership is starting to skew younger, so we'll see how that changes guild politics. As a young writer, I didn't pay much attention to our health and pension plans. Most young writers don't. I was glad to have my medical expenses covered, but I was lucky enough to be in good health, so I rarely needed it. Once I got married and had a child, I realized all our pediatric bills were being taken care of, and then one day I started looking at my pension plan and thought, gosh, I'll have a pretty decent amount of money in there for retirement! But you don't think about those things so much in your twenties or early thirties.

How do gender dynamics play out in the guild?

We are at the mercy of the hiring practices of the companies. We've put a lot of pressure on the companies to hire both women and minorities and have gotten very little out of it. Female membership has crept up from 19 percent to 26 percent, which is still, obviously, not where it should be. Minority membership isn't even as high as that.

Why do you think it's so hard?

In features, the studios hire the writers, and they hire people they know. In television, the person who hires the writing staff is the showrunner, and in the old days (even today) almost all the showrunners were white men. When they hire people they know and trust, they hire their friends—talented friends, of course—but their friends are mostly white men. I'm told some of the late-night shows are notoriously old boys' clubs. I know some women who have written for those shows and have found it difficult. These are funny, brilliant women, but it's just unpleasant for a woman to be in a room full of that much testosterone.

Don't get me wrong. Quite a few showrunners are willing to say, "Sure, bring me a woman I can hire, bring me minorities I can hire, bring me anybody good." But a lot of them say, "No, this is my show, my reputation, my living. I have to trust these people, and I'm not going to hire someone who I don't know and trust to deliver the goods."

Do you think the gender discrepancy is caused by the kinds of films that are being made?

For studio features, yes. The most popular films are action films, thrillers, or horror. It's rare to find women who actually want to write those films, or so the studios say. But women are doing quite well in comedy.

What about race?

Studios pay lip service, but there isn't much progress. If they're doing a movie about African Americans, then they may bring in an African American writer. Studios tend to believe they need to hire a writer who looks most like the desired demographic for that particular film. But Alvin Sargent is in his eighties and he wrote the last *Spider-Man* movie. So you don't have to be a member of the targeted demographic to write a good movie for them. It just tends to be the logic by which they operate.

We've spent some time tracking down recent studies on labor conditions in the industry. We assume the guild tracks this information as well. Does it make any of its studies publicly available?

No. It's all proprietary stuff, for our leadership's eyes only, because it's often used for negotiating purposes. Plus there is some fear that making these reports public can be provocative.

Provocative in what sense?

If a guild gets its members riled up about certain issues, but there's nothing it can do for them at the negotiating table, what's the point? You don't want to stir writers up and say, "Damn it, cable rates are unfair, let's do something about them," when you know that at the end of the day, the guild is not going to strike over that issue.

There's a lot of suffering in silence.

Both in silence and in ignorance. If people don't know how bad things are, they're not going to get upset. As soon as you let them know they are earning 50 percent less than what they are due, they'll say, "That's infuriating. What are we going to do about it?" The guild replies, "Well, there's not much we can do about it, because your work area, say cable, only affects 20 percent of the guild, and the other 80 percent is not going to strike over this issue. They'll sympathize with you. But they're not going to risk their livelihood for issues that don't affect them."

That was the good thing about the 2007 contract. Almost all WGA writers believed the Internet was the final resting place for content, and that the big income stream that would replace the downturn in DVDs would come from the Internet. That hasn't come to pass, but someday it will. Anyway, 90 percent of the guild—across network and cable and features—felt like it was important and the right time to get jurisdiction over the Internet. It's hard to see another unifying issue like that on the horizon.

How do you feel about the way the 2007 strike was resolved?

I wanted us to get more. For a year before our contract expired in November of 2007, we worked with the Screen Actors Guild and the Directors Guild to come up with a unified negotiating position. In the middle of that summer, the DGA told us they had completed a $1 million study that convinced them that the Internet was not going to be worth anything for six to ten years. They didn't want to do anything about the Internet in the next round of negotiations. We said, "Fine, we don't agree, but will you at least back us?" And they said, "We won't commit to that."

As we prepared to strike, we asked the DGA, whose contract didn't expire until July of 2008, "Please tell the companies you will honor our strike and not negotiate your contract until we have negotiated ours." They said no. So at that point the companies were looking right past us to a union that was signaling, in essence, "We don't care so much about these issues, so come negotiate with us!"

I believe the DGA would have started their negotiations with the companies within a month after our strike started, but our strike mobilization was so strong—we had thousands of writers on picket lines every day and all the polls showed the public was overwhelmingly with us—that it gave the DGA pause. They were afraid they would look bad. But about two months into the strike, as the strike moved off the front pages and out of the news, the DGA sent signals to the companies that they were ready to negotiate about the same issues we were striking for. So a group of forty writers who were also members of the DGA put together a petition. They called themselves "WD-40." They got more than three hundred signatures of prominent DGA members asking the DGA to please stay on the sidelines while we tried to negotiate our contract. The DGA leadership was miffed, but they stayed out of it for another few weeks.

Finally, right after the Christmas–New Year holiday break, the DGA started negotiating their next contract. They negotiated about all the issues we were striking over. That was seven months, mind you, before the expiration of their contract. I think it was unprecedented in the history of American labor. One union negotiating that early over the same terms as a striking union? Shame on them!

As we understand it, besides the differences between guilds there are also differences within them, for example divisions within the DGA: there is the feature film elite, then the television directors, and then assistant directors, and so on. From what we hear, the real power is with the elite; is that true?

I think that's correct. As one member of the DGA leadership once told me, "You guys at the Writers Guild are about minimums. We're about maximums." DGA leadership is committed to protecting the rights, real or hoped for, of their A-list directors. A lot of those rights are not exactly codified. Obviously if you're a director with final cut, then basically you have the power to do whatever you want with a movie, but you're still at the mercy of the studio, who might say, "Edit the movie however you want, but if you do things we dislike, we won't release it." Directors want absolute power over the movies they direct, so the DGA would rather give up pressure on minimums and other rank-and-file needs to protect their A-list directors. In both TV and film, the membership seems happy with that. I guess they all think one day they'll be A-list, too.

The Writers Guild, historically, has been the most politicized guild by far.

Absolutely. We've struck more times than SAG and DGA combined.

To what do you attribute that? Does it have to do with the mentality of minimums versus maximums?

I don't think so. The DGA members see themselves as the boss, as management. They don't like to look at themselves and say, "We're a union of workers." It's even hard for a lot of writers to see that. In 2006 we hired David Young as our executive director. He had a background organizing garment and construction workers. A lot of our members were upset with that choice. They said, "We're writers. This guy represented plumbers. He doesn't understand our issues." They saw us as more of a guild—with an emphasis on craft—than a union. I believe we may be a union of smart people, but we still have to use the same strategies and tactics that other unions use or we're not going to be effective in collective bargaining. I just think the DGA has always had a harder time calling themselves workers.

IATSE was originally formed by the companies. That DNA—a company union—has been with them since their beginnings, and in general they can be counted on to do whatever the companies want. SAG could be strong, but they had problems for years with AFTRA undercutting them—a sort of race to the bottom on minimums, pensions, health, and so forth. Now that SAG and AFTRA have merged, their pension and health plans are in such dire straits financially, that's going to preoccupy their collective bargaining priorities for years. And that's going to hurt the WGA and DGA because of pattern bargaining. All the concessions SAG-AFTRA get from the companies will go toward fixing their pension and health plans. The WGA and DGA pension and health plans are in much better shape than SAG-AFTRA's. What will writers get outside of a few improvements in pension and health? I fear not much.

A lot of people don't understand why the guilds can't get along. Why we can't, in some sense, have a one-union town. If you look at Detroit, like it or not, those unions were very successful negotiators for their members. When their contracts expired, the auto workers' unions united to negotiate against one auto company. In Hollywood, it's the opposite. One union at a time negotiates against all the companies.

The DGA and WGA have a long history of bashing each other over creative rights, the "film by" credit, and so on. I've done some DGA bashing myself, and I've had some of their leadership (privately) bash me. But we have so many issues in common. It's time to put our differences behind us and negotiate together for the common good of our members. Together we'd be a powerful, powerful force.

Which guild is the most polarized between elite members and the rest?

Definitely the Directors Guild. They have somehow managed to put in place a governing body that always has operated very effectively for their elite members. Half of the DGA are what Hollywood calls "below-the-line" workers: first assistant directors, second assistant directors, and so on. They are taken care of in every contract, but they don't have a lot of bargaining power within their own guild because all the "real" directors hire them.

Do showrunners complicate solidarity in the WGA in a similar way?

To a certain extent, yes. There have been some discussions about the Writers Guild having a legal weakness because we have management—aka showrunners—in our ranks. But my experience has been that the showrunners care deeply about the writers on their shows and stand in solidarity with them. After all, most showrunners started as freelance or staff writers. They've been there, and they care.

How did it work bringing in an executive director with a background outside the entertainment industry?

It was an intentional choice on our part. Before that we had an executive director who had been a chief negotiator at CBS for twenty years. That did not work out well from our perspective, so we decided to go in another direction. We thought, we are a union, let's bring in someone who knows how to organize a union. David

Young had been working in the WGA's labor organizing department for a couple of years, and he turned out to be just what we needed. During the strike, management tried to denigrate him, to convince our members that he was a glorified plumber, janitor, whatever, and that "smart people" like us shouldn't be represented by someone who only knew how to represent "illegal" workers. For people who were looking for a reason to not support the strike, that rang true.

But anybody who knows David Young knows he is a brilliant, tough, fair, highly educated guy who is more than capable of negotiating against the entertainment conglomerates. My fear is that he is going to get tired of working in what is now, in essence, more of a "guild" environment, and want to get back into an actual labor movement.

Do you have hope that the trajectory will change?

I do. I don't see how we can make progress without it. But I do think we have to get the buy-in from the other unions. Because no matter how united the Writers Guild may be, or how right or righteous we are about what our writers deserve, if the DGA is going to step in front of us and negotiate over the same terms we might be bargaining for, we're done.

5

Allison Anders, director

Allison Anders rode the independent film wave of the 1990s with such notable titles as *Gas Food Lodging* (1992). Although still an indie filmmaker, today she devotes most of her time to directing episodes for television series that range from comedies to police procedurals. Anders discusses the many changes she has seen in the motion picture industries over the last few decades and compares the challenges directors face in film versus television.

If you had to describe your work, what do you do?

I am a couple of things. I'm a writer. I write for film and television, and personal, prose-y things, too. I also, of course, direct, both film and TV. Writing is pretty self-explanatory. You know what is involved with that, but people have very strong misconceptions about directing.

I remember directing a TV episode with a TV writer who was very involved, very controlling. I asked him, "Why don't you just direct?" He said, "Oh, no. I couldn't do that. I don't know lenses, I don't know cameras, I don't know shots." And I said, "Well, I don't any of that shit either. I don't know lenses. That's for the DP [director of photography] to know." There are some directors who know that, but that's not me, and that's not the most important part of the job. When you direct, you are making creative choices. That's what a director does. Yes, I work on setting up the camera with the DP, but otherwise, directing is decision making. It's making choices on casting, on wardrobe, on makeup. It's choosing the paint on the wall. And this writer was very capable of doing exactly that, because without realizing it, he *was* making directorial choices. The following year, he directed the first episode of his own show.

The other thing that directing is about is setting up an atmosphere that is going to achieve what you want. Everybody is different here, but for me, I am going to try to set up an atmosphere of trust on the set, so the actors can give it all up. You want to make everybody feel safe, and then get the hell out of the way and let them do their jobs. Most directors are not like that, but the ones who mentored me are. You guide the process and make a lot of choices, but once you are on set, you've already made them and you trust the people who are heads of their departments to realize those choices. Otherwise, you'll drive yourself and everybody else insane because you're trying to do everybody's job.

On TV you have fewer decisions to make because your episode has to fit with the tone of the series and stay consistent. If I decide to put my thumbprint on something, it may affect later episodes. So you don't want too much of your thumbprint on the episodes you direct, which is unlike my own movies, where that's the whole point.

You started out as a filmmaker during the glory days of independent cinema during the 1980s and 1990s, and since that time you've navigated tremendous changes in the way movies are made, financed, and seen. Can you talk about that arc of change, and how it has affected your career?

It's been incredible. I started with *Border Radio* in 1987. Kurt Voss, Dean Lent, and I made that while we were still at UCLA film school. It was shot on 16mm, black-and-white reversal film, with equipment owned by UCLA. After years of struggling to finish it, we got two pieces of financing. We got a soundtrack deal that was about $10,000. Ironically that would have been crap in the 1990s, but it would be considered great today, because of the way the music business has imploded. We also got some money from German TV. The incredible thing was that German TV helped finance a lot of films at that time. They financed Jim Jarmusch's movies at the same time that we were making *Border Radio*. They had a bigger hand than people realize in the American indie film movement. By the 1990s, when I did *Gas Food Lodging*, there was another important source of financing, which was Larry Estes. We couldn't have existed without this man. He had a program at RCA Columbia that was phenomenal. He green-lit *Sex, Lies, and Videotape* (1989). He green-lit *One False Move* (1992). He was a real champion of the emerging American independent film movement before we even had such a name.

During the 1990s, we had a lot of things in place that are no longer in place. We had had critics whose opinions mattered, so if they championed your film, people went to see it. We had theaters that allowed you to play your film for a while so that you could build word of mouth. We had audiences who went to theaters to see the movies that we were making. And we had actors who were interested in doing something different. Now all of that is pretty much gone. That kind of support system doesn't exist.

Are you saying that today people like Estes aren't in the business anymore? That indie directors no longer have one or two people who can turn the key and make everything else happen?

I don't think there is anybody like that now. There are some people who have survived all of this. Like Andrea Sperling, who produced Gregg Araki's movies and then went on to produce other young, independent filmmakers. She has managed to stay in there and continues to find financing for independent projects with great success. But these films are being made for a whole lot less than what we had back in the day. Today a film like *Gas Food Lodging* would need A-list casting attached to all the major roles, which we didn't need back then, and the director would get maybe $500,000 to make it as opposed to $1 million.

By comparison, how does a film get made today? Do you put together the financing and shop it around at festivals?

Well, yes, but the problem is the rights that they want in exchange for the financing that they give you. When Larry Estes green-lit our movies, all he wanted was the video rights. When HBO green-lit *Mi Vida Loca* (1993), all they wanted was the right to air it on HBO and the video. They didn't want the theatrical. They didn't want distribution rights for the entire world in perpetuity. They just wanted a slice that mattered to them, and they didn't care what we did in other distribution windows. We were on our own for that. Now, investors want everything they can get. They expect to get everything back. They also expect everybody to defer salaries and have skimpy budgets for their departments. It's really harsh. It's a harsh reality.

During the 1990s, there was just enough money to be made in the video rights that things were a little bit softer to negotiate. Likewise with the soundtracks. You could make such amazing deals on your music because in the 1990s that was a huge business. The soundtrack could actually make a lot of money. The soundtrack deal could cover the cost of rights for songs you wanted to use in your film.

When did things start to change and tighten up?

Right around the millennium, when the music business failed and people could start downloading movies. When people stopped going to the movies and stopped buying music, we had a real problem. At the same time, magazines and newspapers started having problems, so we lost critics, too. We lost everything that was supporting the indie movement. Creatively, we also had a shift, as digital cameras became available. I was one of the first people to shoot entirely on digital and go to Sundance with *Things Behind the Sun* (2001). It was great, but there are problems with that, too. We were the last generation to shoot on film, cut on film, and screen on film. I haven't worked on film since *Sugar Town* (1999).

So career-wise, you began to turn to television. Why did that become an important or viable option?

In the 1990s there had been some talk about me doing an episode of *ER* (1994–2009). I was terrified. I didn't know what TV was, didn't know the first thing about it. In the end, it didn't happen, but it was the first time I started to have a conversation about it. Later I met with the people from *Sex and the City* (1998–2004). I was already a fan of the show, and the producers said they loved my movies, so it was exciting. They wanted to get that "Allison Anders thing" in there. But it was a little harsh, because I came to it with the experience of writing and directing my own stuff. When I direct a movie, it's 100 percent my vision. People can give input and I can listen or not, but I make every single decision. When I began to prep an episode for *Sex and the City*, all of the things that make up the "Allison Anders thing" were already decided. The cast was in place, as was the look of the show, the characters' backstories, the type of music they listen to.

All these things had been decided. I was petrified. If all of this is in place, how am I supposed to give them the Allison Anders thing? The decisions are what create that thing. So I assumed the attitude that this is not my baby—and I still feel this way about directing episodic TV. I am just the foster mother, and I am going to nurture this along for the brief time that it is in my hands. I will hopefully impart a little something of myself, my experience, and my love. Then I'm going to pass it along to the next foster home. I don't want to leave too much of myself there, but there will be a little bit. There is one scene where Sarah Jessica Parker throws a Big Mac against the wall at Mr. Big, and people say, that was definitely yours. There was a rawness to it. There's always one scene where I can say, that's mine.

What's the most important aspect of working as a director in episodic TV?

It's working with the actors, for sure. In the worst of shows, there are a bunch of producers all fighting with each other. They say, I don't like the thing the actress is doing with her mouth. Or, that scene is tedious. So they deliver notes [that suggest changes]. That's the dark side of the job. On the best shows, that doesn't happen. Nobody is breathing down your neck, but it's still somebody else's show. Your job is to work with the DP and the editor and the crew. You get your cut, but ultimately you're going to be recut by your showrunner—and that is as it should be. You're trying to keep things in character with the way you understand the series, so you don't have complete freedom. The actors can't do something totally outside of what they've done up until this point. They have to keep consistent. Generally the day before you start shooting, you have what they call a "tone meeting." You go through page by page, scene by scene, with the showrunner and sometimes with the writer, the DP, or the editor. We're all trying to get in sync with what the tone is supposed to be in each scene. If there's something special that they want or don't want, that's the time to address it. It should be pretty clear what you're supposed to be delivering based on that tone meeting. I always take those notes with me to set.

Are you doing episodic to pay the bills? It sounds so different from what you were doing before.

It started out to pay the bills and to keep myself afloat, but now the beauty is that there are a couple of shows that I've enjoyed working on, and it's become a home base. One was *Southland* (2009–13). The other has been *Murder in the First* (2014–16). It's funny that I ended up enjoying working on cop shows, because you wouldn't think that by looking at my independent film work. But I find more freedom there than anywhere else. I think the genre must play some hand in it. For example, the way they shot on *Southland* was more guerilla than I ever worked before, more guerilla than *Border Radio*. They created this show that was, in their minds, a fictional version of *Cops* (1989–ongoing), so they could just shoot out in the streets and, if people looked at the camera, that's fine. People are always looking at cops and wondering what they are doing. It was an amazing freedom. We shot in the streets a lot. We were out there with the Steadicam the whole time. There was one little monitor on a C-stand for me, and the script supervisor, and that was it. It was an interesting way to work. And you have all these great professionals working with you, especially the stunt people.

When I got the first script that I was supposed to direct for *Southland*, it had a big car chase that ends up hitting this woman. I told [showrunner] Chris Chulack that I'd never done a car chase in my life. He said, "That's okay, I'm going to teach you how to do it." It was fantastic. I know how to do that now. That's why I consider Chris my TV mentor. So I don't know how people are learning anything new if they are not directing episodic. First of all, I don't know how they are making a living. And I don't know how they are keeping their chops because the technology is changing so fast every day. TV keeps you up to date. You wouldn't know what's happening out there otherwise.

Then there is the third hat you wear, which is the TV movie hat. Can you talk about that? How do you feel about directing TV movies compared to other parts of your career?

I've done two. First, *A Crush on You* (2011), a Hallmark movie. It was made for a very low-budget company and then sold to Hallmark. It was financed by a guy I never met, but he cuts everything and does all the casting himself—it's a weird situation. I was in a bind and I needed to work. But all those decisions were done. I just went and worked with the actors and a fantastic crew. Great little cast and crew. It was a great experience. But it wasn't the greatest movie. It's probably not something I'd put in my body of work because there is virtually nothing of me in it. Then there is *Ring of Fire* (2013). It was written by Richard Friedenberg, who had been my advisor at Sundance on *Mi Vida Loca* (1993). It was a beautiful script. And it was just so—I hate to say it—in my wheelhouse. That phrase is so overused right now, but it fits in this case. The movie drew on so much that I knew intimately.

It all started because Lisa Hamilton Daly was hired at Lifetime to up their game a bit in terms of their TV movies. They wanted to bring in good directors and make prestigious work. This project came along and, thank god, they wanted me. When I went in to meet with them, I said, "Normally, I would not be so arrogant as to say I'm the right person, but I am the right person for this job. I already know about these characters because I was attached to direct a movie about them before." They were so great to not force any casting on me. They had already been in talks with Jewel to play June Carter, but even then, they asked me what I thought about the idea. They were so conscientious about the director's vision. The music supervisor went out on a limb for me so I could use Joe Henry as the producer of the early tracks. I knew he would get that authentic sound, but he had to do the music here in Los Angeles. They had a tax break in Atlanta, so it meant they wouldn't get the tax break on those tracks. But they still did it for me.

So I absolutely feel that *Ring of Fire* is part of my movie directing career. And there is some episodic directing that I would include as well. Anything I did on *Southland*, on *Murder in the First*, even *Orange Is the New Black* (2013–ongoing). Those episodes feel like me to me. If I looked at that stuff twenty years from now, I would say, that's mine.

To turn to some day-to-day issues you face as a director, let's start with productions being spread across the country, and even around the world. How does that affect your career?

I would love to always be working in L.A. It doesn't get any better, there is no question about it. You have better crews in L.A. We are set up for the greatest efficiency in the world for movie and TV production. There is a certain fluidity to getting around, moving your trucks and setting up locations. To move. You cannot replace Los Angeles for that. And working on studio back lots makes me think it was a stroke of genius for these early filmmakers and moguls to put this shit together. It is the most efficient, glorious way to work. Not to mention the prop houses and the costume houses and so forth.

Having said that, the next place you want to go is New York, because they have efficient crews there, too, although not as efficient as Los Angeles. However, it's difficult to get around. You don't have the same kind of fluidity. Actually, I think Vancouver is more akin to L.A. in terms of moving from one location to the next. If you have to move from the stage to a location and back again, you're screwed in New York if you're inside the city. They do have good stages, though. *Sex and the City* was shot at Silver Cup in Queens. *Orange Is the New Black* is shot out in Orangeburg in this abandoned mental hospital. That was a little bit easier. But in Vancouver, you can get around easily.

Then you have the weather issues. Shooting in Toronto in the winter, what a nightmare! Your day is so short. I love working in Atlanta. Crews are getting a lot better, but I felt bad for my department heads. The crew base there isn't strong yet. But what you do get in those southern states is the most phenomenal pool of actors. Fantastic actors that you can take from Georgia, Louisiana, Tennessee, the Carolinas. They all consider that local hire. That was a real gift.

And there are the tax advantages for productions, you can't deny that, but overall you don't do any better than shooting in L.A.

If you're shooting an hour-long drama outside L.A., how long are you away?

Believe it or not, three weeks total. So you're prepping five or six days, shooting six or seven days, and then you've got your three days of editing. You're done in three weeks. It's kind of beautiful.

How long are your working days?

On prep, it varies. Maybe one day you've got half a day, one day you've got a twelve-hour day. Generally the days are lighter during prep. You find that your concept meeting, your production meeting, and your tone meeting may take up a good deal of time. Casting takes time, but sometimes you do your casting online. A lot of people don't like that, but it doesn't bother me. I like to watch the actors on tape, and I like to have discussions about it through email. So that's what you're doing in prep. Then during principal photography, those are twelve-hour days, generally. If I'm over twelve hours, something is terribly wrong. There's an efficiency problem somewhere along the line. These are always five-day shoots, so you have the weekend. I've never worked on a show where you shot six days. Then you go to editing. A lot of times the editing is done online as well. You see the cut and you give the notes. Half the time I'll go in, but if I don't have time, sending notes and looking at the cuts online is fine with me.

As a director, what are the big challenges? Do you feel like the pressures are exorbitant, or are they pretty well managed?

To be perfectly frank, I think the hardest part is never knowing what you're walking into. I'm booked for two episodes of this new show and I have no idea what is going to be in that script, but I am going to have to deliver it. I would never do a movie where I didn't read the script and care about it ahead of time. You never know if there is going to be something offensive in the script, yet you still have to direct and shoot it. In those situations, you can make certain choices, which I always do, not to be gratuitous. But you're not going to know any of that until you're already booked to go or on your way there. Granted, by that time, you've already seen the show or read previous scripts of the show.

The other big challenge is if there are too many people giving too many opinions on the set. This is a problem that arose out of the Writers Guild giving producer credit to TV writers. That means a writer can tell you how to direct the scene. They might not know anything about directing, yet they are telling you what the hell to do. It's a drag. It's especially a problem with less-experienced writers. Imagine they've been in the writers' room all year long. They are overworked in there. They are all vying for the showrunner's attention. They all want their ideas to become the script. Their work is rewritten so much that by the time they get to your set, they are so possessive about it. And then they are sitting in front of the monitors and they have no fucking idea what they are looking at.

This is a typical baby writer I'm describing. They don't know that we're not getting everything in this one take. Maybe you're just shooting part of the beat and they are suddenly flushing with panic because they're not seeing the whole thing—but that's going to be shot in the next setup. They don't know how it all fits together, and I don't have time to teach them how this all comes together in the editing room. What we're getting are pieces and it's all going to be cut together later. I can't go through that whole process with somebody who's been cooped up for a year and is finally getting to be on set. That's the worst.

Let's get to an issue that has come up in a number of our other interviews: gender dynamics. During your career, have you seen things change for better or worse? What are the gender issues that the industry needs to address?

In terms of hiring, there is no question that things are getting better now. Only three years ago I got a job because they realized, we've never hired many women on this show. On some shows, they hadn't even thought about it. On other shows, of course it's a mandate: *Orange Is the New Black*, *Sex and the City*. I don't think there was a woman director around at the time that hadn't done an episode of *Sex and the City*.

I know of a Tumblr site called "Shit People Say to Women Directors." I look at that and think, I don't know who you're working with, but I have never encountered this stuff in my life. Very seldom have I encountered a kind of boys' club mentality where they've dismissed me because I'm a woman. It has happened a couple of times, but it was years ago with old-school guys. But these guys I work with on *Murder in the First* are feminists. An example is, one of the characters is getting ready for a date. We've never seen her dress like this before. She has on these amazing black leather hot pants, high heels, really done up. They wanted to do the sort of male gaze, tilt the camera up and down her body. I said, "Guys, I hate to use the F-word [feminist] and say this is maybe male gaze-y, but can we just do something different?" They all laughed and said they got it. Maybe I should have gotten that shot, too, but I'm glad I didn't. That's a good example of where they were all right with going with my direction.

This conforms with what we've heard in other contexts. People say that the tone is very much set by the director or whoever is in charge on set. Gender dynamics are signaled by someone at the top and then get picked up on by the crew. It can range from what you just described to a situation where there is a real macho, guy-cult atmosphere.

Right. Most women I know, you wouldn't even try to pull any of that shit with them. My generation fought too hard to get in there. Martha Coolidge and Kathryn Bigelow? Nobody is going to get by with sexist attitudes around them.

The deeper aspects are that women are still not nominated for the big prizes for directing. And historians have left women out of whole segments of film history. I remember talking to a publisher at one point and asking why there are no books about women directors. I wasn't given a satisfactory answer. There are so few books on a single woman director's body of work. Leni Riefenstahl and maybe Sofia Coppola, that's about it.

Nerdism is a big thing, too. They have this in music. Music nerds want to keep that a boys' club. They don't want to let girls into that club of music nerdism. The same with movies. For years, I always wondered, why doesn't TCM [Turner Classic Movies] ever talk about women directors? The only women they ever interview about film are actresses. They don't talk to women directors about film.

When we were talking to DGA President Paris Barclay, he told us that he has seen statistics that show many women go into film school wanting to be directors, but very few of them leave school with the same ambition. Why does that happen? What changes?

I've thought about that as well. I think about all the women I was in film school with and how few of them ever pursued it. I also came up with a lot of women filmmakers in the American independent years of the 1990s who made one film and left. I don't think it's because we don't have the stomach for it. I don't think it's that we decide family responsibilities get in the way. I think there are fewer opportunities. Most people, men or women, don't have an appetite for restarting their career every single time they go to make a new movie. It's pretty disheartening after a while.

One problem that I do see—and I've told women this over and over again—is that you have to be ready with your next movie while making your current movie. If you go to the Sundance Film Festival and you win the top prize and the critics love your movie, but then it comes out and nobody goes to see it—it's not a genre film or they don't know how to market it—then people are less excited about you. Well, you have to get ahead of that. You should already be making the second movie before the first comes out because otherwise you're not going to build a body of work. In other words, get your financing for the second film when people are still excited. Long before you get into Sundance is the time you have to make sure you have the next film lined up, and preferably already financed. Or use your time at Sundance to get your financing.

Another issue is that the "boy wonder" mythology is really, really tough to overcome. People in the film business are always looking for the next boy wonder. They are not looking for a girl wonder. I think Lena Dunham has come the closest to being a girl wonder. But then she stopped doing movies. I hope she directs another one!

Let's talk about the Directors Guild, which represents both an elite group—above-the-line talent who play a managerial role and enjoy profit participation—as well as below-the-line folks, some of whom are fairly low level. Does that create problems?

The guild is pretty effective. It's a fairly small guild, even including ADs [assistant directors] and UPMs [unit production managers]. Some of these issues are like I mentioned with the writers on set, for example. I think that is a problem, and I wish they could address it better, but I don't know how they'd do any more than they already have done. On other issues, you do see some impact. I don't know who has been pressuring people to hire more women directors, but somebody has definitely been on people's asses about it. And believe me, I'm taking full advantage of that. I would love to see women get more involved in the guild.

Another thing I would add is, I wish high-profile actresses who love to talk about needing more women behind the camera would put their money where their mouth is. There are some good ones. Charlize Theron and Reese Witherspoon have hired and worked with a lot of women directors. But there are some A-list women who have never worked with a woman director. Every time I hear them, I just think, yeah, it would be great, so why don't we start with you? Why don't you hire a woman? A lot of people will say that flirtation and seduction between the male director and female stars is as old as the hills. Still, there are a lot of wonderful actresses who are big girls who don't need to be seduced into doing their job.

The DGA always comes on set. There is inevitably a representative who will come on set and ask the director how it's going. An interesting issue came up recently on *Murder in the First*, and this kind of thing seems to be happening more and more: it was my episode, but we had a scene that didn't make sense for me to direct. I was busy with a crew in a different location, and so we decided it was more sensible for Jesse Bochco to direct it, but we had to ask the guild for permission to do that, and they said no. So we had to make a phone call to this guild representative and then I had to write him a letter and say, "I want to do this. I need Jesse to direct this scene because I don't have enough time in my schedule to do it. Also, that particular scene belongs more to another episode even though it is part of my episode." In the end he let us do it, but he said, "These shows are becoming so ambitious"—not like *Murder in the First*, more like *Game of Thrones* (2011–ongoing)—"and we want to make sure that you guys all have enough time in your schedules to do what these episodes are now demanding." That was interesting.

So they're worried that these very ambitious shows are concealing the amount of labor they involve by spreading it around in ways that don't conform to the conventions of the contract?

Exactly. That they are not giving us enough time to do our work. That was not the case with *Murder in the First*. The DGA rep understood that, and that's why Jesse was allowed to direct that scene. But the rep said, "We don't want to end up in the same situation as the Writers Guild, where people are team-writing TV episodes. We don't want team-directing to become the norm simply because the producers and the networks don't allot enough time to do these ambitious TV shows."

Inevitably there are situations that make sense, either because of problems with scheduling a location or scheduling an actor, or there is not enough time to shoot everything in one episode, so another director might have to direct a scene that is left over from your episode. That happens all the time. That is understood. The problem is when producers don't give you enough time to get everything done. So now this person directs a piece of your episode, then you direct a piece of somebody else's episode, and now we have this thing that is nobody's vision. So it's also an artistic integrity issue. It's about making sure that the person who has been hired to direct an episode—and is going to be given screen credit—has truly done the work.

6

Lauren Polizzi, art director

Lauren Polizzi has worked in the industry for more than thirty years as a set designer and art director on such films as *Jurassic Park* (1993) and *Star Trek Beyond* (2016). She has also taught at the American Film Institute in Los Angeles for more than fourteen years. In what follows, she shares her experiences with the shifting workplace dynamics that have resulted from mobile production and increased financial pressures.

What does an art director do?

Art directors are the "first officers," if you will, to the production designer. They assist in the conception and management of bringing an entire film's sets to fruition, from concepts to working drawings, and from construction through filming.

Art directors, and often illustrators, are hired soon after the production designer, and we begin with reference materials, simple 3D models, and/or loose sketches. Getting from there to working drawings requires many additional sketches, illustrations, models, and action plans as well as meetings with numerous department heads, all with the goal of developing the designer's initial concept into a working set of plans that serve both the director's needs and the shooting company's. At the same time, we're making presentations to the studio, the director, and the art department. We're developing construction schedules and creating budgets. Art directors also meet with a number of other departments, including special effects, visual effects, grip, lighting, props, and set decoration, to develop a cohesive way to achieve each goal. Sometimes those meetings inspire new ideas, and so it's back to the drawing board, and the process repeats.

We'll meet with producers and assistant directors to determine when each set is needed and where. We'll then work with set designers to finalize the working drawings for construction. When those documents are ready, we hand them over to construction and other departments, and then supervise that project's progress. When the crew gets there to begin shooting, we'll be there to make sure they have everything they need. If the director and crew are satisfied, we leave to go get the next thing ready. If a set transitions in any way, say there's a "before" and an "after" condition, then we need to be there to keep tabs on any alterations. In short, we talk with a lot of people, propose a whole host of ideas and solutions, answer a lot of questions, and keep all the plates spinning smoothly. There are many, many moving parts at any given time.

What does your typical working day look like?

For me, a typical preproduction day will start between seven and eight in the morning. I come to the office and check in with my set designers, model makers, and illustrators to make sure they are on task with all current information. Once into construction, my day will typically start at seven o'clock on stage or location to guide any developments, and make sure that everyone there is equipped with all the information they need. Then it's checking back in repeatedly with everyone else, to keep it all moving forward. My days will last anywhere from six in the evening, in the very early stages, to nine o'clock or later when things really get going. It just depends on what's needed for the next day. Sometimes there's so much happening in so many places that there aren't enough hours in the day to feel on top of it all. It can feel relentless and daunting, but it always seems to work out.

So you are doing both design and management? What's the balance between the two?

People don't realize how many decisions go into designing environments for a film, even for a small, simple set like the room we're sitting in now. Somebody has to figure out how the action will work in the set, create a plan, pick the materials to use, decide on the colors, and so on. What kind of lighting elements should we provide? Built-in overheads? Shall set decorating provide lamps? What about windows? Where should they go, and what shall we put on them? Blinds? Drapes? What does the DP [director of photography] need? Is this wall going to have to go away so that the shooting crew can get the camera angles it needs? Those are the kinds of puzzle parts to creative design that I really like. But I like the managerial part, too—the meetings—it's a big part of it. When does the set shoot? How much time do we have? Who will draw it? Where will we build it? Which department will provide which pieces? Can we purchase any of it, or repurpose any pieces of previous sets? Is there enough money to accomplish what we want? Art directors juggle all of that, but even that has its creative aspects, too. I enjoy it—at least I always manage to say that in retrospect!—but it can be a very stressful position, as things often have to happen quickly. People can get nervous, and sometimes testy. Managing personalities is a big part of my day as well.

Can you talk about your relationship with the production designer?

Each designer brings his or her own design preferences, workflow, and personality to each project. I come on board to support that designer and try to work within their methods, plus offer mine. It's important that we understand one another, that we work in tandem, with easy and open communication. We have to create and share so much information, and for so many hours a day, we'd better have a good rapport. If not, it can all go downhill quickly. It's key, and that goes for working with everyone on the production. When we each head off in different directions to oversee things, we need to know we're on the same page. The designer will count on me to figure certain things out on their behalf, anticipate trouble spots, and then keep them posted on all developments. It's a real team effort to keep it all moving forward, and stay flexible, but with a cohesive end goal. And on productions with multiple art directors, it's even more essential, as things can easily get missed or overlooked when everyone thinks that another person is taking care of it. Smartphones have helped here—it's so easy to make a call, or send a picture for explanation. As long as you're in a place with good reception!

Are you usually engaged in production for the entire shoot?

My involvement depends on the size of the production, its budget, and where things stand in the schedule. As a set designer I often finish up long before production is done, as the drawings must be done ahead of construction. As an art director, I'm there for as long as what I'm in charge of is still in development, or shooting. I might last the entire run, or I may come onto a show a bit later, as the sets I'll supervise may not shoot for a while. It just depends. But once my sets have shot, I'm done, wherever that lies in the run of the whole production.

What are the frustrating parts of the job?

There are countless frustrating aspects of the job, and I think I've covered a few of them. But the first on my list would be negotiating my rate for a job, and we negotiate every time we take a show. The union negotiates with the producers for a scale rate, a minimum, but does not negotiate for individual members' rates. But as you grow in experience you want to be compensated—and dare I say *appreciated*—for that experience. There are different ways that productions go about deciding what they'll pay you, and those always seem to change. But often you're simply told, "We're only paying scale," or, "We won't pay you more than what you made on your last job." So that rate could last for years.

Another frustrating thing that I always find somewhat amusing is what happens early on, with just about every show. There's an introductory production meeting where we all are introduced, and the producer tells us how happy they are that we're all here, that we're the best team in the business, and how much fun we're all going to have. But not long after, we might get called into their office and pointedly questioned as to what the hell we're doing with our creations and/or budgets. Like we're out of control, or trying to take advantage of the company. What? Just a little while ago I was the best in the business! Ha! I well understand that there's a lot of money at stake, and that they are in charge of keeping track of it. I appreciate that making sure it's being spent wisely isn't easy. But some go overboard and make the process antagonistic—they want to make sure we know who is in charge, and that we're being watched. The best ones are firm, but listen to your reasoning, and then make guiding, informed calls. It's important that we all have a contributing voice and are not just told "no" over and over.

Do you have an agent who represents you?

As an art director, I do not have an agent. A few art directors do, but most don't. It hasn't been necessary for me.

Is negotiating for yourself stressful?

It is for me, and it never seems to get easier. I'm always wary of the process. You never know who you'll negotiate with, their demeanor or their role within the production, what they do or don't know about you. I usually negotiate with a production manager or producer, depending on who is already on board in production. And each one seems to know beforehand what you made on your last show. They all say they don't, but they do. I went to negotiate on my most recent job, where I knew the producer from a previous show. I went in expecting to have some time to talk with him, but he said this time they were doing all negotiations through the controller—he wouldn't be involved. I had to do it all via email. So I sent the controller my requested rate, and he then passed it on to a representative at the studio. I heard back by email that the rate was denied. That's not exactly a negotiation, nor very personal. It became a fight just to keep my rate from the previous show. I almost had to turn it down. But we did reach an agreement—after a third party got involved on my behalf. Afterward I spoke to other people in my department, and it was clear that many of them had endured a difficult fight as well.

Are negotiations becoming more impersonal and less involved?

I think so. You are an independent contractor up against a corporation. Asking for anything above the scale rate is done at your own risk. And anyone on the other end of the conversation can just say that the studio said no. This is the first time that I experienced such a curtailed negotiation, so I will have to wait and see if it will be a trend or not. It's tiresome having to go through this battle each time, which was only made worse this time by communicating only through email. Making your deal with the producer sets in motion how you will communicate with that person over the course of the show. You begin a relationship—for better or worse. As much as I've disliked negotiating my rate on each show, I have at least appreciated this dynamic. As it becomes more impersonal, you have to make quicker decisions because there's no relationship to leverage. You need to decide to take the wage reduction to have the job or walk away in hopes that another offer comes your way. You sometimes have to make quick calls, and gamble on the results. It's stressful—this is your livelihood at stake.

How do you find jobs?

Fortunately I have worked with a lot of people who seem to like my work, and I've been at it quite a while, so my name is fairly well known in feature art department circles. I'll put the word out to my friends when I'm available and looking for work. Also, the union has what they call an availability list, so as soon as you are out of work you can elect to be put on the list as "available for work" if you want to be. But the union does not find the work for you. Anybody who is hiring can request this list. At this point in my career I get more calls from friends looking to hire someone than from people making cold calls off the list. And I get calls to make recommendations on others, too. But it depends. Job offers tend to come in waves—it can be quiet for a good while, and then suddenly a number of calls come in. My last break was longer than I anticipated, about four months. It happens. There are lulls. It's why it's important to save money. During my days of unemployment I can relax and have a vacation. And when I'm ready, I'll email friends and say, "Hey, I'm looking for work again," and hope I get some calls back. Many of my colleagues do the same thing.

Can you usually find work throughout the year?

Yes, mostly. And I think if you are willing to work in television, or travel for features, you can probably work more consistently. There are plenty of projects these days looking to take experienced people to places out of state. Your options also improve if you can do more than one thing—like, I am willing to art direct or set design, and will work on features or television. I'll go for the project that a) has people I like, or have wanted to work with, or b) sounds interesting creatively. But it's the people I'd be working for that gets the most emphasis when I'm deciding on a show. Who cares if it's the biggest show in Hollywood if you're going to be miserable for the next eight months?

Do you think a willingness to travel is an important professional asset?

Yes, more and more. Twenty years ago, the features I worked on were based in L.A. At least the stage work was based here, but you went on location to shoot other footage. You went to Chicago if you wanted that skyline, or wanted to feature some aspect of that city—if it was important to the story. Now tax incentives mean you might be sent to any number of places to film locations *and* build stage sets. And possibly make that location city look like a completely different place—like Toronto for Los Angeles, or Boston for Anchorage. It can be pretty nutty. When you get into it, into the detail of each place, they're a lot more different than you think!

It used to be fun to pick up and go on location for a period of time, but now I have a house and pets, and it's more complicated. What used to be location work for six to eight weeks is now six to ten months. Some people have families and bring them along, and it's a big move for them. Otherwise they are flying back and forth a lot, and that's tough on people. Relationships can suffer. Because of this, many have chosen to switch from working in features to working in television in order to stay in L.A., as it's more consistently local work. Some have picked up entirely and moved to incentive-rich cities, such as Atlanta, where they can feel settled and somewhat secure about work. Again, it's about personal choices. I'm choosing to continue in features, keep my home base in Los Angeles, *and* be picky about where I go, too, so I have to accept that I could very well have more time off work in any given year. I am unwilling, as yet, to move, and that is my choice. My roots—my family and friends—are here. And, as these things have proven cyclical in the past, I don't believe that any one place will last forever as a work haven anyway.

When you end up in these places, how does the makeup of your department change?

It depends on the size of the production, where you're filming, and how many people you are allowed to take, if any. It can become a horrible mess if you are going to a place that is not used to seeing film crews and you are tasked to find local hires. You may end up needing to bring more people from L.A. because there are no (or not enough) locals who can do the work—especially set designers, as that is a more specific job that requires a good amount of talent and organization. In extreme cases, you may be left to do portions of the work yourself because you need something fast, and there's no time to find someone in L.A., fly them out, and familiarize them with the project at hand before the deadline. This is a) not very healthy for you, and you can't endure it for long, and b) against union rules, and the company can get fined if it's discovered. Many productions have gone to New Orleans and Atlanta, and there are more and more people gaining experience in those areas as a result. But if you are the third or fourth company coming into a now-popular area, and all the experienced people are already working, you must then hire less-qualified people, which could end up costing you time and money, or convince production to allow you bring more people from elsewhere. That goes for any city.

Is your position at risk of being filled locally?

It's happening in a number of places. For example, the production we are prepping right now is going to shoot in Vancouver, and Hollywood has trained a lot of people up there for quite some time now. There are well established, qualified, and talented people living there. I'm doing preproduction work here, but my services won't be required in Vancouver as there are others happy to take over the position. So I am out of a job when the show moves there. If the producers had changed their minds and were taking the show to a US location instead, I'd likely remain on the project. Again, it depends on the place and the timing.

Which cities have enough local talent that studios can find people to fill the art department?

I'd say the biggest are Vancouver, New York, New Orleans, Atlanta, and, of course, London—London is busy right now. And soon perhaps Boston. A number of shows have been going there. But again it depends on how many shows are in a city at the same time.

What if you just want to stay in Los Angeles?

These days, you will probably have to work more in television, or be satisfied with piecemeal feature preproduction work. As I mentioned, many are reframing their careers, moving, or even retiring. I also teach at the American Film Institute, which I enjoy, and I've been thinking that in another five or seven years, maybe I'll try to transition back to set design and continue to teach part-time at AFI. I might even consider taking a full-time position there if they had one available. I can train new recruits as well or better from home! As more shows are heading out of town, and getting more and more stressful, I'm starting to feel like I may want to make some of those career-based decisions sooner—for my own sanity and comfort level. You spend so much of your day at work that you can lose touch with friends, lose family time, personal time, and other things that create a quality of life. I don't want my entire life to be about work—as much as I do enjoy what I do. I hear personal relationships can be pretty nice! I'd like to pursue and enjoy other things as well. We'll see what happens.

Moving around the country also poses professional difficulties. You're leaving long-time colleagues behind for a local crew you don't necessarily know.

Yes. I often miss my colleagues, especially when I have to train someone in the way we work. With set designers, for example, it's not just being familiar with a piece of software, like Vectorworks, it's knowing how those drawings need to be created, what our process is, how we build things, and being part of a fast-paced creative team. It's even more difficult for construction, as they need so many more people. And they need to be fast and competent workers. If they aren't trained, and they move too quickly around all that equipment, it can lead to injuries, some serious. And that is not good.

Whether in L.A. or out of state, it's so much better working with a familiar crew. There's a shorthand that has been developed; you're friends. You know what everyone's temperament and talent is, and you all have fun, and can better keep your sense of humor through stressful times. But if I can't take those people with me, I will get recommendations from other local shows and other colleagues who have worked in the area. They'll tell us whom they hired, and we'll start with that list. I have found some gems who are eager and hungry to do the work. They have the skills and enough experience for us to guide them onward. Some new recruits just think working on a movie sounds like fun, and they are only there for that singular experience. Some may have no film aspirations at all. They may be architects or interior designers and want to give movie production a shot, then find it's not really what they want to do. Some of them experience the hours and deadlines and decide it's not what they expected or want to deal with. Some people do end up liking it, and end up putting their heart into the work. That's the point when we know we've just trained another person to take our place!

What do you make of the incentives game? Do you think there are a lot of hidden costs associated with moving from location to location?

I'm sure there is quite a bit going on in this tax-incentive game that I don't know about. Most of us can't fathom how the incentives are actually worth it. I asked this question of our construction coordinator—the same guy with whom I worked on *Mockingjay, Part 1* (2014) and *Part 2* (2015) and *Star Trek Into Darkness* (2013). We spent about $50 million on construction for each of those films. They sound like equivalent figures until you understand Lionsgate received 30 percent back from Georgia for each *Mockingjay* film. That's millions of dollars, and sounds like quite a deal! Still, to reach our goals, we also had to bring in more than a hundred additional people *just for construction* in order to get it done on time. Other departments needed additional crew as well. All that travel, housing, car rentals, and per diem adds to the bottom line. Plus, you have to factor in the additional shipping costs to bring in the necessary equipment and goods. It's mind-boggling. Isn't it cheaper to just stay at home? How does this not offset that 30 percent subsidy? I don't see the overall budget. Producers do. They must come out ahead somehow. But to us, it's all additional and unnecessary stress, headaches, training, and trial and error. It's already difficult and complicated work. Why make it that much tougher?

Right now Atlanta is investing a lot of money into their production infrastructure, praying that the filming will stay there. Pinewood has built a new complex right outside the city. I hear it's pretty nice. There's even a dedicated Home Depot on the lot! But Hollywood is fickle, and will shift work elsewhere at any time if it means additional money to them. Why wouldn't they? Many states already have found this out. Hollywood leaves, or isn't generating enough revenue or jobs to justify governments making it easier for productions to remain there. For those of us based in L.A., it gives us a bit of hope that some work will eventually return home, though that's only a partial victory. Sadly, studios have been downsizing their Los Angles back lots as well. They've been closing their mills, staff shops, scene docks, and other support services we've always counted on—they don't want the overhead anymore. Those buildings have been torn down and replaced with new parking structures and office spaces. Certainly not soundstages. I have no idea who's occupying those big new spaces. Development and marketing divisions?

Television and cable shows now dominate the stages on these lots. I fear that even if features do come back to California, we won't have good spaces for them to use. We'll be forced to use the same kind of limiting and frustrating warehouse space we've had to endure in other states. It'll be interesting to see what happens.

You mentioned the headaches of shooting on location. Can you give us examples of that? What causes additional stress?

Obviously we are under pressure to use local goods, services, and talent. And it is more convenient to do so, for all concerned. It also improves on the production's rebate when your expenses are local. But it can also pose challenges. For example, local vendors are not used to our types of requests, or our timelines, and most vendors don't stock inventory like they used to. It's common for us to order a lot of different material samples to compare their suitability—how the textures and colors appear under lights and on camera. But local merchants tend to offer only limited selections. And for so many of the futuristic sets I work on, we're looking for more unusual things. So we have to get the things we want shipped from elsewhere, usually Chicago or L.A. if we're in Atlanta. When I worked on the original *Jurassic Park* (1993) in Kauai, just about everything was shipped in from elsewhere. And of course we may need to see samples of things first, but those samples might arrive damaged, or maybe the company makes a mistake and ships the wrong thing, or the wrong color. And because we're doing all this from a distance, it's more time consuming. Delays in shipping are common. And we don't have much time to spare. You can't slow down the production train, so you compromise on things you otherwise wouldn't under what we'd consider normal circumstances.

Then there's the weather. There's a big reason the film business is in Los Angeles, and it's the weather. It's often sunny there with mild temperatures. I'm both frustrated and entertained every time I see a national weather report. I look at Boston, Atlanta, New Orleans. When I see rain or snow or freezing temperatures I think, "How's that working out for you?" When I left to work in Atlanta I prepared myself for hot humid weather, and what I thought would be a temperate winter. Because I like to be prepared, I took snow boots with me—my friends thought I was nuts! But need them I did, and I had to buy additional gear, too. We were building a lot outside, and in open buildings without heat. It was freezing, an absolute nightmare, and I felt bad for all the guys working out in it the whole day. They could barely function in the cold, and equipment would shut down; paint would freeze. Plus you can't build outside in snow or rain. We lost a lot of precious time, and stressed out about finishing our sets on time. Sometimes production can change the shooting schedule to circumvent the bad weather, but often it just comes down to putting more people on more overtime and on weekends to finish. We still lost two shooting days due to ice and snow—that storm in Atlanta even made national news. But the sets got done! I have a plaque on my office wall that reads, "We don't believe in miracles . . . we rely on them."

Are we getting to the point where the whole logic of shuffling the pieces around the world is starting to affect one's ability to be creative?

Absolutely. It's hard for talented people to do their best work while constantly on the move. They're getting tired of it. It's hard to keep your life together when you're on the road that much.

What are the three biggest concerns art directors face?

I'd say time constraints, productivity pressures, and budgets. I often say that we teach studios the wrong lesson every time. It seems we are constantly given less time and less information to accomplish what we need to do. "Well, you had twelve weeks to build the set last time, so now we're giving you ten weeks." And we'll manage to figure out creative ways to meet the new deadline. For the next project they'll give us eight weeks. Once again, we will manage to pull it off but we'll need more overtime and perhaps produce less quality. But the studios continue to tighten the timeframes without adjusting their expectations. They know we'll produce. They know we don't want to fail. They know we want it to look good. They know we want to maintain our reputations. But at a certain point we have to remind them that their expectations are unrealistic. There are times when we have to say, "No way, it can't happen," as no amount of people or overtime can accomplish what they want. You can have the set look good, cost little, or be done quickly. Pick any two.

If I can add a fourth concern, I would say incomplete scripts on feature films. Sometimes we'll start with just an outline for the film. An outline is often enough to get us started with concept illustrations and initial set designs. But as the director becomes more involved and new script pages arrive, we may need to accommodate new ideas and actions, so set concepts may change in some form or another, or even disappear. If construction has already started, they need to tear down and rebuild. I've been on shows where months of work were wasted because the original action or concept was thrown out for new, updated material. And the schedule doesn't always change, so now you're repeating the process (sometimes several times) but in much less time. It can get crazy. Everyone on the crew is on top of one another to solve problems and get work done. It can feel impossible to plan anything in any kind of mindful, let alone financially prudent, way. There's a saying: where there is chaos, there is cash. It seems increasingly rare to be given the proper time and budget to accomplish the tasks at hand in a well-thought-out manner. We're always going into overtime rather than planning efficiently from the start. Yet somehow there's always money to do things over when ideas change.

What drives the unfinished scripts?

It's hard to answer that from where I sit. If a production has a main actor attached with a script outline and a release date, that's often enough to green-light a project. Our department will start from there. We try to proceed cautiously with a skeleton crew—just the bare minimum to get the work started. If the release date is sooner rather than later, planning and implementation need to happen quickly. There's no time to waste. Sometimes that strategy works out all right. The initial outline provides an adequate framework for us to do our jobs and then expands, and the script adheres to that initial idea. But I've worked on other productions where sets change drastically, and multiple times, and end up costing more in terms of both cash and sanity.

As an example, on *Star Trek Into Darkness*, we had a big opening scene on a primitive planet where all the vegetation is red. It was a huge, complicated chase scene for which we were going to build a village, a temple, pools, and a landscape that the characters worked their way through and down. They were to run through a forest, down a mountain to a beach, and then swim back to the *Enterprise*. So we scouted Hawaii. But after figuring out how we could make it work, and tech scouting with the director, it was deemed too expensive. Over the next months they cut the scene down to a fraction of what it was. In the end, we went from big set pieces and beautiful Hawaiian vistas spanning much of Kauai, to a 40-by-125-foot handmade set on a platform in a parking lot in Playa Vista. It worked, and it worked out well, but it was reimagined, re-scouted, and re-budgeted *numerous* times, and also went from what was to be the first set shot, to nearly the last. It's just one example of the time, effort, and money gauntlets we go through on these big productions.

7
Mary Jane Fort, costume designer

Mary Jane Fort has more than two decades of experience as a costume designer on feature films such as *Mean Girls* (2004) and television shows such as *Grounded for Life* (2001–5). In this conversation, Fort explains the little-known aspects of the costume designer's job as well as creative collaboration, emotional labor, and gender dynamics on set.

Tell us about your job. What does a costume designer do?

A costume designer is a visual storyteller. We are at our best when we help the actor visualize the character and enable the actor to become his or her character. It's not about clothes or fashion. It's about contributing to a larger vision: Who are these characters and what is this story? My job is to capture that larger essence by breaking the story down into smaller components. How will all these parts work together to create the whole? I approach my job like a painter approaches a painting or a decorator approaches a room in a home. Each element you create helps deliver something bigger and more cohesive.

When do you join a project?

I come on pretty early in the preproduction process. I'll join the project after the director, director of photography, and production designers. They are my key collaborators. I work with them for quite some time to help design the overall look of the film or television show.

And when is the cast involved?

Casting is often done at the eleventh hour, especially in television. It adds another element to my job. I can work with the production designer to coordinate a character's wardrobe for a particular space. He or she will tell me that the building's facade will have a green door, and I'll coordinate the colors to ensure that the characters stand out appropriately. Buildings don't talk back, but I'll have to adjust and negotiate my plans when the cast joins the project because oftentimes the talent won't feel comfortable in a particular color or outfit. They'll say, "I'm not going to do that." It adds an element of psychological or emotional labor to my work. I'll have to try to figure out how to make the actors more comfortable so they can do the job they were hired to do. I have to reassure them. I have to figure out how to translate our original plans in a way that makes sense to the actors and helps build their confidence instead of diminishing it. I have to understand how the actors want to approach the role and respect their creative process by incorporating their ideas into the overall vision. I think of it as layering as I bring all the ideas together.

Can you talk more about the emotional labor?

After I've had conversations with the director and the production designer, I'll meet the actors and talk. "How do you see this person? And who do you think he or she is?" Usually these people are all on the same page, and we'll talk about colors and shapes. I'll ask, "Is there anything that you hate or like?" After that we start the fittings. They'll come to a first fitting, and you start looking at things, and then you end up essentially finding the character. That may not happen during the first fitting, but often I'll say, "This is not quite right, but maybe something like this," or they'll say, "This doesn't make me feel right," or, "This kind of shoe, that does it!" And then I start editing out what didn't work. Most of the time the actor and I won't show anybody any options until we have it narrowed down to what we want. Then we'll show the director to get his or her input.

It's a process that sometimes runs more smoothly than other times. Through this process, we discover the character, and then I start breaking that out into the different changes we'll need to make according to the script. I also have to think about the environment. I'll join the production designer and set decorator to start looking at what I've done and what they've done. The DP [director of photography] then looks at all of it, and we'll see how it all works together. We have to talk about all the little things. "Does this work? Is that lamp's texture going to conflict with this shirt?" There are so many details.

So it's a very creative collaboration, but also an intimate one. Actors are very vulnerable with you.

Absolutely. I see them without makeup. I see them without clothes.

How do you negotiate their insecurities and vulnerabilities?

If the actor doesn't feel comfortable with me, then I'm not doing my job. I've done something wrong somewhere in the process. Actors aren't fragile creatures. Some are, but most of them are there to do the job. They have no problem taking their clothes off in front me. [Laughs] There's always a dressing room, but no one uses it.

We're all invested in breathing life into this character. It's my job to protect the actors from being made to feel more vulnerable or less confident in their abilities, which can happen if I put them into costumes that accentuate insecurities. The actors may look perfectly fine to me, but I don't know what's going on inside their heads. If they don't feel like they look good, then that's going to get in the way of their best performance. Of course there are times when the actors need to look schlumpy or need to be in an ill-fitting suit. They understand that. But it doesn't do anyone any good to send them to the set in something that isn't working for them. I'll say to the director, "She's not feeling comfortable in the dress we chose. Can we try another one?" No director is going to say, "No! Let's make our star miserable!"

It's about how you communicate with the production team and the talent. If you disagree, then it's about working through that process. Perhaps you compromise and agree to see how the costume design looks on camera first. "Are you sure this is comfortable? Let's try it with this jacket before changing our minds, or maybe we should tighten it up here." Sometimes their initial instincts were correct. Sometimes they'll agree with me. Whatever the case, I want to make sure they are 100 percent confident in our choices before they go in front of the camera.

When do you take on assistants for a film?

I like to have them on day one, but it all depends on what the budget allows. For a midrange movie, you'll have about eight to ten weeks of prep time. I'll be there for two weeks to meet with my collaborators and gather ideas. Then I'll bring on a wardrobe supervisor who is the real brains of the department. That person manages every single logistical element in the costume department: budgets, supplies, materials, script breakdowns. I can't do my job without a good wardrobe supervisor.

*Your most recent project was **Project Almanac** (2015), a sci-fi feature film. What does a film like that require from the costume department? Help us get our heads around budgets, characters, costume changes, et cetera.*

Project Almanac was a midrange feature with a budget of approximately $12 to $15 million. I think the first six or seven characters on the call sheet had about fifteen to twenty changes each. Any adjustment qualifies as a change. A character may wear one thing in the morning but then add a jacket for dinner or change into a bathrobe at night to brush her teeth. It was a relatively easy project to handle because we were dealing with discrete chunks of time as the characters traveled through time—a few weeks here in this world and then a few weeks there in that world. Compare that to something like *Mean Girls* where we had to accommodate an entire academic year. So *Project Almanac* was relatively simple, while *Mean Girls* required many more changes. The latter was so very, very, very detail oriented. I had so many subtleties to track. You have to have an excellent group of people around you.

All of these details and changes are ultimately my responsibility. I may not do the breakdowns, but if something is done wrong, I'm the one who has to say, "Sorry, we did it wrong." Surrounding myself with great people gives me the freedom to be creative. I think one of the things that I love so much about the medium of film is that everyone truly depends on everyone else. If one element is missing or goes askew, you can't do it. Everyone has to work together. It's what makes it so much fun for me.

At this point in your career, do you have a team that you work with consistently?

I have my team, but they aren't obligated to work solely with me. Somebody will inevitably have another commitment when I'm working on a project. So you have a roster of people you know and trust. Sometimes your entire dream team is available. Sometimes you have to bring on somebody new. It can be a lot of fun, or it can be a nightmare. You never know!

Do you do the hiring?

Yes, indeed. I hire the wardrobe supervisor. I come with people, and generally he or she has people as well. Together, we decide who is right for a particular project and we budget who and what we need. That is our core group, and then for different days that are big or particular parts of the script that are challenging, we have extra "man days." Although it could happen, I've never had production oppose someone I wished to hire.

How big is the department on a midrange feature film?

I'll have a core team of eight to ten people, with additional help occasionally coming in throughout production.

How did you become a costume designer?

It happened by accident. I studied as a painter. I have a bachelor's degree in fine arts. I'm from a small town in Tennessee, and I wanted to move to New York and work in fashion design on Seventh Avenue. I didn't know how. I didn't study fashion design, but it's just what I wanted to do. So in the late 1980s, I moved to New York. I was designing T-shirts for Swatch, and then the head designer left because of some conflict with the company. Production ceased, but our contracts wouldn't let us work for anyone else. My friend was an assistant to Jonathan Demme at the time. She asked, "Can you work for free?" He was producing a short film that needed a costume PA [production assistant]. I did that for no fee and absolutely loved it. So I thought, "How do people do this?" No one could tell me! Someone said, "Read the trades." Remember, this was before Google. Jobs were advertised in the trade magazines. I ended up responding to an ad in the *Hollywood Reporter* for the Whit Stillman film *Metropolitan* (1990). I got it. I had no idea what I was doing, but I was doing it for $200 a week. I used my own clothes, my own resources. I kept everything in my apartment in New York. I took it to work each day in a cab that I paid for. It was Stillman's debut film and it ended up doing really well, so an agent called me to ask if I wanted representation. Again, I had no clue what he meant. But he explained it, and I was like, "Sure!"

It's a funny way to get into the business. I never came up through the ranks. I was never an assistant. I've always been the department head, which means I've made lots of mistakes. I've lived. I've learned.

When did you start doing television? Why?

I started doing television about ten years ago. Television allows you to have more of a plan. You know when you'll have holiday time. You know when you'll be at home. It's less of a gypsy lifestyle, and it was at a time in my life when I wanted that. At least that's how television production was ten years ago when we were making television in Los Angeles. Now we're making television in Atlanta, Dallas, or Philadelphia, and television is as much of a gypsy lifestyle as film.

When did that start to happen?

I didn't start leaving the area for long periods of time until five years ago. I've worked in Philadelphia, Atlanta, Dallas, New York, Nashville. And Canada, of course.

How does that feel?

It can be fun. You get to see different places, though right now being in Atlanta is like being in Los Angeles. You almost know more people in Atlanta than you do at home because so many people are moving there to work. It's also challenging to work in these different areas. I honestly don't know how it saves the production any money. You can never find local crew who are skilled enough to do the work you need. You end up bringing people with you, but it's still a logistical nightmare.

You start with one assistant and your wardrobe supervisor—that's who you can bring on from the beginning—but then you have to staff your department with local hires. We are obligated to try. You talk to the local union, and its staff reassures you that it has all these great people who are eager to work. The area may have eager people, but those people either lack the proper training or they just want to work "in the movies" without actually doing the work that's required. I've had people steal money or walk away with clothes. It just adds so many hoops to jump through. I don't want to disparage local crews—they simply haven't been doing it long enough, and there aren't enough of them. It'll change in time.

Or maybe not.

I don't know. I did a TV series in Philadelphia. Because of the incentive program, we were supposed to hire local crew and purchase our materials locally. No one wanted to take the job! No one wanted to make a long-term commitment! We interviewed people, and they would say, "I can work for a month then I'm going to make a music video. But I can come back." It just doesn't work that way. Do you want a job for this amount of time or not? We already had a small labor pool, and then we couldn't find anyone to hire. I ended up bringing five people with me. I had the same experience when it came to purchasing. We ended up doing most of our shopping in New York. Philadelphia stores didn't stock what we needed. If there's a sweater available in September, it'll still be there in January. We needed more variety for this particular show. It took so much labor to prove our point, and finally, the producer just said, "Okay. Bring your people and purchase in New York."

Do you ever just throw up your hands and scream, "Not this again!"?

I don't, because I know it will all work out. I've never had somebody say to me, "Well, that's just too bad. I know these people are unqualified, but you have to deal with it." No one wants to ruin the project. Everyone has a boss. A line producer doesn't want to look like she mucked it all up any more than I do! A smart line producer will let me hire the people I need to ensure the best possible outcome. If

I can't do something because I don't have the staff, then the line producer will look bad, too. We all want to do our best.

Where is the disconnect?

It's with the people who sit in buildings somewhere far away from the set. We laugh about it all the time. You never meet these people. You never see them. They're like little ghosts who develop universal formulas that may look logical on paper but not in practice. For example, during pilot season, there's a process called "the pattern." It basically establishes the prep times for each department. I'll get three weeks for prep. It doesn't matter if it's a pilot for *Lewis and Clark* or *Three Men and a Table*. I get the same prep time. It's laughable. How can I prep this historical period piece in three weeks? They'll spend more money to make it fit into the formula than to develop a new formula. They won't give me a month prep time. Instead they'll double up on crew. Everyone works seven days a week, fourteen hours a day, for three weeks.

Doesn't that take a toll?

Of course! But you know it's going to happen. You know it's going to be crazy. You know it'll get done. It's only three weeks.

How are you compensated? Hourly?

Not me. I'm paid by the week, and I work a five-day week. For days six and seven, I get time and a half and double time. But for my crew, it's hourly. Again, it's time and a half and double time when you get into long hours. I think a wardrobe supervisor might make more than I do. They work hard.

Ultimately everything gets done, but it does open the door to exploitation, yes?

It does. I care about the art of it. I care about the craft. I want to do a good job. So I continually prove I'll get it done under the conditions they create for me, no matter how many hours it takes.

You have an excellent temperament for this job. Are most costume designers like you?

I have heard that sometimes people can be so attached to their vision that they can't let go of it. But again, that's not my philosophy. It's not about me. It's about what I can bring to the table.

If the director sees something differently, I can argue: "I don't agree, and I think we should do this, this, and this." But if somebody says, "Absolutely not. I want it this way," I'm not going to throw a tantrum, yelling, "I worked so hard on this. I can't believe you don't want to use it!" I have other things going on. I don't want to say it's not important, because it's all important, but it's not worth it. It distracts you from the bigger picture. I'm already juggling so many details that I'm not going to stomp around when one of them doesn't go my way. Ultimately, it's not my movie.

It's almost a necessary philosophy when so much of your labor is invisible. Yet you have an artistic vision that contributes in meaningful ways.

Yes, absolutely! My job is to help visually tell the story through what the characters wear. If I do my job well, I don't draw attention to that process. It would be distracting and contrary to my objective. Yet I help guide what you see in particular scenes. I help create meaning. Who are these characters? What are they thinking or feeling? How are they evolving? It's an integral component to the overall vision of the film. Creative collaboration is a challenge, but I find it a rewarding one. I love it. I can't imagine doing anything else.

Do you work a lot? Do you have downtime between projects?

It all depends. I had years of overlap when I was doing two things at once, and then I sort of developed a life. Things happen and you need to take a little step back, and then you'll get back onto the treadmill again. I can't do a million things at once like I used to be able to do; I don't enjoy that anymore.

I used to do a movie and a TV show at the same time, but then the people around you suffer and your quality of life suffers, and the job takes a toll. I'm good at taking time off, but I'm also fine with working a year or so straight and then taking a break and jumping into it again. I know some people who never take a minute off.

You're not anxious about the next job?

I think everyone is to a degree. I probably should be more anxious!

Have you had the same agent for your whole career, or have you changed?

I was with Gersh for a very long time, and I changed to Innovative two years ago.

And why was that?

I loved the Gersh agency, and I love the agents there, but they don't have a strong focus on television. It's kind of crazy to me because everybody's doing television now. And so I made the decision to change, but I do miss them.

Does the agency play an important role for costume designers?

You have to have an agent.

Really?

Yes, unfortunately. [Laughter] Everyone has a love-hate relationship with his or her agent. You like them as people, but after a point, you're doing so much repeat business with employers you already know that you forget whether you met them by chance or whether your agency made the connection. Over time you meet people, and after a certain point you'll work with them over and over again. You have your people who call you, and then every so often your agent will get you something new.

How does compensation work with your agent? Does the agent only get a fee when he or she brings you something?

No. They negotiate your deals and most of them take 10 percent whether the job came through them or through a personal connection. But, in their defense, negotiating often becomes so much more complicated than it sounds. The same day I signed with Innovative somebody called and asked me to do *Project Almanac*, and the agent helped me protect my credit, travel, accommodations, and all those things. They're sort of a necessary evil.

What are the gender dynamics in costume departments? Are there more women than men?

There are many more women in the department than men. I have worked with one or two great guys, but the core group I've kept together over the past ten years is women. It wasn't intentional, but we ended up becoming close and forming friendships.

Do you think that's because you spend a lot of time together?

It's a miserable experience if you can't work together. You need to get along to do this job well. One sour lemon can ruin the entire experience. It's horrible.

How do the gender dynamics affect the department's relationships with other crew on the set?

It certainly factors into the way other people interact with us, and it bugs me. I can't stand it when I hear someone call for "the vanities." Really? No, that's not what we are. I also take offense when I hear someone call us "Wardrobe." Again, that's not what we are. Of course, the actor comes to the set followed by a makeup artist, a set costumer, maybe a hair stylist. So, maybe it looks like that's all we do, but I've just spent the past hour telling you everything we do! There's so much more that goes into this profession. I feel like people can be demeaning to the costume department, and I take great umbrage to that.

They call you the vanities?

An AD will say, "Where are the vanities? We're getting ready to shoot." So the makeup artist will come in and powder a nose, and the set costumer will tweak the collars. It's just rude. They have names. They're professionals. You can say, "Where's Sarah, and where's Elizabeth? We're getting ready to shoot." It's not just demeaning; it's also dismissive of our craft.

And this is happening in front of a crew that's 80 percent white men.

Yes. What they're really asking is, "Where are the girls?" Don't get me wrong. There are some fantastic male costume designers, makeup artists, and wardrobe supervisors. But the department is gendered as female and feminine. That's how it's seen.

Do you think there's a need for change as far as gender dynamics on the sets?

I hate to sound like I'm complaining. I don't want to whine about it. I want everyone to have the job he or she wants. I've never wished to be a DP, and I don't know a DP who has ever wished to be a costume designer. And I think the film industry is open to that: do what you want to do, and no one will stop you if you're good at it. The only place I know where the male-female ratio is off is with line producers. While the industry has some excellent female line producers, there are not as many, and they make less than their male colleagues. And I'm talking about line producers who work on major tent-pole movies. Only like a handful of female line producers work on that type of film. That's where you see the inequality, because it's a boys' club. Women aren't perceived as authoritative enough or aggressive enough to handle the responsibilities and to wrangle the crew and budgets and whatnot.

But it's not just a matter of numbers. It raises questions about value and about whether the set is an inviting space for certain people.

I always feel welcomed. I've never felt unwelcomed.

Interesting. We've been told that sometimes stand-ins are treated horribly by crew. [Stand-ins are hired to take the place of actors while cameras, lights, and rigging are set up for a shot. On some sets, women who perform these tasks are subjected to inappropriate comments and overtures from male crew members.]

Oh, absolutely! It all depends on whom you're working with. Some projects have completely horrible, sleazy people, and other sets have some of the most wonderful people in the world. Every set has a different dynamic and vibe, but it's a trickle-down from the top, because that vibe comes from the people who put together the crew. So if you have a great director and a great line producer and producer, for the most part you're going to have a crew stocked with admirable, respectful people who are good at their jobs. But if you have a director and producers who do not have very high standards for themselves and say whatever they want, then they generally don't mind when somebody else behaves inappropriately, and that's when situations get very frustrating.

You knew immediately what we meant when we said "stand-ins."

Of course. I have witnessed some bad things. I have had some bad experiences. I've been lucky to work with wonderful people more often than sleazy people. But they're there.

*One last question about gender dynamics, which is more of a structural question. Do you think the industry is particularly challenging for women because of the way work is organized? The long hours, the constant mobility—is that hard for someone who wants to have a career **and** a family? Women still face a different set of cultural expectations than men: they're supposed to shuttle the kids to soccer practice and manage the home. Does that make it hard for women who are working in production?*

It's very hard. A lot of people make choices at certain times in their lives. Perhaps they decide they're not going to travel for work. Perhaps they try to figure out how to make work more accommodating. If their children are young, they can bring them to work for a certain amount of time, but then the children reach an age when they're in soccer, and they don't want to go to work with mom. Everyone makes different decisions. I've even known people who have left Los Angeles. They just weren't able to make it all fit together. So, yes, it is difficult.

For me, my parents were older and not living near Los Angeles, and they had needs. My father died, my mother had surgery scheduled, and somebody had to be with her. I needed to be able to plan when I could do these things. Everyone has things like that, and you hopefully work with people who will try to cover for one another. I did have that support.

Say you need to leave on a Thursday and be gone until Monday morning. Hopefully your department will help you work it out. As far as the people who work for me, I try to be respectful of balancing their time commitments and needs. Let's say that on Thursdays someone has to drive carpool. All right, we'll figure it out, and she won't come in until nine o'clock. We try to all work together. Nobody else knows how we balance schedules or even that we do it. There was one woman who worked with me who put her child in a daycare near Fox, which was where we were working, but the daycare closed at six. She would run to get her, bring her back, and everyone would pitch in to help. We had this beautiful baby with us in the evenings.

But again, nobody is aware of any of those exceptions. I don't think you could do that if you were in the camera department, or if you were a grip. It depends on your job. It isn't that there aren't great women DPs, but there just isn't a support system.

Exactly. It isn't intentional, but it plays out structurally.

It takes individuals who are willing to make those exceptions. "You can go a little early if you need to pick up your kid from daycare."

And structurally, workplace expectations aren't the same in every department.

They aren't. Really, it's about the people you work with. That plays a huge part because it's long days and hard work. It's stressful and it's hectic. You need personalities you can work with, and you need generosity, kindness, and professionalism. It's a great set when everyone shares those values.

8

Anonymous, makeup artist

Anonymous has worked for more than fifteen years as a makeup artist on various film and television projects. In this conversation, she illuminates the invisible labor of makeup artists, including the intimacy they share with actors. The conversation also touches on the enduring value of organized labor despite the ongoing erosion of traditional protections and benefits.

Tell us a little about your job.

I have a lot of variety in my work. I do a small number of features, primarily low-budget union shoots. I also work on episodic television and a lot of commercials. I book a lot of promos and up-fronts, which are my bread and butter. There's always a lot of demand for that work. And then I grab the occasional gig that comes my way: celebrity work or print work. Most makeup artists specialize. They work on features or episodic television. I am fortunate to have some variety, and I really enjoy that.

What accounts for the difference?

I do a lot of day playing, or day checking, which means I make myself available to work for a production that needs additional artists on a short-term basis. You fill in for a few days or, if you're available, a week or more. It allows you to jump from job to job.

What's a typical working day like?

My day starts pretty early. In television, a standard call time is 5:30 a.m. In commercials or up-fronts, it starts a little later, around 6 or 7 a.m. I get up between 3 and 4 a.m. depending on my commute. We all have call times on the call sheet, which is when you're scheduled to be at the location. But my philosophy is that call time is work time. If my call time is 5:30 a.m., I am there with my gear unpacked and ready to go before 5:30 a.m. I don't want to be shoving a breakfast burrito in my mouth when talent shows up. So I always arrive about thirty minutes before my call time. I'm usually at work for anywhere between twelve and sixteen hours. A typical day is fourteen hours, but I've worked a twenty-two-hour shoot and any number in between.

What kinds of information do you get before the shoot?

It depends on the job. If it's a feature, you have preproduction time to break down the script before shooting begins. How long depends on the budget. I primarily work on lower-tier features with budgets from $5 to $15 million. There isn't always that much time or money, which means preproduction isn't going to be lengthy. I'll have a few weeks to look over the script, prep, and figure out supply costs. I do a lot of high-budget commercials. I typically have a week or so to prep those, though that doesn't mean I'm getting paid for that time. I'm reviewing storyboards and special requests to best assess what the project will require and make sure that my kit is stocked with the right materials. In general, we're expected to be ready to go with guns blazing.

And you maintain your kit on your own dime?

It depends on the show, but whatever kit fee you earn often doesn't cover what you're expected to provide. It's mostly a courtesy fee they provide us. In television, we'll sometimes receive a kit fee of $25 per day. In commercials, it's roughly $50 per day. You negotiate everything in the features world, so there isn't a consistent figure. When you're doing things like music videos or promos, it's at the discretion of the production coordinators.

How did you become a makeup artist?

It's different for everyone. I was trying to make the transition into production in the late 1990s, early 2000s. I worked full time as a national artist for a makeup line. It paid a modest salary with nice benefits. I would travel around the country promoting the line and training other artists. I worked out a schedule where I could travel Sunday through Thursday. This kept my weekends free for spec work, offering my services for free. It was common at the time for working directors who wanted to transition into another medium—say from commercials or music videos to television—to put together a modest budget for some work on the side to help them make the transition. I'm talking about budgets of around $40,000 or less. I was working full time to pay my rent but jumping on every spec shoot I could find to build my professional network and get more credits under my belt.

I did that for a couple of years before I developed enough contacts to finally leave the cosmetics world. It was like jumping off a cliff. I was saying goodbye to a really successful career to become a full-time freelancer. I was saying goodbye to my salary and health benefits. I was starting over from scratch, often working for people who were younger than me. It was hard. But I was following my passion. I wanted to work in production. I was very fortunate that my husband was supportive. He said he didn't know how we were going to do this, but that we'd figure it out. Within six months, I was working regularly.

Now I get most of my work through personal recommendations. Those come from producers or coordinators or directors specifically asking for me. Sometimes a friend will be double-booked and they'll refer me. As you gain experience, you rely on those recommendations. People know you. People trust you. For example, I did three different shows this past year because I'd become closely acquainted with the department head and key makeup artist and they felt very comfortable having me as a third to cycle into their shows. On those shows, it wasn't a director or coordinator saying, "Oh, your department needs a third or fourth person. Let me go get them for you." It's the department head saying, "This is how I want my department to run and these are the people I want to be hiring this week."

What's an aspect of your job that outsiders might find surprising?

Makeup artists become so intimately acquainted with the cast. We form very tight family units with one another and with the actors we see for so long each day. We're seeing them at four or five in the morning, at their most vulnerable. Maybe they didn't have much sleep. Maybe they had a nasty breakup. Maybe they're puffy or hungover. We see them in ways that they don't normally let others see them. It's our job to finesse them to a place where they're calm and ready to work. So a big part of my job is getting them into the right state of mind. And that involves a tremendous amount of emotional labor. People can be nervous, uncomfortable, edgy, or antsy, but I almost always find a soft spot or avenue to conversation. I get in there and soothe them. We're not therapists, but it's our job to get them in the right mood. If they're not focused, calm, happy, or at least comfortable in their skins, they can't do anything for the director. It doesn't matter if it's a thirty-second commercial or a two-hour film. They're just not in the right headspace. It's my job to help get them there. I find it very natural and quite easy. One of my directors used to call me the talent whisperer because I could get even the angriest person ready to go to set.

How does it feel when you're not working?

Awful. It's the worst part of this job. There is no length of time that is good for me to be out of work. I get nervous after more than five days.

Why is it so awful?

There's nothing worse than having no control over your destiny week by week. You can only do so much to make it rain. You can call your peers and say, "I'd love to get some union hours. I'm looking for anything you can throw my way." You can call producers with whom you're friendly to remind them that you're ready to work. My friends who are salaried don't understand how I cope. No matter how miserable their jobs are, they say, "We don't know how you get through these times." I don't either! I lose my mind. It's terrifying. It's so disconcerting because there's no actionable thing you can do to change it. You're helpless. All you can do is remind people that you exist. You put yourself in the back of their head, and that's it. You're at the mercy of others. You're contingent labor.

I think it's even harder in the entertainment business. When you love what you do and you're in a creative industry and you're also a freelancer, if the phone doesn't ring, it feels very personal, whether it is or not. You start doubting your work and wonder whether you're ever going to get called again.

Do you think this is typical?

I don't know if anything is typical anymore. Some of the people who were my journeyman mentors, who taught and trained me in these classes when I entered the union, had worked in the studio system many years ago. There was a consistency in those days. You'd go in there and you'd be there twelve hours a day, five days a week. That was that. Whatever it called for. These days, nothing is typical.

Would you have liked to work in the studio system of the old days?

I think it would have been an extraordinary education. It would have been regular and consistent work. I also like that socialized work environment. But on the other hand, I like doing a lot of different things. I like bopping around because the working conditions have changed a lot. It can become a little tedious, and so many corners are cut these days. Once you're in a production for a month, you start seeing where all the little gaps and problems are and how they affect you. It becomes less fun and glossy. You get anxious to move on and do something new, to get a mental break from it.

What kinds of cost cutting really get to you?

The stuff that is penny wise and pound foolish. It's hard to pinpoint because examples sound so silly and mundane. It's not paying a couple hundred dollars for someone to have a partial prep day for an elaborate prosthetic, but then ordering $200 of some bizarre vegan meal that the actor absolutely has to have on a given day. It's not putting in place things that will make production run smoothly, but instead indulging people with difficult temperaments who suddenly need this or that. Instead of doing what seems the most logical, we'll have elaborate discussions about where we borrow from Peter to pay Paul. A unit production manager or production coordinator will say to me, "I know your department needs it. I'll figure out a way to do it, but you have to give me time to rework this and figure out how to flip another line item." Why not just budget for the overage? I'll ask for boards, a breakdown, and a schedule, and I'll look at it and go, "You want us to get eight talent ready, plus twenty featured background actors? Listen, guys, we can be an hour late or you can spend $450 for union scale and get me a swing assistant. And I think you'll be happy to extend that money. You can put them on an eight and skate. And at eight hours they'll skate off for $375. How does that look to you?" It just doesn't make sense to me why simplicity is often greeted with resistance.

Is there generally less work today than there was five years ago?

Absolutely. So much work has left Southern California for other places. Louisiana. Georgia. Michigan. The Carolinas. There have been some efforts to slow the exodus, but even those efforts have been destructive. Unions have negotiated for what they now refer to as ultra-low-budget contracts, which are designed for ultra-low-budget movies (and also new media productions) as a way to make them local union shoots despite their meager resources. This is important, because crew can stay here to work on a union shoot and earn the hours they need to remain active union members and most importantly keep their health insurance. But the pay is often pretty bad. You earn something not too far above minimum wage.

My understanding is that the negotiated rates were designed with the idea of stopping runaway production from leaving California. So they approve all of these super-low-budget union movies at rates that would never have existed even a couple years ago *because* of runaway production in order to *slow* runaway production. For these kinds of shoots, highly skilled craft workers are earning not too much more than fast food jobs just for the privilege of working near home.

In the union's mind, I guess, the alternative is not to work at all. So the agreement is taking an already difficult situation and making it worse. However, with the new tax credits going into effect this year, the hope is that more regularly salaried work will return home.

Are you tempted to work outside Los Angeles?

I prefer to make it work in Los Angeles. I have a friend, however, who has been living in Detroit for eight months with his wife. It's easy for them. They don't have children. They don't have pets. They just get up and go. But when you work out of state, you end up in this bubble. You eat, live, and breathe that project. If you're in Los Angeles, you're at least going back to your home after you're done for the day. There's more of a work-life balance. Well, there's at least *some* distinction between work and life!

I can't imagine being gone that long. Some people love it and thrive on it. I don't think it's for me, personally. But also on an emotional level, it's extremely sad to see so much business leave town. I don't want to be a part of the process that keeps pulling work away. This is what we do. This is where we do it. We are the entertainment capital of the world. Why work anywhere else?

Do you think your working conditions have changed? Given what you've said about runaway production, are there tensions or pressures that manifest on set because of the loss of work?

There are two different consequences that are somewhat related. First, the era of big personalities—what you might consider diva behavior—in hair, makeup, and costume seems to be over. At one time, certain artists could commandeer certain jobs at certain rates, no matter the budget. I think that era is gone. The industry doesn't allow for it anymore. There isn't that kind of elasticity of money anymore. The only time I see this happen is when there's a celebrity request that is hard and fast, and they will not use anyone else. We're worker bees now. There's no time or money for divas. Secondly, and in general, the department is being asked to do more and more with less and less, which in turn makes it feel somewhat less glamorous than it did not too long ago.

Some of what I'm about to say, of course, also has to do with industrial changes and financial pressures in the music business. For example, when I first came into this business there was a lot of cachet associated with working on music videos. When I started working, the big music videos were made with A-list talent. Makeup artists were going in and getting up to $4,000 a day to work with the big-name artists. Now we're working for less. You're lucky if you get $300 for doing a twelve- to fifteen-hour day. We have to tap into our kits a lot more. They don't reimburse us or offer kit fees. They might want some very elaborate hair and makeup that calls for a lot of things that normally would be budgeted but aren't now. And you have less and less time to get people ready. It's just a series of things that have made that work very unglamorous. It's gotten to the point where makeup artists avoid music videos. They'd rather collect unemployment than do a music video because they know the hours are long, productivity pressures are extremely tight, and it's just—not what it used to be.

Why did you want to join the union [Make-Up Artists and Hair Stylists Guild, IATSE, Local 706]?

When I first started out, I didn't know if I would ever be able to join the union. It seemed so distant and difficult because it is a rather closed club and many of the loopholes or back entrances to get in have quietly shut over the years. Local 706 seems harder than any other IA local to enter. It's also one of the most expensive.

I'm a bit of a socialist at heart. I thought the whole idea of the union is strength in numbers. You want to get as many union members as possible. Yet 706 keeps new people out as much as possible because they're trying to preserve the work for their core union members. It's a very weird double-edged sword that I haven't heard of with any other IA local. I believe in organized labor, and I want more union membership, not less.

How do you become an active member of the union?

The simplest answer is that you need to earn a certain number of hours and then pay your dues. Literally. It's thousands of dollars to join. And then quarterly dues are at least $250. But there's a catch-22. To get in you have to work a lot of union hours, but you can't get union hours unless you're in the union. So it's extremely difficult.

There are basically three ways to get in the union. They sound very easy, but they're absolutely not. The most straightforward way to get into the union is to work thirty days on a nonunion film that flips partway through the production to become a union signatory. It's tough for makeup artists, though. When you have a small makeup department, there are two or three people. We can't flip a production because the producers will know it's us and can retaliate. But if you have a big group of ten to fifteen crew members, it's more difficult to pinpoint who initiated the flip—it's always good to have the grips and electricians on your side. They have a little bit more power because there's more of them to hide the whistleblower.

It's always a terrifying thing when a production flips. The union reps come and shut it down. Then the production is given two options. First, they can flip to union, which means you've got to go back and get more money. Sometimes it just can't happen, so the show dies. Everybody leaves and you have to start all over with a whole new crew. What traditionally happens is you don't try to flip a show until at least two thirds of it is in the can, so they don't want to replace you with scabs for continuity reasons.

The second way is called the 60/60/60. You have to have sixty production days in a year, three out of five years in a row. It doesn't sound like much, right? It breaks down to five or six days a month. The problem is that it has to be feature film or television and most of us don't work in that capacity alone. Our working days also come from press junkets, music videos, or on-air appearances, but you can't use them to qualify for 60/60/60. It's a very limited calculation. It's also a hassle to prove: you have to request a letter from every single payroll company and every single production company to document that you did the work. It's hard, and the documentation is time consuming.

The third way is to do ninety union commercial days in a year. That of course is a lot more days per month. I know a lot of people who initially came in on commercial contracts because back in the day, a nonunion artist could still work union commercials; it was kind of a back-door entrance. That loophole has since closed, but there was a time in which production would willingly approve nonunion artists for commercial jobs. It also helped if those artists had agency representation and the clients specifically asked for them. (There was also one soap opera that had a specialized contract that allowed nonunion members to work. But since it was also a back door, everyone wanted to get on that soap. Imagine a department head with a list of fifty eager artists all vying for the chance to sub in on that one show for eligible days!) The biggest challenge with this path is that your days don't roll over into the next calendar year. They expire. So it could take years and years to join if you fall short annually.

For me, after years of qualifying my hours I became a trainee, and finally a journeyman, in my union. That elevation involved years of work even after I joined the union. I had to continually document my days on various productions, and take months of weekend classes. I am now technically at the highest level that I can be in our union. It used to have a lot more meaning. These days producers don't care. They'll hire a trainee, but luckily as a journeyman, there is no project I'm barred from working on. For example, commercial artists cannot work on episodic television in our union. They have to elevate to a trainee position in order to do that. And some shows only want journeymen to work as department heads, although there are no longer any hard-and-fast rules about that. On a personal level, it feels great because I never thought a dozen years ago I'd ever get into the union the way I did. I never thought I'd be a trainee, and then when I was a trainee, I never thought I'd be a journeyman. I'm always shocked and pinch myself. I'm a journeyman! It's still remarkable. But it doesn't get you the same accolades that it would years ago.

What do you need to do get your health benefits?

My guild requires eight hundred hours annually. It keeps going up. But when you have the benefits, they're spectacular. You can have a family. You can have a partner or a spouse or children or other dependents all covered, virtually for free. It is remarkable. You get the same health insurance as Julia Roberts. But the problem is that you've got to earn those hours every year. And you start at zero each year. If you work more than eight hundred hours in a given year, you can bank up to four hundred hours for the following year. But any more than that, you just lose the hours.

I remember going to my first meetings where there were so many people who were jokingly called the "old timers." They had been in the union forever. They had gotten in fairly young and had been working for thirty to forty years. Many were now up in arms about changes to the health plan (the requirement was moving from six hundred to eight hundred hours). The contract stipulated more hours for less and less coverage. They were frantic and angry. But I was young, and it all looked so glossy to me. I felt I had made it. I was looking through the eyes of someone who was so delighted to be finally invited into the union after so many years of working. Now, looking back on those conversations, I understand why the process made the "old timers" so frustrated. It also hasn't stopped: our health care and pension qualifications and coverage have continued to erode, particularly in the last five to ten years.

You have a level of labor consciousness that seems rare among your generation. What do you think about your peers? When is the last time you saw more than twenty 706 members in the same room?

It's sad, because we have a couple thousand members and maybe thirty to sixty people attend a union meeting. It's sad because it reduces the opportunities to talk to one another within the union about our experiences on set. Unfortunately, the culture of our union has made it that way—no one talks.

I'm still learning from other great makeup artists who also are journeymen. I try to do it for other up-and-coming artists. It's so important to our craft and our collective future. It doesn't seem like there is enough dialogue. I think it's because runaway production makes things tight for everyone. Nobody wants to share information or resources. It also leads to fewer people coming to you for help or advice. In union meetings people aren't talking about it all that much. Everyone is very concerned about their livelihoods; everyone is concerned about whether they can stay here or if they have to move. So nobody wants to pass on and share information as much as they used to.

Do you think there's a mentality that, by keeping the membership limited, it protects members in some way?

Yes. I don't think it actually works, but I think that's what the union thinks. But if it works so well, why do we have these new union contracts that pay us next to nothing on certain projects?

If you could wave your wand, what's the change you'd most like to see in the motion picture industry?

I would make sure union signatory companies never run anything nonunion. I've worked for a number of union signatory production companies that mostly specialize in commercials, promos, like cable TV and reality TV. But they run 50 percent of their jobs nonunion. They'll give the production a different name, even though it's the same address. Every time the union calls them, the union says, "You know you're in violation of your contract." But the producers somehow get away with it by simply changing the name of this one-off production entity. If they get a big enough budget, they do a union production. If they're desperate to get a client, they'll do it nonunion even though they use a union crew. It's very frustrating. And the union certainly tries to protect its members by calling them out. But there are dozens of jobs going on daily around the city and they can't hunt down every job, every day, to penalize the production. There isn't enough manpower for that. At a certain point, you wonder why the companies even signed the union contract. We lose our union rates and our hours every time we have to do a nonunion job with a union company. In fact, I probably lose 50 percent of my hours every year to signatory companies that violate their contracts.

Do you think that's something that has increased?

Absolutely. Because nobody wants to pay for anything anymore. When budgets are tighter, production companies find running the project nonunion helps keep everything on track. They can pay us a few hundred dollars less. They don't have meal penalties. They don't have health care costs.

I also would wave my wand to ensure that it's much more tenable for crew to join IATSE. We don't have enough collective bargaining power to improve conditions in Los Angeles.

It's taken me a second career and a lot of time to get to this point where I'm a journeyman and I can do the jobs that I enjoy doing, and I'm still trying to get to that next level, trying to secure work on higher-tiered contracts, trying to get bigger celebrities on my client list. I know it's a matter of time. It's perseverance. It's putting in all your effort and your hours. It's advocating for a strong union to better protect us, so that things like ultra-low-budget contracts wouldn't exist.

You do all that because there is no magic wand.

9

Stephen Lighthill, cinematographer

Stephen Lighthill, ASC, has been a camera operator on film and television projects since the 1960s. Formerly head of the Local 600, the International Cinematographers Guild, he now oversees the cinematography program at the American Film Institute. Here he outlines the many challenges camera personnel confront as they build their careers, and speaks about union efforts to manage the changes taking place in the motion picture industry.

What are the key issues confronting cinematographers today?

I would put pay rates at the top of the list. All cinematographers, except those in the very top ranks, say they are earning what they earned twenty years ago, even less. And you see it across the board. You see it in documentaries. You see it in independent features. Every employer is worried about the bottom line, and everybody is trying to pay you less for your work. Even when we find a job that pays slightly over scale, we're pressured to waive other conditions of a standard contract, like overtime or turnaround time [the rest time between one day's work and the next].

I recently discovered that the International Cinematographers Guild has worked out tiered contracts, which are basically designed to give low-budget producers a break on wage rates, but still require them to make retirement and health care contributions for members. So, although these cinematographers are earning wages that are well below scale, they're still accruing hours that allow them to qualify for health care. The result, though, is that the guild was forced to give up any kind of standard wage structure for cinematographers when they work on low-budget productions. For instance, I recently talked to an experienced friend who used to make a good living shooting relatively low-budget movies with budgets between $2 and $12 million, working at scale or a little over. Now those jobs pay less, with some of the lower-tier contracts offering only $1,000 per week, which is about half of normal scale for a forty-hour week. Most people have a basic fee that is considerably higher than that.

Lower-tiered contracts are a killer for people who have families. So, now my friend is working in television as a camera operator where he at least gets a regular paycheck. He can go home and take care of his daughters, and he's not so worried about money all the time. He'll go back to being a cinematographer when the conditions are better. This is an experienced guy with great credits. We're moving backward in terms of wages.

I think cinematographers also worry about work hours and safety. The hours we work would be jaw-dropping to other Americans, particularly on one-hour television dramas. I talked to a cinematographer last week who said she had an eighty-hour week over the course of five days. That was normal.

Budget pressures have also threatened a lot of the traditions that give cinematographers their creative authority, including reasonable preparation time. Sometimes producers will let the cinematographers review their budget line items and negotiate—for example, the cinematographer can give up some lighting in order to get a more expensive camera lens—but that's not always guaranteed. Now you'll see producers make decisions very early in the production process because they see it as a way of controlling their budgets. Cinematographers may want to talk with directors to figure out what's appropriate for the story, but the producer would rather dictate the terms and the technology to save money. Or the director will just decide that specific things will be done in postproduction rather than on camera.

The relationship with visual effects would likely round out our top concerns. For us, it raises important questions about our role and what we contribute to filmmaking. When I was president of the American Society of Cinematographers, I had a big meeting with lots of cinematographers who also worked in effects: Dean Cundey, Richard Edlund, and others. I said, "Okay, the academy is pressuring us to establish two categories: visual effects cinematography and traditional cinematography." We kicked the idea around, and I quickly came to the conclusion that this is a very bad idea—a dead end for cinematographers. Ultimately it would ghettoize the people who shoot in a traditional way.

Let's talk about the big picture. What has changed in the industry?

Everything has changed and maybe nothing has changed. People still love stories. People still watch film and television. But what do they watch more? They watch TV more. They go to movie theaters less. I don't care what the box office says, people are going to the theater less. The middle-aged parents who used to be the bread and butter for the industry are not going to the movies because they can't afford it. A trip to the movies with a family can easily cost $50. It's expensive to go to the movies. People are watching TV more, people are watching on their cellphones more, people are watching on their iPads more.

There's still a voracious need for production, but the employment landscape is not what it used to be. You see new entities getting into the business to fill the need for content, but what does that mean for cinematographers? In the case of Netflix, the jobs pay pretty well, but in many cases they don't. For example, YouTube is establishing a presence and it now has a production facility in Playa Vista where crews are earning $10 an hour! They're getting paid checkout-stand wages because YouTube will subsidize a guy and say, "Okay, come on out from Madison to L.A. and work with us. We'll give you a little training and some equipment to help expand your channel." But these creators are responsible for putting their own crews together and can't afford to budget anything other than rock-bottom wages. This puts enormous pressure on traditional wage rates, categories, and the way L.A. does business. And the bigger picture is that even though L.A. remains a center for talent—acting, writing, and directing—many producers are going to go elsewhere to shoot because of government subsidies and lower wage rates.

Another big pressure comes from technology. If you look at any profession—architecture, medicine, surgery—craft is being seriously undermined by the introduction of computers. Whether it's computer-aided design, computer-aided surgery, or what's happening to us in production, things are changing. A producer comes out and sees me shooting with a digital camera, pulling a card out and shoving it into a computer and thinks, "Screw it, my son can do that."

Technology is making our filmmaking tools so much more accessible—I don't like the word "democratization" because it implies a new reality—but filmmaking has always been an art and craft that requires study and experience, and still does. People can go to Best Buy and, for a couple grand, buy a 70D DSLR camera and a laptop to make a movie, but they probably are not telling good stories. I'm sorry. They're just not. To be a storyteller, you have to develop certain skills that define what's good and what's not. Of the thousands of entries that Sundance is getting, very few are good. How many sales happen because of Sundance? Not many. Are there any more sales than there were twenty years ago?

Let's talk about globalization. Are there other places in the world outside of L.A. with deep pools of talent? For instance, if a producer decides to shoot in Prague, is it possible to find good cinematographers there? Or does the globalization of production mean talent from L.A. is now shuttling around the globe?

Obviously everybody's career is different. Many cinematographers have a home in the L.A. area. They don't work here. They work in Atlanta or they work overseas, but they come back here because the producers and directors are here. Very early in my career I knew I had to build my professional life in Los Angeles. I had an agent here, an address here, a phone number here, but I lived in San Francisco, and my agent and I saw very quickly that that doesn't work. You have to really be in L.A. You have to always come back, no matter where the work takes you. You have to be seen. You have to go to screenings, go to the various events, and be involved in the organizations that are part of the industry. And you have to be here so that if producers have extracurricular things they want you to do, you're ready.

I think there's still a lot of pressure to keep the center of cinematography in L.A. At the same time, there's certainly great cinematography in different countries, but it's not as robust or as saturated as it is in L.A. It also depends on where you're going. If you're going to Munich, sure, but if you're going to Prague, maybe. If you're going further into Eastern Europe, the answer is no. You're going to bring your cinematographer. If you're going even further afield in the Middle East, the answer is again no. You're going to bring your cinematographer.

In your estimation, what are the top ten cities for cinematography talent?

In the United States, you have New York and Los Angeles. That's it. London would be another. There are exceptions, of course. People live in Mumbai or Mexico City. And Stephen Goddard lives in San Francisco, but he never works there. Honestly I don't think I can identify ten cities. Poland is filthy with cinematographers. Are they A-list and known to everybody? No. But they're great because Poland has a really active independent scene thanks to their state-sponsored media funds. The United States doesn't have that type of support available, and it's a tragedy. I'm not talking about incentives for producers. I'm talking about support for artistic endeavor—to recognize filmmaking's potential as a meaningful and provocative creative exercise as well as a commercial activity. Germany knows this; the Netherlands knows it; all the Scandinavian countries know it. And they have a deep enough understanding of this industry that they'll finance coproductions all over the place.

But the United States has always been very blind when it comes to the arts. In the 1980s I made a good living shooting sponsored documentaries about social issues like organizing labor unions, the Spanish Civil War, and other topics. These were generally funded by the National Endowment for the Humanities. I would do a couple of those a year. I made a great living because of those films in the 1980s. Then Ronald Reagan said, "We can't do that anymore. We're competing with Hollywood producers." Well, the Hollywood producers would never step in and fund a documentary about labor unions in the 1930s. That has to be a passion project for a director who works for five to ten years putting it together. I shot a film about Berkeley in the 1960s, and the producer literally worked on that film for more than a decade. You should subsidize that kind of thing, and we don't do it. And that's a tragic disservice not only to those issues and debates, but also to my students who no longer have the opportunities I once had to hone their craft and make a living on those productions.

What makes an A-list cinematographer?

A-list cinematographers have achieved recognition from their peers, whether it's from the Television Academy, the Academy of Motion Picture Arts and Sciences, or from the ASC or the British Society of Cinematographers. They have also surpassed conventional standards, and the work they've done has made peers say, "Wow, that's exceptional." Then, of course, you can look at how much they've worked. I think there are a lot of cinematographers who haven't had much recognition, but they just work all the time and consistently deliver what's asked of them. It's difficult to make categories. People are hired for all kinds of reasons. I think the pool of talented and capable cinematographers is deep. I think it's way deeper than the stock of available jobs. The ten-year, ten-thousand-hour rule seems to apply: it takes that much time and effort to make a great artist and craftsperson in film.

What role do agents play in all of this?

They don't play a role. Agents have never played a big role for cinematographers. They may play a big role in negotiating for the very top professionals, like Robert Elswit, whose phone will be ringing all the time. They may also help clients pick future projects, but in general, agents do not get you work. Your network gets you work.

Music videos and TV commercials are a whole different world, though. Those agents are going to the parties, looking for the jobs, trying to sell you. But those are very fashion-oriented kinds of businesses where you can go out and sell. You're basically selling a guy or gal for a three-day shoot, and the producer, director, or art director is desperate for something different. In those kinds of situations agents can help you find jobs and mold your career. When you're dealing with feature films, it's all on you. It all comes from what you've done and who recommends you.

Ask any cinematographer: he can trace how he got every single job in his career. He knows how his name got put in the hat, why it came out of the hat, and how he got the interview. And, because it's all a big network, the strangest people recommend you. A second art director who you were nice to on a set is suddenly a production manager. And he says, "You know, give him a call." It really is focused on personal contacts. In fact, you're much more likely to be suspicious of an agent because you might worry that the agent is just trying to make money by selling you to some guy who may or may not be so good for you or your career.

Let's talk more about the importance of professional networks. Do cinematographers find themselves working with the same people again and again?

If you're good, your network is something you've worked on for a long time. You get work from your network, but you've also built your network on your own. For instance, you make calls [to potential employers], and you keep track of your calls so you don't bug people. You get involved with a mentor, someone who wants to help you. People don't succeed in this career without someone else wanting them to succeed. The whole business is a process of finding those people, being in touch with them in an appropriate way, and paying attention when someone calls you on the phone. You don't say, "Oh, you want to hire me? Great, thank you." You say, "Gee, how'd you get my name?" Then you send that person who recommended you a thank-you note, and you keep track of the fact that that person recommended you. If you have an opportunity, you also find out exactly why he or she wanted to recommend you. Anybody will tell you that the key to a successful career as a freelancer is working on your network, developing your network.

Are there certain individuals that cinematographers must keep in their networks? Directors? Producers?

Sure, but it depends on where you're looking for work. In the television industry it's all about the producers. They're the ones who make those types of decisions. There are no directors involved at the beginning of the game when they're thinking of who will be handling cinematography. In bigger-budget feature films, many people make cinematography decisions. A director may want you, but a producer may not, and they have to agree at some point. Also, the bond company may say, "I'm not going to trust that person. They've never done a $100 million movie, so I'm not going to bond it." Then you have to have a producer who's willing to go to the mat for you, or willing to ignore pressures from the bonding agent.

And that will happen?

Oftentimes the bond company will say something along the lines of, "Okay, but if he or she screws up, it's on you." Sometimes the company is worried about the cinematographer's experience, but the most common concern is substance abuse. The bond company will have concerns about someone who has done something on a set at some point in the past. They'll say to a producer, "If something goes wrong, we're not going to pay for you to find another guy or to pick up the days that were lost. That's going to be on you."

How has the union [International Cinematographers Guild IATSE, Local 600] changed over the course of your career?

Early in my career it was a very nepotistic organization. There were seniority provisions that worked in very exclusionary ways. It was known as the Roster, and it consisted of three groups of people, like an A, B, and C group. You couldn't work if you weren't on the Roster. You couldn't get on the Roster if you didn't work. Finally, the Justice Department said, "You guys are using that to control who is allowed to work. Get rid of it." So they got rid of it. That was a big change.

And there's now a much more serious investment in safety—that's a huge change. There's a passport safety program. You actually have a little card that indicates you've taken the required classes. Everyone has to take them if they want to work. It's especially intense for grips, who must know a range of safety protocols: how many people can be on a camera cart, how many can be on a scaffold, and even how much weight a room can hold. Their training involves a lot of intense geometry and engineering. The studios are on board with the safety concerns, so it's been a great change.

The guild also takes its commitment to training very seriously. As new technology is introduced—whether it's cameras or recording media—crews get trained. If a producer goes to the union, he or she can expect to get somebody who's properly trained and knows best practices. That's a big advantage.

You've mentioned concerns about lower wages and longer hours. How is the union organizing around these issues?

Most of the work is freelance, and that makes organizing tough. It's also very hard to organize productions. A production will be up and running inside a month and then be gone. Still, the IA [IATSE] isn't totally powerless. Many producers say that they're going shoot using nonunion workers, but when they go out and hire people, they're hiring union people. There's just nobody who's any good who is not in the union. Many workers will sign onto a project without saying they are union. Then when they get on the set, they call their local. The union comes down and says, "You've got union people on this, so we've got to turn it into a union contract."

Then those people have to sign a card and follow the regulations of the Labor Relations Board, which require that a union representative write a contract for you. The response is not automatic by any means, but of course you're in big trouble with your local if you go and work on a nonunion site without telling the local that you're there.

Leadership will do an actual organizing drive. They'll get everybody together after work and they'll say, "Please sign the card indicating us as your work representative." They have to do that. So when a union person takes a job that's on a nonunion site they let the union know, and then the union is going to try to organize the site and make it a union production.

If the union can't organize the site, will the person work there anyway?

No. That's nuclear war.

Is it valuable having the union on site?

Absolutely. It maintains wage rates, which would otherwise be quite low. The union comes in and asks the producer to pay wages that they're currently paying but also to pay back benefits, which is 15 percent or 17 percent of pay. So the producer can still pay grips $75 a day, but they're getting their health insurance paid for and they're getting a little bump in their retirement fund. We have one of the healthiest retirement funds in the country. We don't get paid residuals like writers do. Residuals all go into our union's retirement fund, which actually helps mitigate the pressure on wages. People at least can say that they'll have something there for them when they're in retirement, even though their wages may not be so great today.

But in some ways it has exposed the union as kind of a paper tiger. Wage rates have been deteriorating, but employees do get their benefits. And when the union organizes a production, it sometimes finds nonunion employees who then join, making the union even stronger for the next time.

How many people are in Local 600?

Today the guild is huge—it went from a small local union in Los Angeles to a national local with about 6,500 members. So if it's ever pushed to the wall it has a serious ability to defend itself. It's got a beautiful website and a beautiful magazine with substantial readership. And it has a full professional staff. So the guild is very careful about tracking what people do: who's working and whether their dues are paid. And those people keep bringing new business and attention to the guild. It has helped make us as powerful as the Directors Guild. Anybody above the line is very powerful, but below the line it's a different story. You have to have numbers and you have to be organized. Because of our power, we play a leadership role on the set. This is crucial because producers will intentionally or unintentionally cut every corner they can. For instance we have a standing agreement that if a person feels that they're too fatigued to drive home, a producer has to pay for a hotel room so that worker doesn't have to commute that night. That's something that has to be watched. Producers must understand that they've got to do that.

You said that the union is the leading force in organizing below-the-line labor on sets. Is this true in other places, or just in L.A.?

There's nothing our union can do in Prague. But in places like, let's say, Wilmington, North Carolina, the union will be able to organize productions because you're in a remote location. The producer has no alternative. There's nowhere to turn. The IA can come in and say to the producer, "Now you're union." They'll go in with the cinematographers and the grips and other groups and say, "Look, this is the labor pool in Wilmington, North Carolina, and they're all in the IA. Make an agreement with us." When people are in a place like New York, it's easier to hide from the union for a few days. But we'll find out about them some way. Even in new locations that pop up in response to incentives, the guild will open offices as soon as a labor pool starts to develop. Our representatives are in place and keep track of everything.

In most places in the United States, you can't hide. Plus, remember, we aren't the only union members on the set. Actors. Directors. Teamsters. They won't do a nonunion production in the United States. SAG-AFTRA is a very powerful group, and it uses that power very carefully, but it ends up being good for us. After twelve hours, actors have to be done. When they leave, there's nothing to shoot, so we go home, too.

Does that change once you cross national borders?

Yes, it's a radical change. But the change is not as stark when you cross into Canada, where we have very powerful locals and the government is a fairly progressive supporter of unions. When I went to shoot in Canada, the immigration guy asked why I was there and then called the local union [to let them know I would be working in Canada]. After that call, I worked under a work permit for a certain period of time. I had to leave the day after the permit expired. They watch you very closely, but they're also very supportive. So you're not going to escape from the union structure in Canada.

Once you go into other countries, though, you're in a whole other world.

If increased mobility is a new reality and you're finding yourself shooting in distant places, how does that affect the way you put your camera crew together? Do you often find yourself working with foreign crews?

A cinematographer has relationships with the people he or she works with, and those relationships develop over many years. So when you get a job, you pick up the phone and your first call is to your gaffer. Then you call your key grip, then your personal assistant, then your operator, your steady camera operator, the people you've worked with before. You may have people you work with in L.A. and people you work with in London. You may be okay leaving L.A. without somebody, but you'll find people you're connected with all over the world now.

Sometimes cinematographers go overseas, and they come back and say to me, "I had a wonderful crew. I had a great experience. I'd love to work with those people again." Just as often they come back and say, "I'd rather die than work with that crew again." Sometimes you're in another country where most people don't speak your language and you're dependent on an interpreter or some similar scenario. Other times directors help you, but basically they're using pidgin English to get through the day. It's very difficult. When you're on the set you sometimes hear conversations that have nothing to do with you, but they give you clues or warnings about how the work is going and what may be ahead. When you don't get those clues [because of linguistic or cultural barriers], things can become very difficult.

Do most cinematographers try to keep their preferred team intact when they travel abroad?

Yes. Part of the problem is that under the basic agreement [with the studios and major producers], if cinematographers take more than three below-the-line people, that triggers a clause in the contract that requires studios to pay residuals to the IA. Most big productions will honor an A-list cinematographer's request for certain crew but then quickly dig in their heels. They'll say, "Gaffers? Sure. Anybody else? No." Then the cinematographers have to make a bunch of quick decisions. They have to decide whether to call their agents to talk for them or whether the director can help at all. Put simply, the question is: How do I best control this situation to get what I need? It can easily become a big political mess. You have to negotiate your way through it very carefully. Some cinematographers simply walk away. It happens all the time.

10

Calvin Starnes, grip

Over the past two decades, Calvin Starnes has worked as an assistant director, a grip, and, most recently, a screenwriter. This interview focuses on his work as a grip, a career he recently quit due to his frustrations with changes in the industry. In what follows, he recounts his concerns about diversity, safety, training, work hours, and relentless budget cuts. Starnes blogs about his experiences in the industry at writercalvin.tumblr.com.

Describe your career in the industry. Where did you start? Where did you end up?

I went to Boston College from 1990 to 1994. During my junior year I was interning at the Coolidge Corner Theater and this movie came through, which I think was the first US-Russian cooperative film after the Berlin Wall came down. It was called *Banya*, produced by Mark Donadio. He gave me my first job as a production assistant, which got me started working in the Boston film industry. I did PA [production assistant] work on commercials and movies and worked on student films and low-budget productions as an assistant director or a grip or an electrician.

I came out to L.A. in 1996 and did AD [assistant director] work for three years, but burned out quickly. You typically have the same arguments over and over again, especially in the lower-budget, nonunion world. You always have a UPM [unit production manager] or line producer who tries to cut corners, like skimping on the transportation department or failing to hire a location manager. They make those cuts without realizing how important the jobs are and that somebody has to do those tasks whether you hire someone or not. So, in those situations, the AD often ends up doing those things on top of their main responsibilities.

In 1999 I had a friend who was doing this Ken Loach movie, *Bread and Roses*. Ken is very pro-union and the show was going to start nonunion, but was guaranteed to flip. If I signed on to grip for Ken, I would get all of the days I needed to join the union. More money? Less responsibility? Sign me up. I threw all my AD stuff in the trash and gripped from 1999 to 2014.

At the time, being a grip seemed attractive. Once you got in the union, you were able to work on bigger shows and make more money. Back then, you didn't have as many low-budget shows and the tax incentives hadn't destroyed the L.A. industry yet. If you were good at your job, you always had work. And I was fortunate to work a lot and make good money.

What does a grip do?

Not all grips do the same thing. You have canvas grips who mend and sew all the flags and rags. You have construction grips who might work with the art department or be on loan to another department. You have rigging grips, who generally come in before shooting to set up these massive green screens or steel towers and scaffolding or build tents or anything that is labor and time intensive.

Then you have set grips, or "show ponies," as some like to call us, who work the set. We're the sister department to the electrical department. They set the lights. We shape, color, diffuse, and cut the lights with various flags and frames. We also design and build rigs for lights when they need to be in places that you can't put a light stand, like on the ceiling or off the side of a building.

Or if they want to put a camera on a roller coaster, motorcycle, boat, or car, we're the ones who have to figure out how to do it. We also do all the camera work in terms of dollies and cranes. That's the dolly grip. Dolly grips are unofficially part of the camera department because even if they wanted to help us they are often chained to their dolly and their camera operator.

It sounds like grips have their hands in a little bit of everything. Does that make union classifications and job functions complicated? Do the boundaries between departments ever blur when it comes to who does what?

Officially, each kind of grip has a specific list of duties, but we always end up doing more than what is officially written into our contracts. If other departments show up not having done their work or are unprepared, they will probably call grips to fix it. There's an old set joke: "What's the heaviest piece of equipment the grip department carries? The art department." But it all depends on the department head. I had a boss—a key grip—who was a yes man. He presented himself and his grips as the guys who could do anything. And I understood why. He wanted to make himself look good, which in turn makes him more hirable. The flip side to that is that he got to look great saying "yes," but we had to do the extra work.

Of course you also get other key grips who refuse to do anything outside their specific responsibilities. They don't care if other departments aren't prepared or don't have the right equipment. These guys just say it isn't their job. And I can definitely see that side of it, too. It depends on who you work with. There's a delicate balance between being a team player and doing someone else's job for them.

Do you think producers want to film in other parts of the world because they can escape union work rules and regulations?

It's probably naive to say they aren't a factor, but labor cost is a small fraction of your budget compared to cast, location fees, and equipment. So it's a factor, but subsidies are a much bigger factor. Studios are not choosing to go Louisiana because labor is cheaper. They are going to Louisiana because Louisiana is going to give them a big bag of free money.

What are some of the complaints that producers make about work rules and job categories here in L.A.?

Producers want to do more with less. There's no doubt about it. How can we do this for less money? How can we get rid of more people? If they can do it with six guys instead of nine and make them work longer, they will do it. In the 2012 contract negotiations, the studios wanted cross-utilization between the art department, electricians, and grips. Cross-utilization would allow the studios to hire fewer people and make those people do more work. But not everybody can do what a grip can do. Not everyone can do what an electrician can do. I can't. Asking us to do more for less or do something we're not trained to do ultimately creates an unsafe work environment.

Not every executive or producer wants this. There are some genuinely great producers and execs out there who get it. But this is often the cost-cutting mentality of the people driving the negotiations. Clearly they have no clue what anyone does on the set because if they did they would never ask for this. But, far be it for an executive to step over a dollar to pick up a dime.

Do they actually see a lot of cost savings in cross-utilization? Or is it a bargaining chip? Is it something they throw in to muddy the waters so they can later say, "We'll take this off the table if you take that off the table"?

It's tough to say. By all accounts the lead negotiator of the AMPTP [Alliance of Motion Picture and Television Producers] does not seem like a pleasant person, and during the last negotiation she didn't give a shit about anything that our side had to say. I wasn't there, but those were the reports coming out of the negotiations. It dovetails nicely with the subject of income inequality and the fact that corporations don't care about labor at all. Basically they say, "If you break, we'll get a new one. You are replaceable." So I do think cross-utilization was a legitimate request, especially when you look at the latest Writers Guild of America negotiations, where studios asked for an obscene amount of rollbacks. Of course you're going to ask for more than you're going to get. That's negotiation. But I think it says a lot about what they think of us when they ask for *so* much. It just seems there's this new cruelty coming from their side. We're in negotiations right now. I've heard that after the 2012 negotiations, our health plan is in good shape, so this round we're focused on working conditions. I think this next contract will be very telling. It will illustrate whether the union is willing to hold the line or if working conditions will continue to decline.

What do you think is driving the decline?

Media conglomeration. Six companies own 90 percent of *all* media. Nine tenths. I don't think you can point to a particular individual on a set and say he or she is responsible for the decline in working conditions. But you do feel the effects of media conglomeration. It's too easy to chart the rise of the multinational corporation alongside the decline of our protections and entitlements. Multinationals rolled in with more money and more lawyers. We have money and lawyers, too, but the guys running my local union are grips. They didn't go to business school. They didn't go to law school. It was just a bunch of set guys trying to look out for one another. Now they're facing a wall of corporate lawyers backed by lots of money and education.

 The multinationals are using their power to reshape our contracts in a way that benefits them way more than it does us. We consistently lose during negotiations. For example we have a lot of contracts stating we don't get double time unless we work more than fourteen hours; as a result fourteen-hour days have become standard. Five fourteen-hour days, plus lunch, is a seventy- to seventy-five-hour workweek. Everyone's tired. It creates an unsafe working environment. And it's not just the low budget-productions that are doing this and benefiting from this.

 Up until recently, HBO for example had a sweetheart deal. HBO! You might have heard of them because they have a couple of popular shows on the air. Initially HBO executives got a special deal because it was a new network, but they've had this deal for many, many years—even after establishing a track record of hit shows and high profits. You can't help but wonder how this all happens when you're driving home late at night after working a fourteen-hour day on *True Blood* (2008–14) for lower wages.

You've mentioned safety several times. Describe some of the safety concerns on a set. Have you seen those concerns increase over the course of your career?

The biggest concern is fatigue. Everyone needs to watch Haskell Wexler's documentary *Who Needs Sleep?* (2006). He's made "long hours" his cause, and I'm sure glad he has. I understand that if you're in your twenties, a seventy-hour workweek may not seem like such a bad thing. You're young. You're resilient. You're still in the romance phase. You're in love with the glamour of working in this industry. But you're going to get older. You won't want to work seventy-plus hours a week forever. You'll want a life, a family.

Plus, it's horribly inefficient. If you need to shoot a TV show in eight days but you're asking us to do it in seven, you'll need to bring in a second and third unit to get it done. That may create more work for more people and it may cost more, but if you don't do it, everyone gets beaten down. You're overworked. You're exhausted. Your health declines. Your family life declines. Your entire quality of life declines. Again, I'll point to *True Blood*. They will finish at eight in the morning on a Saturday, only to have to be back at six or seven in the morning on a Monday. Your Saturday is fucked because you can't function. Sunday you're barely back to normal, and then you're heading to work on Monday. And they're paying you less money than you deserve.

There are great unit production managers and line producers who know that more humane schedules actually make the crew more productive, more efficient. They would love to schedule ten-hour days. But the overlords who control the purse strings will only give them fifteen days to shoot something they know really needs twenty days to do properly. There is this misconception that shorter schedules mean greater efficiency, but that's not always the case: you're paying more in overtime. You have to bring in additional people. You have potential injury costs. You have lower quality of work because everyone is rushing. You're missing shots. Ultimately, it lowers the product's quality.

If you're working on a great show, you're willing to give so much of yourself. If you feel that they care about you, and they are not beating you down because of the bottom line, you will go that extra mile when it's necessary. But if I feel they don't give a fuck, which is often the case, then I won't give a fuck. I'll do my job, but I won't give them anything extra.

Have you worked outside of Los Angeles? How do those experiences compare?

I worked in New Mexico. I did two movies there. I also worked in Atlanta. The labor pool I was exposed to at the time didn't measure up to what I was used to working with in Los Angeles. There's a local top tier that is great, and then there's everyone else. As the town gets busier, the qualified people get snatched up and you end up with kids you can't trust to do certain things. They might hurt themselves, damage the equipment, or hurt somebody else. We did *Due Date* (2010) in New Mexico. It had tons of car stuff, tons of car rigs, and you need to be able to do that type of work efficiently. When you're in these new locations with kids who might not know how to do certain things, you have to double-check their work or not ask them to do it at all. You might have to ask them to just stand there and hold your wrench.

At this point, some locations are beginning to train more and more people. That's because they have a lot of work, so they've developed training programs of their own. They're probably getting better every day. But the bulk of people in L.A. are professionals. They are going to get it done well and fast. And that's the critical difference. It's the trade-off production companies are willing to make. They can get all kinds of free money when they leave L.A., but the quality of work often suffers.

You said "kids"?

When I say "kids" I mean the level of experience, not necessarily age. But in New Mexico there did seem to be a lot of grips in their twenties and thirties. Same in Atlanta, but also some in their forties. You don't see a lot of older grips working on set. You see a few in their fifties and sixties working sets, but it's a young person's game, especially with the hours we have these days. There is some ageism. You might not get hired because there is a perception that you're weaker or slower. Gripping is hard work. It's hard on your body.

Let's talk more about the -isms. How have you seen racism, sexism, or ageism affect working conditions?

I'm a young, white, straight guy, so I don't get any abuse, but I've seen and heard a lot of offensive things. I've worked with homophobic guys. I've worked with racist guys. I've worked with guys who say horrific things about women. Film sets can get very "high school locker room" very quickly. You look to producers to set the tone, especially in television. Directors come and go, but the producers are the constant fixtures.

The cast also can play a role in bad behavior. Male cast members are often the worst. If they begin to misbehave, then it becomes okay for everybody else to misbehave. And if nobody shuts it down, like the producer, then the bad behavior gets out of control. Certain decorum is ignored. Bad behavior becomes the rule of the day. Comments that shouldn't be said are said.

I think a lot of women would like to say something, but don't come forward for fear of losing their spot or for fear of looking like they're "difficult." But they should come forward. I know it's easy for me to say that because I'm not the one who has to deal with this stuff. And to be fair, men should also come forward to confront someone who is saying or doing something they shouldn't. Just because someone like me doesn't get any abuse doesn't absolve us of responsibility to step up when we see it happen. Only by coming forward do we even have a shot at changing the environment or reducing the number of times it happens. Right now everybody does it because everybody gets away with it.

Of all the people on set during your career, what percentage have been white, straight males?

I would say like 70 or 80 percent. Probably more. You have a lot of women in certain departments: makeup, hair, wardrobe, the art department. I would say there's a sizable percentage of lesbian and gay people within the industry as well. That said, I've never met an openly gay grip. It's weird. Sometimes you spend your day on set talking about random, benign stuff then all of a sudden someone will say something homophobic and you realize not everybody thinks like you do.

I've only been in a position to hire and fire a handful of times. At the end of the day, I don't care what color you are or if you're a woman. If you can do the job, great, that's what I want. But not everyone operates that way. I'm not suggesting that anybody has an evil motive or goes out of their way to never hire people of color or women. Maybe they just want to hire their friends, and all their friends happen to be white males. That said, I know there are racist or sexist people who would probably never hire people of color or women.

Do you think this trend has anything to do with the way crews are put together at the beginning of each production? Do cohorts develop and then tend to stick together?

Definitely, you have to fit. You spend more time with these people than you do with your family, so you have to get along. It's tough to break into crews that travel together, no matter what color or gender you are, because there is a preexisting core. You can come in as a day player and then come in more regularly, but once you have your team, that's it until somebody leaves.

There's no way to establish top-down hiring policies that would make teams more diversified because that would break up the logic of how crews form and travel. Teams have to create their own affirmative action plans. If you're forcing me to hire someone, you're creating a situation where I don't know if I can trust them, and I don't know their skill level. You're also telling me to hire an unknown over someone I already know and trust.

Here's the thing: technically, the unit production manager or line producer hires and fires. But they tell us, "Bring in your guys because you know who you like to work with." If production gave us a team of their own choosing it would be inefficient. It would potentially cost them money and could create an unsafe environment. We would have to start over with each production—getting to know each other and how each person works, and then building up the trust that's necessary to do the job well. As I mentioned, we're already under a massive amount of pressure to do so much in such little time.

You don't want to bring in inexperienced people, but every member had to break into the crew at some point, and as a relative unknown, right?

Well, yes. There are a few ways to get a spot on a crew. One, you all started in the business at roughly the same time and came up together. Two, you have someone who will vouch for you. I have a handful of guys that I will vouch for. If you come with a vouch, it's like *Goodfellas*. Somebody is speaking up for you. You're trusted.

Sometimes you lose a guy due to sickness or family emergency. Or suddenly production just added something to the schedule and you need to bring in guys immediately, so you end up having to call the [union] hall. When you call the hall you never know what you're going to get. We call it "quick picks," like the lottery. And sometimes you get lucky. I made a great friend who is an awesome grip from a hall call.

Other times you get guys who are drinkers or don't want to wear a radio or have attitude or just aren't good and never will be no matter how great their attitude is. They demonstrate the imperfection of that system. In the purest sense, unions can't put one guy over another. We're all supposed to be equal. But we're not all equal. You build your reputation, and your reputation precedes you. If you are great, that reputation goes forth and people call you. If you're difficult or bad at your job for whatever reason, then that reputation goes forth and people won't call you.

But if the set is 70 or 80 percent white already, when people are crewing up, they only are thinking about people they've worked with before. It becomes a self-perpetuating system that excludes people of other ethnicities. I don't know the answer. I don't know how we break that cycle. How do we make sets more diverse without forcing people to hire new and unknown people?

If just one person on your crew had to be someone new who was not a white, straight male, that might be a way to get started. It could almost be a lottery, so you don't know what you're going to get. The downside would be that the new guy would take a spot away from a core team member. I'd have to tell my friend, "You can't work because I have to hire this guy."

I think a good starting point might be if you could create an additional spot on a crew. But that is something that would have to be created by production. For example, we were told to hire the brother of the UPM of this TV show we were on. But we didn't have to lay anyone off. He was going to be an extra guy. So we said, "Sure, bring him in." He didn't know anything, but he was a good guy. He wanted to learn and he worked hard. We taught him a bunch of stuff. That's the perfect scenario. If it's an extra person who won't take a spot away from a core team member, give me whoever you've got. It diversifies the crew. It creates more work for more people. And it trains a larger, better workforce because it's putting the new guy among a solid, experienced group of grips.

What are the top four things that keep grips up at night?

Tax incentives. Tax incentives. Tax incentives. Tax incentives. Is that four?

In my opinion, they are destroying the industry. It's a race to the bottom. Everyone is trying to figure out what they can do to attract productions to their town. But incentives should be for a start-up business, to help it gain a foothold and become sustainable. But these are billion-dollar companies. The make a net profit *every* year. Even at the height of the recent recession, they were profitable! And yet they're getting money from all these states. To be fair, I don't blame the studios. If someone wanted to give me money, I'd take it. Who wouldn't? But after these temporary communities are built on incentives or subsidies, the state legislature could determine the tax incentives aren't beneficial, which they aren't, and shut off that money and production would just leave. You would then have all this infrastructure gathering dust and people without jobs who invested in a career that no longer exists.

For thirteen years Louisiana has been enticing productions to shoot there with huge handouts, and production would stop almost overnight if they turned off the tap. How long have we been shooting in L.A.? More than a hundred years? Maybe in one hundred years Louisiana can be sustainable, but right now in 2015 it's a false economy propped up by taxpayer handouts to billion-dollar multinational companies.

Tax incentives and subsidies bribed so much of the work in Los Angeles to other states and countries. And California is having to bribe them to come back with our own massive tax incentives. I have potholes the size of the Grand Canyon on my street. But instead of fixing my street and our infrastructure, we get to give our tax dollars to profitable media companies just to keep them in town—that is, until someone offers them even more money to shoot somewhere else.

I don't know. I made a good living as a grip in L.A., but I don't know how much good work is left here. TV pays well, but the features were destroyed by incentives. Back in the day, you had huge features shooting in L.A. all the time. They were taking anyone off the street to fill crew positions. Those days are gone. I would advise anybody looking to get in the business to be very wary. A booming production hub today could easily become a ghost town tomorrow. Look at Michigan.

Some years during your career, you were doing a TV series as well as a feature film or two. That seems like a hefty schedule. How did you manage that workload?

It depends on the projects. I did *Scrubs* (2001–10) for many years. Those were five-day episodes, anywhere from eighteen to twenty-two episodes per season. If you run that schedule all the way out with twenty-two weeks of no hiatuses, that's still only five months, which leaves you seven months to play with. There were years when I needed to work all of the time. And there were years I could afford to be a little lazy and not work so much.

It's really about what you can stomach. If you can handle working that long, go for it. If you land all the right shows and work quite a bit, you can have a big year—a six-figure year for sure. That's not everybody, though. For anybody breaking into the business, I would say that's not the norm.

What would you estimate is the average gross income for somebody who works a reasonable amount of time over the course of a year? We know what the hourly rates are. We know it gets adjusted for overtime. But on average, what do you think people are making annually? Are there any figures out there?

No, there aren't. IATSE should be compiling this data. It is tough to narrow it down because there are so many different rates. If you work thirty weeks a year at some of these lower rates, you're not making that much. The tier-one rate is $17 or $18 an hour. It's obviously well above $15, the gold standard in minimum wage debates, but $18 an hour over thirty weeks a year is not a ton. It ends up being like $39,000. It depends on what your overheads are. I think during my biggest year I grossed $95,000 or $96,000. That was a combination of one particular show that was just brutal, along with some other work. It wasn't fifty weeks or anything like that. It was just a lot of hours crammed into a short period of time. It's referred to as "blood money." You're happy when you get the check, but you hate when you're earning it. The scars are there. You had to work hard for that. Some of the younger guys are enthusiastic: money, money, money. Or people who make poor financial decisions and need to work those hours because they have seven boats, two ex-wives, and fourteen kids. They need to work eighty hours. In my opinion those hours shouldn't even be an option.

Let's talk about your career transition. Why did you quit?

It's a great profession, and I don't mean to hate on it at all. There are a lot of great men and women who do it, and they love it. I wish I could be that person, because I would have continued doing what I was doing until I was sixty and had my sixty thousand hours. But there was this constant feeling that "they" didn't care about us. It beat me down. I felt like we were machinery. I needed to get out. I just didn't know what to do after that.

Then, one day my wife and I were watching a movie and this idea for a story evolved. I decided that I'd try to write it, with the naive hope that maybe I'd get lucky and sell it and I could get out. Well, I got lucky. And once I got my foot in the door, I thought maybe I would give writing a go. I'm fortunate enough that my wife works and makes money, so I can give it some time without having to worry about money. If I don't have any further success, I'll have to reassess. But for now my tool belt is hanging in my closet, hopefully never to come out again.

What's an example of something that happened on a set that made you feel like you were just viewed as a machine?

I've had UPMs turn off heaters even though people were freezing because they needed the heat for the night exterior we were shooting the next day. It was complete cluelessness. I've had UPMs who would nickel and dime you over every single thing. They would ask if I really needed everything I asked for. Well, no, *I* didn't need it; *they* needed it to shoot *their* show. You want to say no? That's fine, but then you tell the DP why I can't do what they're asking me to do.

It's a general lack of awareness of the bigger picture on the side of production. I've been on shows that did way more hours than were necessary. Not because of maliciousness; it was just inefficiency and incompetence on the part of the people running the show. Some producers and ADs don't have their shit together.

There might be times that you'd be standing on set waiting for something to happen. Finally a crew member would ask, "What are we waiting on?" And the AD would say, "Oh, yeah, I guess we're ready." If you add up all that standing-around time, and I've done it, you realize the amount of time wasted when you're not running a tight ship.

Every show is different. But I've seen far more negative than positive in my experience, and I've been on film sets for twenty years. It's a pervasive feeling of "The crew doesn't matter." The crew is often the last consideration after the budget and the actors.

How concerned are you about safety?

I'm curious to see if there will be any changes in the industry after the Sarah Jones tragedy. I was very unhappy with IATSE's response. After she died, they made all the right noises and gave speeches and had marches, but did nothing to enact meaningful change. In fact, I had friends who were behind the Pledge to Sarah website and they designed their own web app to address safety concerns on set, but they met a lot of resistance from the camera guild. There was a petition for IATSE to set up a national safety hotline, and on the day the petition launched, the president of IATSE, Matt Loeb, released a statement saying that they indeed had a national hotline in the works. I'll be interested to see if it ever materializes. Creating something like a national hotline would be a stand-alone thing that could provide an additional layer of safety for people to have at their fingertips. Hopefully IATSE is true to its word.

The tragedy seemed to bring these issues out and put them on the front page. Were you surprised?

I wasn't surprised at all. There are so many factors that went into that particular accident. I haven't read all the transcripts or reports, but you could easily see how it happened. You have faith in the ADs and production: if we're here, we must have permits. We must have this and that. I don't know the experience level of the people who were there, but maybe they didn't know any better. I have heard stories like that with more innocent scenarios. The mentality is, we're just going to pop a camera here and get it real quick. It's no big deal. A lot of times it isn't, but in this case, it definitely was. Just three weeks prior to that event I had to shoot pickups in the L.A. Metro tunnels for *Godzilla* (2014). I had to take a special class and get certified to be on the train tracks. I learned about all the stuff that could happen, like how fast you can get killed even if you know what you're doing and you're a railroad employee.

At the independent, lower-budget, and nonunion level, filmmaking can be very Wild West, either by choice or by ignorance. You need people there who are experienced enough to know when to speak up and who are willing to speak up. I read in some of the interviews that there were people saying prayers to keep them safe. So they knew enough to pray before getting out there but not enough to say, "I'm not fucking going out there." I also understand not wanting to speak up because you don't want to lose your job. Some of these people were women, so again they are faced with the added weight of potentially being seen as difficult. Maybe Sarah had reservations but didn't want to speak up. Or maybe she was dedicated and believed that if her boss, the director of photography, was out there, then they were safe. I don't know. I wasn't there. But when I read about it, I could see it. Anyone who has spent any length of time in the industry understands exactly how the accident happened.

Have you felt unsafe on sets?

Yes. One time I was in a condor [an elevated work platform, like a cherry picker]. A condor has a big base, big wheels, and a long articulating arm. We'll often rig twenty-by-twenty-foot frames onto them with grids to diffuse the sun. We had two of them, and we were working in a neighborhood. The wind was up. We were under power lines. I had been up there for a while, and I had to pee. It was my first time ever peeing in a condor. You bring a water bottle up with you because you could be up there for a while. I had my blanket around so nobody could see me. It was a very delicate procedure because you have a small bottle and the wind is blowing. All of a sudden my radio starts blowing up, they're calling me, "Calvin, are you okay, are you okay?" I'm like, "What the fuck? *Now* you're calling me?" They're like, "Bring your condor down. Bring your condor down!" I looked and the wind had bent part of the rig that was holding the twenty-by-twenty frame and now I'm bobbing up and down even closer to the power lines.

One production company, which I think is now out of business, specialized in low-budget action films and their sets were notoriously unsafe. They had a stunt guy die. I saw them prematurely blow a cannon roll, which is when you essentially set a bomb off under a car to flip it over. And on the same show the *next* night I was almost hit by a flying windshield from a semi truck that they blew up. Very unsafe. And always because they were rushing.

Whenever I was in charge, I was always the guy who erred on the side of caution. If it was too windy, I would be the first one to tell you to take it down. A lot of other key grips, probably well within the range of safety, would say it's fine. Then there are ones who probably keep it up longer than they should, especially when they get in a high-dollar situation, like commercials. There's this underlying pressure to keep going until you get the shot. And that pressure comes from the top down.

There's also stuff that happens within departments. There was the electrician on *Selma* (2014) who got electrocuted because they were rushing. He was working on swapping out a bulb on a lamp and another dude energized the light and zapped him. From what I hear, he's physically wrecked and unable to work. I've seen guys who rush, rush, rush. But you have to take the time to do it right; otherwise people get hurt.

11

Steve Nelson, sound recordist

Steve Nelson has more than thirty years of experience recording and mixing sound for film and TV projects like *Fast and Furious* (2009) and *Inception* (2010). Nelson has worked on sets and locations across the United States as well as in Jamaica, Hong Kong, Moscow, Thailand, Mexico, South America, and Japan. In this interview, he describes the rewards and challenges of the job, as well as the pressures posed by tighter budgets and production schedules.

Describe your job for us.

I'm a production sound mixer—a soundman—recording sound for movies and television, which makes me the head of the sound department. I also am a member of the International Alliance of Theatrical and Stage Employees [IATSE]. Local 695 has jurisdiction for sound, video, and projection engineers based in Los Angeles.

As a department head, I interface with the people above me, like the producers or directors who give me the job. I make the deal for my department and me, though there's not a lot of dealing to be done anymore. I read the script and discuss it with the producer and director. I do the breakdown and analysis of any given project to determine what might be required to get through that production. I am responsible for putting together the sound crew. The size of the crew is contractually determined. At minimum, according to the union contract, there must be three people in the sound department. There's a mixer, a microphone boom operator, and a sound utility technician. The department can grow from there to include additional boom operators, playback operators, even another mixer and crew for a second unit, but that's generally what you'll find on any given day.

Once the production starts filming, I show up with my equipment. I own it and maintain it. I rent it to the production while I'm doing the work. My crew and I are responsible for capturing the sounds, primarily dialogue, that happen in front of the camera. At the end of the day, we deliver a mix of individual component tracks to postproduction.

That sounds pretty focused and intense. Describe a typical workday.

We work long days, usually no less than twelve hours, but often a lot more than that. We may only be rolling for three or four hours in a full day's work (sometimes more, sometimes less), but with rehearsal, setup, location changes, putting mics on actors or around the set, testing audio, and correcting audio, it's a very busy day.

We get a call sheet at the end of each day, which is a road map of the next day's work. It tells you when to show up and where to go. It indicates what crew are needed and when. It indicates what actors are needed and when. It also tells us what scenes are being shot. It includes a weather report and all kinds of notes for different departments. Basically you show up and set up your gear. On a good day, we'll shoot the call sheet and maybe even some more. It's your reward for being efficient: "We're going to give you more scenes to shoot since you finished early!" More often, we are rushing or working overtime or trying to catch up the following day.

The director and actors might start with a private rehearsal. Once they get it worked out, they'll bring in a few key people to watch. This is when my boom operator and I start to finalize what we'll need for sound. Sometimes when you read the script, your vision of how the scene will play out doesn't match what the director, cinematographer, or actors have in mind, so we think, improvise, and collaborate on our feet. We have to deal with various questions throughout the day. How many cameras? Where are the lights? Where are the actors' marks? Once the filming starts, I push the record button and the sound department listens like no one else. We're making sure we are capturing what we need as things evolve.

What are some of your biggest challenges?

We spend a lot of our time on any given day eliminating extraneous sounds, which, although "natural," will cause problems later in the postproduction process. It can be a real challenge. Producers want to keep moving relentlessly forward all day long because there are 150 people on the clock. Directors want to make their schedule. Every second costs money. So, problem solving costs a lot of money.

But when my team is trying to capture this very fragile thing called "production sound," we often have to intervene to rectify a problem that only we can hear at the time, a problem we know will cause much bigger issues later in the process if we don't fix it right now. I don't think others on the set fully appreciate that work. If we hear a noise, we have to figure out what it is and where it comes from. What is that squeak? What is that humming? What is that buzz? Maybe it's somebody's shoes. Maybe it's a generator. Maybe it's a lighting rig. Maybe it's the dolly wheels. Little bumps. Little rustles. Little scrapes. I'll hear something that the director doesn't. You can't hear it with your ears, but the mic is picking it up. So, the director will say, "What? I don't hear that squeak. It's fine." Or, "Don't worry. We'll fix it in post. We'll fix it in the mix." We hear that suggestion quite often. Or an actor will say, "I love to loop" [re-record dialogue in postproduction]. Really? No you don't. You're working hard to get a performance here—let's capture it.

Sometimes it feels like I'm reinventing the wheel every time I'm on the set. I'm like, "People, really? You're going to put the noisy fan right there next to our mic?" But it's my job to make sure the desired sound is crystal clear and there is no unwanted noise on the tracks. It's my job to speak up when there is a problem and correct it. For instance, I may have to tell the director or others to move the generator or ask craft services not to make cappuccinos while we're filming. I may have to suggest we put down some carpet so we don't hear the clickety-clack of the actors' shoes. It can get really complicated: we have to fix that, move that, adjust that, then, crap, something has created a shadow or shows up in the frame. So we fix it again, move it again, and adjust it again. It can cause a cascading series of problems to get the sound right.

It's a delicate process that requires a deft touch with other folks on the set. We have to maintain good relationships because we can't do our job without their help. I need to know if the actor is going to whisper that line or scream it while throwing furniture. If I ask someone to move the generator, I know it's going to require him or her to shut down power to the entire set. That's a big deal. It requires a series of conversations with a number of individuals who have to understand why it's important to move the generator. These things can make or break a recording, and we have to figure out how to get what we need without irking our colleagues.

It sounds like you need a thick skin to be a sound mixer. You have to intervene when there are problems that nobody else is noticing. You're breaking their momentum.

Exactly. I often am the bearer of bad news. Nobody wants to hear about it because it's perceived as an impediment. But it's not the same for other parts of the production. They'll light a scene for hours! If the set isn't quite right, they'll fix it. They'll repaint it, even. We will literally watch paint dry. They will change costumes because they don't work with the lighting. All these things can go quite noticeably wrong but our [sound] problems are largely imperceptible to other crew members. Yet you can't go home bitter. It's not personal, and, in the end, I'm there to make a suggestion to help improve the quality of what we're doing. That's why they hired me. When we get it right, we have made a significant, if unnoticed, contribution to the success of the project.

The hardest moment is when the director says, "Cut. That's great. Move on," and we've realized that the particular take didn't work for us. I have to yell up to my boom man to stop everything. Then you have a debate with the director that lasts thirty minutes. "I didn't hear it. Did you hear it?" "No, I didn't." "I heard it." And so on. Well, if we could have just done it again, we would have been done with what we needed in the time it took us to debate.

At the end of the day, if I go home and know I have done everything I could to make the best possible sound track, then I know I have done my job well. If I'm constantly getting the door slammed in my face, I'm still done at the end of the day. I turn in my stuff and it's someone else's problem. I've been trying to make this production better, and if those decision makers spurn my offerings, it's on them.

Let's switch gears a bit. How do you land jobs?

Workflow is the big mystery, and the root of all that's good and bad in our business. How do you keep the work flowing? You get jobs by word of mouth, from people you know, by recommendation, by luck, and maybe from an agent who every once in a while finds you something. One job usually leads to the next if you did your last job well. All of our jobs are short term, so we go from job to job. That's the good news and the bad news. If the job is great, you wish it could last a long time. If it's not a great job, you're happy to be out of there. But you're always worried about where you'll find your next one.

Is everyone in your union an independent contractor?

Pretty much everyone on the set is an independent contractor. We are hired at the will of our bosses. They can let us go at any moment. We're guaranteed payment for the day we show up and whatever the contractual minimum is for that day— eight or nine hours. Guarantees are pretty minimal when you're a below-the-line worker.

But—this might be interesting to those outside the industry—we aren't contracted with the studio. A payroll company employs us all. That's our employer of record. When the production ends, we fill out our unemployment papers with the payroll company, not the production studio. When crews are hired for a production, the production studio—Universal or Warner Bros. or Company X—will contract the payroll company to disperse salaries to the crew.

So not only are you an independent contractor, but you're also at arm's length from the actual production itself. The production company takes no responsibility for you at all?

Well, that's not exactly true. There's another layer of bureaucracy called the Contract Services Administration Trust Fund. It's another third party that's responsible for ensuring that the terms of our labor contracts are administered appropriately. These groups mediate the terms among the production companies and the workforce. They approve the work roster; they make sure the crew is approved to be on the work roster; they make sure everyone keeps their I-9s updated. All of that paperwork flows through contract services, which acts as an intermediary between all the parties involved in a production. We sign a deal memo at the beginning of the production that includes the name of the production company, but all the administrative logistics of our contracts, salaries, and benefits are handled through these third parties. It's become a huge business, and it's still growing. You can tell when the business is starting to get big in other locations because these services will establish offices there. I just came back several weeks ago from a job in Albuquerque with paychecks from a company I'd never heard of before.

*How has your **craft** changed in the last thirty years?*

It's amazing to me that the machine hasn't changed that much. I think the parts are changing, for sure, but there remain the same departments, the same crafts, the same jobs. Focus pullers used to have their hands on the lens but now they can do it from an entirely different room. But "roll sound," "clap," "action," "cut"—that's all pretty much the same.

The biggest change for the sound department—any department, I'd guess—is technology. We have new parts for this big moviemaking machine. When I started my career, I was using quarter-inch analog tape through a wonderful and legendary Swiss-made recorder called the Nagra. In fact, I have one displayed on my mantel at home. But now it's all digital. I'm recording nonlinear digital tracks onto a hard drive.

Is that good or bad?

I think it's good. I miss my Nagra. It had a sweet sound, and was a beautiful and precise machine and very innovative. But it only had one track. We had to mix multiple sources onto that single track. That was the mix! If I forgot to open that guy's mic, then it wasn't on the track. Or if I had one mic turned up and caught background noise, it ended up on the track. You couldn't separate your sources.

Eventually there was a stereo Nagra that allowed you to record two separate tracks with a time code. That's when we started mixing sound to a multitrack master. I had a mixing board with four inputs. Today, there are so many more sources. My mixer has sixteen inputs. A scene might have multiple radio mics, boom mics, microphones hidden in the set. Ideally you're working with one sound source. You set your levels for the boom mic, and you're ready to record. But those days are rarities. Generally it's far more complicated, and that's when I start to do my job. I sit there with my hands on my knobs adjusting levels—turning this mic up, that mic down, trying to re-create something that's going to sound like what you'd expect to hear in the theater.

How many more sources of sound are you dealing with now as opposed to then?

Now, with the advent of nonlinear digital recording, you're recording each source onto its individual track. You're mixing up to thirty-two tracks into a master mix that you then turn over to the production company on a small flash drive. Normally I'm working with ten tracks. Reality television often requires more, but god help me if I'm ever recording all thirty-two tracks at the same time. I think that's my cue to retire!

*How has the **business** changed in the past thirty years?*

I've been doing this a long time. I live and work at a certain level in the food chain such that I don't have to obsess about the trades or obsess about changes in the business at the corporate level. We often live in our own world anyway. We know the business through our experience of it. Look, this business has always been about the money, but it's become more and more about the money throughout my career and less and less about enjoying what we do. I can't pinpoint any specific development, but I think I started to feel this shift most noticeably since 2008, around the time of the WGA strike and the collapse of the economy.

Historically there has been some truth in the image of Hollywood as a place of glamour. We're making movies. We're playing with imagination. We're the best at what we do. Let's have some fun while we're doing it. You struggle for so long in this industry doing low-budget, independent productions that once you reach the higher tiers of production, you expect to enjoy some of that old Hollywood glamour. We're supposed to treat ourselves well, and there's nothing wrong with that because you earned it. Why not live up to that image? I'm not talking about coke and blowjobs (well, that was the 1980s) but about capturing some of that spirit. Sadly, a lot of the fun is gone.

I'm not sure what happens on the operational side, but budgets are tighter, even on the high end of the production spectrum. Contracts are less protective, too. Maybe that's why it doesn't seem as fun as it once was—it's no longer, "We're in this thing together, let's get it done, and let's enjoy doing it." At one time, the business felt much more like a family business. If you went down to the studios you'd see all these neighborhoods built up around the lots. People lived in those neighborhoods; they raised their families there. And at the end of the day, you went home. That's not the case anymore.

I remember my first union job. We were working late one Friday night and the clock passed midnight. Suddenly, everybody around me was cheering, blowing up balloons, bringing out party favors. It was great, but I was so confused. When you work a nonunion job, you work until you're done. Nothing changes because of the clock. When I asked what was happening, they said, "It's midnight!" It was Saturday, the weekend. Weekends were protected in the union contract. The contract protected a sacrosanct notion of leisure time that was separate from your working time, so you actually had a weekend. If you had to work into the weekend, your rate of pay doubled or tripled or quadrupled! The union even had pay rate increases for working later into the evening. Remember, this isn't supposed to be an expected benefit to the workers but a way to hold managers and employers accountable for how they make use of time. It is a penalty for employer inefficiency.

We no longer have a weekend clause in our contracts, and once you give up something in your contract, it's nearly impossible to get it back. Sure, there's a vague notion of a weekend, but the sense that work stops Friday at midnight and resumes Monday morning doesn't exist. I've seen a lot of what they call Fraturdays, which basically means you'll work until the sun comes up on Saturday morning and then maybe your weekend starts. *Buffy the Vampire Slayer* (1997–2003) was famous for their Fraturdays; the show was known as *Buffy the Weekend Slayer*. So too was *True Blood* (2008–14). Maybe it's a warning to stay away from vampire shows.

It seems like there are two things happening here. One is that the technology has made it possible to generate and store much more raw data. The other is that the boundaries around the workweek aren't being controlled like they used to. Does this mean that the people who plan and manage the productions are perhaps less disciplined than they were in the past? Or does it mean that people are willing to push themselves to work harder and longer to generate better material?

That's where it all starts. In designing the whole production. I'll just say it: some producers are inefficient. Granted, there are a lot of factors to juggle, but some producers and their overlords narrowly focus on the bottom line. They lose sight of the bigger picture, which might lead to greater efficiency. Moreover, some disregard the toll that inefficiency takes on their employees. But as long as it doesn't cost any more, it doesn't show up on the bottom line, and it is acceptable.

And it *does* take a toll. It's a risky wager to shoot fourteen, fifteen, sixteen hours a day, and it happens with great regularity. And it shouldn't happen. How much money is it actually saving the production? And at what costs come those savings? There's got to be a more efficient and safer way to plan the schedule. We've been trying to limit workdays for the past fifteen years, ever since the young camera assistant Brent Hershman was killed in a car accident after working a nineteen-hour shift. Yet extremely long shifts still happen. Just in the brief time that I was in New Mexico, a teamster was killed in a car accident. This wasn't a worker on my show, but on the other show that was shooting there at the same time. He rolled his car on the way home from working a seventeen-hour day. Nobody wants that to happen. There are times when people will say, "People, this is going to be a long day. We know that to reach our goals, we will need to work a sixteen-hour day." They plan for that, and I think that's wrong in so many ways. I mean, a twelve-hour day is a generous workday already. And that's what we assume as a starting point. Name one other business where employees expect a twelve-hour workday. Whereas we're *advocating* for a twelve-hour workday. It's ludicrous.

Why doesn't anyone refuse?

Contractually we can't. If I said, "No, it's been eight hours, or twelve or sixteen or twenty, that's enough for today," that would be a violation of my contract. That's the case for other employees as well. It would be a wildcat strike. We're getting paid and these are the terms of the contract. If nobody has made it prohibitive for the bosses to keep us on the clock then somebody is going to take advantage of the situation.

So you can't refuse as an individual, but should your union be saying no?

The union negotiated the contract.

Why are they doing that?

There you go! Why? I don't have the answer, but it gets worse. Did you know the number of hours we need to work to keep our health insurance active actually increased in our union by 33 percent a couple of years ago? We have to work 33 percent more time to keep our coverage active, and it's less coverage! Go figure.

Part of what's driving these changes is the overall diffusion of the production business around the globe. Right now, for people like me, the biggest threat to continued employment is the siphoning of our jobs off to other places in the United States and Canada and England. Places like Santa Fe or Albuquerque or New Orleans or Shreveport or Atlanta or wherever in North Carolina or Rhode Island or even Canada all have union locals now. These grab bags of locals, which include the stagehands and everybody else, used to be pretty small, but now, as the work has spread throughout the land, they've grown and they have their own agreements forged by the international union. They're called Area Standards Agreements. The contractual terms are different for each local according to its particular agreement. For instance, what hours you work, your overtime, your annual wage increase, and how many hours a year you must work to keep your health plan active are different for various locals. Area Standards Agreements allow producers to film in other locations with a local crew that will work in very different wage structures than we do. They also have very different pension plans and health coverage. And these are union contracts! If you're a producer, you can use those agreements to ensure your labor costs are kept at a minimum. It also forces our local to make more concessions—how else will it keep its membership competitive with labor in other locations? So we give up a bit of our health care to lower our costs.

Of course, it's not just the union that has created these issues. The state governments have also decided they are going to pursue motion picture work through tax incentive programs. All of these states are trying to undercut each other, and I think it's just one big race to the bottom. A 30 percent cut! A 35 percent rebate! We'll do it for free! Maybe it works out. Maybe it doesn't. For every study that says a dollar spent is a dollar earned, there's another that says a dollar spent is a dollar lost. You can make the numbers work any way you want because they're just numbers.

Tax incentives look good on paper, so Hollywood heads to those areas. A lot of times executive teams don't even create a budget for a production in L.A. anymore. They'll go to Louisiana or Georgia or anywhere but here and work with anyone but us. So that's one of the biggest changes, and the union isn't doing anything to stop it. They're actually enabling it. In the last five to ten years, there has been a strong disinclination to work in my geographic area and a bigger disinclination to bring me on staff. Now it happens that we do travel—they'll bring us, especially when a location lacks the necessary skills—but as these locations host more production, local crew are learning the required skill sets. Productions won't need to bring me anymore.

How much is a sound mixer paid?

It has changed a lot. When I started, there was one contract: the "basic agreement." If I'm doing a job today, I have to determine which contract it is under. We have basic cable, other cable, long-form TV, and one-hour episodic contracts. There are so many different contracts. Which one is it? What is my rate of pay? How many hours until I get double time? Do I get holiday pay? All these things have been negotiated away depending on which contract. The contracts also have tiers: tier 1, tier 2, tier 3. There's even a tier 0 where there are no numbers written in. This is for some of the new media stuff, and the terms are "as negotiated." We're talking about people being paid what they would be for flipping burgers. People are getting minimum wage for some of these jobs. If I'm making full basic scale on a basic daily rate, my hourly rate is roughly $68 an hour for my straight time.

As you look back over the last thirty years, what has happened to the income of someone at your level? Take a senior sound mixer back thirty years ago and compare what he or she was taking home then to what they're taking home now. What's the rate of deterioration?

If we're lucky, we've held our ground. If I'm making $68 an hour, that's a good rate. But think of it this way: if you call a plumber because you have a leak in your house and it's the middle of the night or it's Saturday night and your toilet is overflowing and the plumber finally stops laughing before he agrees to come over, what would you pay? You'd pay that guy a lot of money to come out. But as a Hollywood movie crew, we work for the same low price in the middle of the night or on a Saturday night as we do when we show up on a Monday morning.

That's one of the things that has changed. We do the same work no matter the day or time. It's as hard as it ever was. It's as challenging as it ever was. We have to go to the ends of the earth. We've got to work in the blazing sun, in the freezing cold, on the water, in the desert, for the same or less money that we always have earned.

Take my equipment rental as another example. That's not negotiated by any contract. But it's a significant part of my income. I provide a big pile of the best equipment. I keep current with technology. It's good stuff, and it works. I'm responsible for it. I keep it in tune. It's a big investment. You know I've got a couple hundred thousand dollars invested in sound equipment. My collection has grown, and it's grown relative to what people expect on a movie set. Today producers and directors expect me to have *a lot* more gear. When I was starting out more than thirty years ago, you could get $1,000 a week for a pretty minimal package. Today I can get up to $3,000 a week for my equipment if I'm working on a big movie. But for TV, like if you go to work for ABC or some of the television networks, you may get $1,600 a week, $1,700 a week, or maybe $1,800 a week for the same equipment package. Over the span of thirty years, that's not a lot of growth considering all the gear they expect you to bring. The rate of increase has not kept up with the realities of what we do.

I live in Santa Barbara, and my wife makes a pretty good salary, and her retirement package at the University of California, Santa Barbara, is a lot better than mine. That's for sure. I looked at my retirement package and there's some cash in there, but if I retired at the appropriate age and stopped working now, I think I would have maybe $1,500 a month as a pension. That's not very much for thirty-something years of work. It shows how much ground we've lost. We've lost all forward motion. Until very recently, our annual rate of pay was decreasing rather than increasing. In the most recent round of negotiations, it was restored to what it was previously: it went back to 3 percent after being at 2 percent for quite some time. Woo-hoo!

As a production sound mixer I'm one of the highest-paid people based on contractually negotiated pay rates. Camera operators and sound mixers are pretty much at the top of the pile. But with the cost of movie production skyrocketing, we're clearly not part of that increase.

More than thirty years of work and your pension is $1,500 a month?

Well, in all fairness, not all thirty of those years were union years. But I've got more than twenty years invested in the union.

Do you think that media conglomerates have played a big part in what has happened to workers?

Yes, I do. Like all businesses, they have become more concerned with shareholders and stock prices. It's more about the money and less about anything else. Conglomerates have played a large role in destroying any sense of community in this business. I hate to harp on that, but there was a time when there was a community here. Now, as the conglomerates get bigger and bigger and further removed from what it is that we do as content providers, there's a much bigger gap between the powers that be and those of us on the set. Even on a more local level, there are people who sit in offices in the various studios who are less engaged or more detached or less knowledgeable about what we do than their predecessors were. The leadership seems much more numbers oriented and much less involved with the nuts and bolts of how the process works.

So the squeeze is on. They're thinking numbers. They're thinking quarterly reports. They're shuffling pieces around the globe, and as they do that, conditions for the production community in Los Angeles are deteriorating.

And they're deteriorating everywhere. You can go to other places and see the same issues. When I was in New Mexico people complained a lot about the money they made or didn't make.

Talk about that. When people discuss runaway production, they're thinking that the glamorous jobs are taking off to other places. People think the folks in places like New Mexico are doing great. Is that the case?

I worked with some people in New Mexico, and they knew what we made and what they made. There was a big difference, and they could feel the difference.

They knew they were working for a fraction of what we were making—about half—and that that's why we were there to shoot. We don't shoot in New Mexico because studios are being generous. Executives sense a better deal, and they go to where the money is. And then they figure out how to make it even more cost effective. New Mexico is interesting in that sense. Like a few other states, it has two production centers. There's Santa Fe and Albuquerque. They're about an hour apart, and people live and work in both cities and are considered local hires even if they live in one city and the production is based in the other. If you're part of the out-of-town L.A. crew, the studio is putting you up in a convenient and comfortable spot close to the filming location. They're taking care of you because the contract says you require accommodation and a per diem and other compensation. But if you're the local hire, you have to go home every night. You don't have the same protection because your contract is different.

My boom man was complaining about this very distinction. He lives in Santa Fe. The production was based in Albuquerque, but we were working in a third location, like the third point in a triangle between the two cities. In New Mexico, you can't just drive in a straight line between two points—sometimes you have to go sixty miles out of your way to get to your desired location, which was the case for my boom operator. But because he was a local hire, he had to go home every night. There was no hotel room for him. Instead, he had to drive 110 miles back home after a thirteen- or fourteen-hour workday in the desert.

What advice would you give to students interested in a career in sound?

How I feel about my career at any given moment is directly related to my state of employment. Right now I feel pretty good. However, when I talk about my career, I try to be straightforward about what we do. I try to be the guy who tosses a cold bucket of reality in their direction, and the reality is that this business is a hard way to make a living. It's hard on your personal life. It's hard on your family. You can't even plan a vacation. The craziest thing is when I see people on holiday checking out of a hotel, and making their next reservations a year in advance. They know that they're going to be back. I could never do that. I don't know where am I going to be in a year. I don't know what job opportunities will come my way. Whenever I plan a major vacation, like going to Europe for three weeks, it's inevitably going to overlap with some work. I'll plan something, then hear about a job happening at the same time.

Something has to give. I'm now at a point in my career where I won't give up vacation time with my family anymore. It's an earned privilege to say "no" to work when it conflicts with what other people consider normal life! But it's hard to do that, especially for people who are just starting out. So, for young people who value job security and stability and need to predict what they're going to be doing and where they're going to be, this is not a job I'd recommend. This job requires a spirit of adventure and improvisation and an open mind and a valid passport to make it work. Oh, and they'll need understanding and flexible relationships in their lives as well. Absolutely.

Here's a great example I like to share: I've lived in Santa Barbara since 1996. In that time, I've done one job where I could come home at the end of the day. Even if I'm working in L.A., it's too far to drive back every night. It's a hundred miles each way. So I spend most of my week in L.A. It's additionally hard to have your kid growing up while you're gone all week long. Anyway, the one job I did in town was a TV movie for Hallmark. I unexpectedly came home in time for dinner after shooting one day. Both my wife and daughter were a little shocked. My daughter—she was only six years old at the time—looked up at me, stared, and asked, "Daddy what are you doing home? Did you get fired?"

12

Rob Matsuda, musician

Rob Matsuda is a violinist who has contributed to film and television scores since 1996, including the feature film *The Horse Whisperer* (1998) and the blockbuster television series *Lost* (2004–10). A member of the Union of Professional Musicians, Local 47, in Los Angeles, Matsuda recalls the heyday of motion picture musicians and describes the ways in which producers have moved much of the work overseas or resorted to licensed pop songs or computer-generated music.

How did you get your start with orchestral soundtracks? Your first film was **The Horse Whisperer***, correct?*

I did a film before that in which my friend put together the musicians for a Pauly Shore movie called *Bio-Dome* (1996). Interestingly enough, the residuals for *Bio-Dome* went on, and on, and on. At the back end, it actually paid better than *The Horse Whisperer*. I'm probably still getting checks for *Bio-Dome*. It was officially my first movie project.

How did you get your foot in the door?

When I was a teenager studying the violin, I had a teacher, Mr. Chassman, who was part of the Fox orchestra back in its heyday. You can see him in the Marilyn Monroe movie *How to Marry a Millionaire* (1953). He would tell me about playing for the movies while I was at my lessons. It sounded like a really great thing! You'd be playing your instrument, and it would allow you to make what I assumed would be a comfortable middle-class living. I knew that was what I wanted to do when I grew up.

Bio-Dome came out in 1996, and I got that job after about ten years of going around playing for concertmasters and contractors and trying to get my foot in the door. When people ask, "How do you get started?" I have to disabuse them of the notion that there's a clear-cut way of getting into this kind of work, at least what's left of it. And it's different for everybody, because it's not like applying for a job at an insurance company.

I got the *Bio-Dome* job because I was a friend of the contractor who got the job because he was a friend of the composer. They both attended the same high school when they were younger.

That got you started. What kept your career going?

I had a good stretch of work after *Bio-Dome*, until 2006. I got my position on *The Horse Whisperer* through a connection with the composer's family. I had been working with volunteers for about ten years at the Los Angeles County Museum of Art (LACMA), and the word got around that I was a violinist. One of the volunteers was related to the composer for *The Horse Whisperer*, and she put in a good word for me. I owe that job to her. Then, once I was playing for him, I started getting hired to play on his other films and things expanded from there. It's critical for instrumentalists to end up on a contractor's list. They are responsible for hiring people to play in the orchestra.

How do you get on a contractor's list?

It's a nebulous process. There are so many ways! You play for people, like the lead violinist, who is called the concertmaster. Of course, those people have an inflated sense of their own power. People have to play for them; they're the gatekeepers who make recommendations to the contractor. My entrée was through a family-work connection. The composer then told the contractor to contact me. And of course people know each other from school, "Oh, I went to Juilliard with so and so." They recommend you to the contractor. People even say there's a casting couch.

When composers are young and they're trying to make it, they need a reel. They need projects to work on, and they often seek out student filmmakers at film schools. The composers don't make much money, which means they can't pay the musicians much, if anything at all. Oftentimes they will ask musicians to volunteer: "I don't have a lot of money, but I'll buy you pizza. Can you help me score the short film I'm working on?" Musicians will agree to do the work in the hope that the composer's profile in the industry will rise and that they'll take you along for the ride. But that doesn't always work. In fact, a major beef with my colleagues is that they'll play for free! Worst of all, when people you play for become more successful, they tend to forget that you once did them a favor. Of course, I imagine that if there's a lot of money on the line and if the young composer has a choice between working and not working, they'll say to the contractor: "Okay, fine, just take care of it. I'm sorry I have to leave Robert and his friends behind, but, this is my chance." So, it's a complex process.

By the way, the same can be said about contractors. They might use you once—if it is helpful to them—and never hire you again.

So the contractor is a central gatekeeper.

They're like Saint Peter, they are so powerful. In fact, there are one or two who are enormously powerful and influential. For a long time during the 1970s, 1980s, and 1990s, there was one woman named Sandy DeCrescent who controlled access to 90 percent of the work. She retired, and one of her assistants, Peter Rotter, took over. Then he controlled 90 percent of the work. At some point after the transition, Sandy and Peter got into an argument over some business or personal matter. Now she's back in the game, and they're mortal enemies! I've never seen them. To me, they're like the Wizards of Oz. I'm not in the 90 percent world. I'm in the 10 percent world. And for a good stretch of time, 10 percent was pretty good. But now, that amount of work is so much smaller that it breaks down to almost nothing.

Do contractors tend to hire the same people? Do orchestras stick together from film to film?

Contractors put together an orchestra for each film. And there are contractors who attach themselves to certain composers. So this creates a degree of expectation: if you played on one composer's film, you will likely play for all of their films. Composers like to work with people they know and trust; so do contractors. But there are no guarantees.

When contractors reach out to people, are they asking for an audition?

No, they know you already. They know they want you. It's more of a conversation about money, time, and availability.

When you were working consistently, how often were you working?

Before I did *The Horse Whisperer*, I was working at LACMA, so I didn't live on my music work. I would do community orchestras, weddings, and any kind of live music work that I could get. Even after *The Horse Whisperer* I still wasn't getting enough work to quit the museum, but by that time I had accumulated so many sick days, vacation days, and free days that LACMA wanted me to take days off. That was great because I would get a paid day off and be able to do a movie.

I met my mentor, Harris Goldman, on *The Horse Whisperer*. I was very fortunate to meet him; he had great relationships with many different composers and orchestrators. Orchestrators are important because they often write the music for a film based on the composer's ideas. Orchestrators possess the technical know-how to translate those ideas into sheet music. Connections to composers and orchestrators are helpful—obviously they're both powerful, and they can make recommendations to the contractors. Harris introduced me to Graeme Revell, who has since retired. He also introduced me to a young composer named Michael Giacchino, who is huge now. I think I did his first non-video-game project, which was the TV series *Alias* (2001–6). *Alias* led to *Lost*. For a while, *Lost* and *Alias* were on at the same time, and then he started doing movies—Pixar movies like *The Incredibles* (2004), *Ratatouille* (2007), and others.

So, right there, I had access to Thomas Newman on some good films. I was doing Pixar movies and any other movie that Michael Giacchino was doing, and during a brief period, I was doing both *Alias* and *Lost*. One week I'd go in and do *Alias* and the next week I'd do *Lost*. And then *Alias* went off the air, but I still had *Lost*.

Can you describe a typical day?

For episodic television, it's a short day. An episode of TV for an hour-long show like *Alias* or *Lost*, which is called a single, usually requires three hours: typically from ten in the morning to one in the afternoon, with a ten-minute break at the top of each hour. For a motion picture, there's more footage that needs to be scored, so depending on the nature of the film, it could be one day, known as a double session. That could mean about six hours with a lunch break, or it could mean a whole week.

Do studio musicians need a second income?

I would say the most successful people have a regular flow of studio work across film and television. But they also teach and play in other orchestras, like the opera or the Los Angeles Chamber Orchestra. However, they always have studio work at the core of their career.

How much can you make in a recording session?

If it is a standard budget, a rank-and-file musician can make about $80 an hour. That's not bad, and you get money on the back end as well. There is also low-budget, and now something called low-low-budget, which pays considerably less.

What is the back end?

Some office in Encino tallies it up, and it's predicated on things like video sales, DVD sales, and what happens overseas. They tally all of the projects that you have worked on and your percentage of royalties, and then you get a check in the summertime. You get one check for film and television, and a smaller check the next month for any kind of phonograph work you've done. (They still say "phonograph" even though it's an incredibly outdated term.) It refers to work you've done on commercial music, like albums or singles.

With your check, you get a long itemized statement, and it behooves you to look at it closely to see if they missed anything. It happens. But it's also really interesting to see the different trends across the film and television you've done. Like I said, I'm still getting money from old projects like *Bio-Dome*. It's maybe $10, but it's money! Other films have a huge drop off. For instance, *Star Trek* (2009) made some good money at first, and then the next year it went down a little, and then down, down, down, down very quickly. It was a rapid drop.

Both **Lost** *and* **Alias** *made a lot of money in international and ancillary markets. Over the course of time, how much money could you expect in residuals?*

It was pretty good money. It wasn't astronomical like it is with some movies, but it was always a nice check. I don't recall exact amounts, but the back end on those shows could pay your rent for the month. It's always surprising what pays well on the back end. Some projects that you think wouldn't do well end up paying you the most.

For example, I have a friend who did a sidelining job on the movie *I Love You, Man* (2009). He was playing in a quartet at the wedding at the end. Sidelining means you appear on camera, almost as an actor. Usually you're miming to prerecorded music; you're just there as a visual. And nobody wanted to take the job! You had to go up to Malibu every day and be there really early, and it just didn't seem like a terribly good job, but because there was no other scored music—every other song on the soundtrack was a pop song—they got this large sum of money! Divided among the four of them, they got really, really good money on the back end.

Another friend, a bass player, had an appearance on a Chili's commercial. He was playing the bass with a jazz singer. When he first heard about the job, he wasn't going to audition for it, but we convinced him. I think when everything wrapped up he probably made $10,000 for that, which is excellent for essentially one day's work.

When you look at the itemized list of residuals, what have been some of your biggest surprises, other than **Bio-Dome**?

A movie that paid very well was *The Incredibles*. We knew that it was going to make some good money because it was very successful. But it was worth thousands of dollars for me! Everybody was asking about it: "Did you get your check for that?" Because, you know, not everybody is in that top echelon of musicians, where they're working for everyone all the time. A lot of the musicians in Los Angeles are just like me, waiting for that elusive studio call, which has become more and more rare.

What happened? You said you started to notice a change around 2006 or 2007.

What happened was just an acceleration of trends that were already in place. Costs all come out of the producers' pockets. I only make scale, but other people in the orchestra, say a section leader, get double scale. And if a contractor hires someone we call a doubler—someone who is hired to play more than one instrument—scale pay is automatically higher. Plus, the contractor could be making double or triple scale. So it all starts to add up before you even calculate the back end, which also increases depending on your scale pay. I think producers began to say, "This is an unnecessary expense. Let's go overseas. Let's go to London." They have nationalized health care so there are no benefit costs for producers. They don't pay any residuals. There is no union. The musicians just get paid their hourly rate for their time in the studio.

George Lucas has all of his films done in London. He has always been virulently antiunion. On the other hand, Thomas Newman has always been committed to scoring his films in L.A. He comes from a film music dynasty, so I think he has a strong sense of loyalty to keeping business in the city. He is loyal to musicians here. His father was Alfred Newman, his uncle was Lionel Newman, his cousin is Randy Newman, and his brother is David Newman. Nevertheless, he got the *007* franchise, and that does not leave England, so now he has to go over there and use their musicians.

Of course London has a lot of incredibly talented musicians. But if you're already in the London Symphony Orchestra, you have that work, so film jobs are just extra cash. Even if you're not in the London Symphony Orchestra, or the four or five other orchestras there, there are lots of opportunities. From what I understand, Abbey Road and Air Studios are open night and day, seven days a week. It's incredibly busy. Freelance musicians are scoring films or video game soundtracks. Video games are a huge market now! Some of them have better production values than motion pictures. I did some of that ten years ago. I started working on Call of Duty and Medal of Honor. We basically created motion picture soundtracks, using a big orchestra. But the video game companies have become even more tightfisted about residuals and in negotiating with the unions. They're basically saying, "We don't need to do this anymore."

Whatever pugnacious tactics the unions had unfortunately weren't enough to prevent studios from going either overseas or out of state to find musicians who would accept their terms. I think Seattle was the first city to break away from the national union.

How pugnacious was the union when this trend started?

I think it was mainly verbal. I don't think there was a lot of punch behind it, compared to the other [motion picture] unions. The musicians' union doesn't have as much power. When writers go on strike, you have no content, so things grind to a halt. But when musicians go on strike, they say, "Well, we'll just go out of town."

Why is it so easy to go out of town? Don't directors and producers want to be closer to the action when they're in postproduction, to oversee the development of the soundtrack?

You would think, but then you have to consider the money, and that's all the producers and studios are worried about right now. A studio is just a distribution channel owned by a much larger global entity. And because they're multinational corporations, they have to answer to the bottom line. The executives who run these multinational corporations likely have no interest in film music or where it is done. They just have to answer to shareholders. Accountants have much more power than they used to. Can you save money by going to London, or the Czech Republic, or Macedonia, or Seattle? If so, we'll do it!

Where do they go? We know about London and Seattle.

The Czech Republic is very big.

Why the Czech Republic?

It's an incredibly musical place. Mozart in his time was more popular in Prague than in his native Austria. The country has a rich tradition of symphonic music that includes Antonin Dvořák and other Czech composers. And the cost of living is lower there, so wages are lower, and producers don't have to pay into health care. They don't have to pay the back end. You just have to pay the musicians for their time in the studio.

What other places?

Well, that's enough to sink the ship. But London is the biggest, by far. Dreamworks Animation is 100 percent London. Until the latest *Star Wars*, George Lucas did his recording in London. The new one was done here in L.A., but I don't know why.

Besides the battle over payments, what else is making jobs disappear?

I think our tastes in music have changed. When you turn on the radio now and listen to Selena Gomez or Katy Perry, oftentimes you're not even hearing real instruments. Those songs are purely electronic productions done by producers. People don't expect strings or real instruments backing up the artist. Recorded music also has good sampling. A very good producer or somebody with a suitable keyboard can get what passes for a good string sound, and the samples are getting better and better. People don't expect to hear a natural, acoustic-sounding backdrop when they hear popular music these days. Those jobs used to be important sources of money when you weren't doing film or television work.

Now you only expect to *see* violins or symphonic instruments, as a visual. If Michael Bublé is doing something on PBS, you may see actual instruments and musicians like me. Or if they're doing a studio session, I might get a call. But when it comes time to do it live, they don't want to see me. Directors will probably try to get a pretty, willowy, young, white, blond woman to put on the set. Somebody's getting the work, at least, but it's not me.

We had no idea this transition has been afoot. It's startling, especially when you consider the significant role that music plays in most Hollywood films.

Oh, there's no reason to apologize. Musicians are invisible, so things can happen to the musicians and the general public doesn't know. That's why I'm so eager and willing to go on record, or talk to people about changes in our business. I don't want to be in politics or anything, but I do want to tell people that musicians do exist, and I want to emphasize that when you hear music in a motion picture, it's played by real people. Sometimes the music is done so incredibly well, like with Thomas Newman, that it becomes part of the narrative. The music is essential for propelling the narrative of the film.

I think the whole transition has been manipulated in very clever ways, even through union negotiations. Like I said, unions don't have a ton of power, so when they capitulate, they often turn around to frame it as a benefit. They'll say, "We have this new agreement with the studios where a certain amount of work has to be done in town." On the surface that sounds great! But the studios still determine what work stays and what work goes. So they'll do a bunch of films like *Attack of the Killer Tomatoes: Part VIII* in L.A., and take prestige projects elsewhere. There's a very tangible difference for musicians between working on a low-budget feature versus a big-budget prestige project.

In another interview, you were quoted as saying that access to job opportunities is now extremely political. Can you elaborate?

We had various watering holes in our business. I had my watering hole with a few other animals. Other animals were at different watering holes. I was at the Thomas Newman–Michael Giacchino watering hole. It turned out to be a good watering hole to have, but now these other watering holes, which provided a lot of work, have dried up and those animals are coming over to my watering hole, and the more politically and powerfully connected musicians have the ability to push me aside, if they want.

What kind of scoring work is still done in L.A.?

Luckily for me, two of the composers who still score here are Thomas Newman and Michael Giacchino, and there is some pop music that needs strings. If you Google my name you'll see some of the sound—not soundtrack but phonograph—work I've done. I'll do work for artists like Beck. Beck's father, David Campbell, is an orchestrator. So, right there, Beck has an in-house person to do string arranging for his records. But that type of work is increasingly rare. Today it's mostly when a producer wants some strings to make something more romantic. They call it sweetening. If a popular artist like Katy Perry does a ballad, that's good for us because we might get the call for that, but again, that doesn't happen all that often. It's just not the predominant sound in popular music. They needed strings more often during the disco era. My god, you listen to a disco album that was recorded in the mid- to late 1970s and everything has strings.

 A lot of the work that made for a middle-class living was not particularly prestigious. It was just work, and there was a lot of it. For instance making commercial jingles for Safeway, and things like that. Back then they used real musicians for jingles. The only time you'll hear an orchestra on television now is when you watch *The Simpsons* (1989–ongoing), *Family Guy* (1999–ongoing), and maybe one or two other animated things. Animation seems to require real musicians. *Desperate Housewives* (2004–12) used an orchestra when it was on the air, but since the demise of *Alias* and *Lost*, I don't think there's been a lot of orchestra work for non-animated TV.

 It's just not looking good for musicians. People are taking early retirement and taking their pensions. All it requires is that the musician not accept any work for a year, and then he or she can start getting pension payments. If work does come in after that, you can take it, but that means we are essentially bankrupting our pension fund. My royalty check is being taxed at 1 percent, which then contributes to the retirement fund, which is currently in the red. Hopefully the union can rebuild the coffers, but right now we don't know if there will be any money left when my peers and I are ready to retire. I just assume I'm going to somehow continue working when I'm ninety years old. Let's hope I'm able to!

What are you doing today?

I'm lucky that a couple of my friends made a financial intervention. They took me out to lunch and reminded me that I inherited my parents' house after they both died in 2011. Since then, I had been living in their house and slowly going broke. They said, "You live in a great house. You have a swimming pool, a view of the city, and you're in Los Feliz. Fix up the house and rent it." Even though I was still grief stricken, I said, "Okay, I'll do it." I got a loan, fixed up the house, and got a realtor.

There were a couple of offers that fell through and then somebody I had heard about and liked from the entertainment industry came and loved the house. He was a novelist for many years prior to becoming a showrunner. One of his stories got made into a TV show and that totally changed his life. Now he was working on another show, so he decided to move to L.A., and he rented my house. I'm not out of the woods, but at least I'm able to pay for an apartment down the hill from my house and start paying off my debts. I hope he stays there forever; he's a great guy.

So the pressure has eased somewhat. Now I view myself more as a landlord than a musician sometimes. Some musicians say you have to do things like that, and a couple of players I know became real estate agents, but that profession is also subject to the market's whims. Some older players have also invested in property, so I have this little thing with the house and hopefully there'll be a point where I'm no longer paying off the debt. I'm getting money from whatever is left from my movie, television, and phonograph work. I'm sorry I can't paint a brighter picture for you guys, but hopefully this was helpful in some way.

13

Global Machine

Editors' Introduction

From a studio's perspective, the mobile logistics of screen media production result from a logical calculation of creative costs. Consideration is given to the nature of the script and the types of locations it requires, but no less important are the range of local subsidies and infrastructure, both physical and human, on offer from a number of production hubs vying for Hollywood's attention. A competitive exchange rate doesn't hurt, either. Such factors partially explain how Hollywood has transformed its mode of production into a global machine that assembles film and television projects across an established but largely interchangeable list of locales. As the interviewees made clear in the previous section, these top-down calculations may benefit the producer's bottom line, but they extract significant tolls from the hundreds of workers employed on those sets. While we often hear this dynamic framed as "runaway production," the commentary thus far offers a critical reminder that there also is a quotidian dimension to the spatial reconfiguration of screen media production.

The interviews in this section, which include a studio production executive, service producers, and location experts, continue in a similar vein but broaden the geographic scope of the conversation to include workers in Atlanta, Glasgow, Dublin, Prague, and Budapest. They explain that job responsibilities on sets in their cities are divided between local hires and transient crew, with most of the latter flown in from Los Angeles or London to serve as department heads. We learn from these interviews a great deal about the increasingly complex logistics of global film and television production, which involve a tangled mess of creative demands, local bureaucracies, thorny finances, and cultural differences, a complicated riddle that globe-trotting producers demand their local counterparts solve on their behalf.

More fundamentally, however, these interviews push back against the tendency to pit screen media workers in Southern California (who are losing jobs) against workers in other locations (who are "stealing" them)—arguments about "runaway production" that simply serve the interests of the studios and distract from the structural forces reshaping conditions for all film and television workers, no matter where they are based. While those structures may be experienced differently in different places and at different times, they are no less responsible for the increased pressure workers in distant locales face when securing work from Hollywood. Hearing from some of those "distant" voices is a vital component of the larger conversation we are pursuing in this book.

This section introduces the broad notion of "service production," which has its origins in the commercial video industry but is now a prominent feature in foreign territories playing host to large-scale film and television productions. Often operated by expatriates who are experienced line producers with Hollywood credits to their name, production service firms are responsible for mediating between the needs of visiting producers and the intricacies of local work cultures and bureaucracies. They budget costs (sometimes in multiple neighboring territories) as part of the bidding process to secure contracts with interested producers. They scout and secure locations and book available soundstages. They lock down local services, from catering and hospitality to drivers and dry cleaners. They negotiate access to historical sites; fill out applications for street closures; ensure compliance with local laws and labor regulations; and somehow balance the often-contradictory interests of studio producers, local politicians, and neighborhood residents. Service producers furthermore supply local production managers, office coordinators, accountants, location scouts, and various runners and assistants who work closely with visiting line producers. They are responsible for hiring local crew members to satisfy staffing needs in the camera, sound, costume, makeup, and construction departments, among others, who then are assigned to work under foreign (largely Anglo-American) department heads.

Sometimes when production takes place in more familiar environs, such as London or Vancouver, the labor of the service producer is redistributed to individuals in the production office, location department, and local film agencies. Much like service producers, then, production managers and location experts also find themselves responsible for managing an astonishing number of details, both large and small, that help suture mobile production to particular locations. Production managers, for instance, know whom to call when they need to find the best focus puller; similarly, location experts are masters of arcane details who, for example, help to secure permits for firing semiautomatic weapons in an affluent suburban neighborhood, while also gaining consent from local residents to launch a shootout in their backyards.

Yet these jobs are more than just middle management and paperwork. As discussed throughout this book, the shifting demographics of most film and television crews today pose some particularly illuminating challenges for screen media workers, arguably even more so for the professionals who must somehow solder together foreign and domestic work cultures when Hollywood comes to town. As global interest in locations has intensified and extended to new territories, the escalation of mobile production has exacerbated many of the tensions and complexities in these emerging production hubs.

The social relations of production, for example, are rife with structural inequities. Opportunities for upward mobility for the hair and makeup artist in Prague or the location scout in Atlanta are limited at best. On the other side of the equation, producers now seek out department heads and other technicians who "travel well," industry slang for workers who are comfortable leaving behind an entourage of trusted colleagues in Hollywood for the opportunity to collaborate with technicians and trainees in distant locales. Moreover, basic assumptions about wages, job titles, and professional experience are complicated by the different union structures in places like Atlanta or Glasgow. Cultural tensions arise as well, since local work routines and job categories are often governed by a division of labor different than the studios' usual mode of production. Massaging these differences is an important responsibility for service producers and production managers.

Even the incentives that are designed to attract Hollywood producers demand detailed attention, since they are marked by iterative change and myriad contingencies. No two government rebate schemes are ever the same. A location's fortunes rise and fall as a consequence of those differences. Accordingly, these service producers lobby their governments for more subsidies, making arguments to politicians about economic impact and job opportunities in hopes of sustaining the flow of high-budget work into their respective territories. As small business owners with overhead to consider, it's no longer just their personal fate at stake but also the livelihoods of the administrators and crew members they have brought into the fold.

For production managers and location experts who have built a global reputation, they face a dilemma similar to their counterparts in Los Angeles: while some of them may enjoy hopscotching between Albuquerque and Atlanta, London and Dublin, Glasgow and Budapest, they're also aware of the toll that professional jetsetting takes on personal relationships and family life back home. This dynamic is especially true in locations like Glasgow, that are largely disengaged from the global machine, which means that production and location managers who hail from there must permanently relocate or spend much of their lives on the road.

Global film and television production is therefore exceptionally complex and multifaceted. As one of our interlocutors confided, the work requires you to be a stellar line producer but also a lawyer, a lobbyist, an accountant, a negotiator, a mentor, and a cultural translator. Service production and the affiliated responsibilities of production managers and location experts demand logistical resolve, creative agility, local resourcefulness, and an oversupply of resilience. At all costs, the labor these individuals perform must keep the production on track, and yet the demands they face underscore the fragility of the whole enterprise—one hiccup, large or small, threatens to bring the whole production to a grinding halt.

Therein lies the precariousness of this labor. Given the distance from Los Angeles, the enduring appeal of a foreign production hub hinges on its reputation for a seamless experience. And thus the careers of those individuals who live and work there are subject to both its perceived amenability and the demands of international producers, no matter how extravagant or complicated. We learned that a common strategy is to say "yes" to requests in the first instance, and then figure out how to resolve them later, often out of earshot of visiting producers who aren't always interested in "logistical complications."

This drive to please is certainly a reflection of personal ambition, but it's also a logical consequence of the ephemeral and itinerant nature of global capital. A location's international standing is vulnerable to even the slightest suggestion of trouble, be it an unstable incentive, a difficult crew, or an uncooperative public agency. Much of this work, then, is proactive and preemptive, squashing problems before they pose a genuine threat. At other times it is reactive and immediate, making peace among a squabbling crew or knowing whom to call when the city throws up one too many bureaucratic roadblocks. It's a challenging and risky business, and yet ironically, much of the labor required to maintain the impression of seamless and transparent production must remain invisible. Returning business is contingent on that frictionless experience, and as these interviews make clear, it takes a tremendous amount of labor to ensure that the global machine runs smoothly.

14

Anonymous, studio production executive

Since 2004, Anonymous has been the head of production for a major television studio, overseeing scripted, reality, and first-run syndication programming. As outlined in this interview, studio budgets are a balancing act between creative production issues and the financial parameters of each project, which these days are significantly affected by the choice of production locations and the associated subsidies.

At what point in the development process do you start reading scripts?

Over the course of a year, the studio will hear at least a hundred pitches. As those ideas start to gain a little heat, I start reading them. I start talking to the showrunners about what they envision for the series. Between the conversations and the scripts, I am pretty good at figuring out ballpark costs. No one really knows how much money I spend but me. When television viewers see the New York skyline on their TV screens, they think they're seeing New York. They don't know how much it costs to make Los Angeles or Atlanta look like New York. Most show creators don't know those costs, either. I spend a lot of time giving them an idea of what their show is going to cost and how we might bring it in line with a more feasible budget. Can we shoot this scene at night instead of day? Can you set the story here instead of there? Can we film the series here instead of there? I'm showing them what they gain or lose, creatively and financially, in those various scenarios. This process becomes more and more fine-tuned as the script continues through development.

What aspects of the script jump out at you? Is there a method to the madness, or is each script different?

I immediately look at location and action. I call them toys. If a show proposes big-name talent whose characters fly all over the world in precarious situations to blow stuff up, that's a nightmare. We simply can't afford to do it the way it needs to be done in order to maintain the level of quality we expect. Obviously, this entails a careful examination of the pilot script to remove extraneous elements or creative flourishes that pose significant impacts to the budget. I'm always asking the showrunners: Are these elements absolutely necessary to the story? It may be exciting to blow up three buildings in the pilot episode, but we can have the same impact with a third of the cost if we only blow up one.

Do scripts have casts attached when you review them?

No, but they usually have names in mind. I can get a sense of who is on their mind and what level of talent we're considering. For me, it's important to know: Are we talking name talent or no-name talent? Generally they'll want God, and I have to tell them we can't afford Him.

So those are the "toys." What about locations?

I'm immediately thinking about locations. The process entails a careful consideration of the space and place of the narrative—what locations are required for the story and where they are available. This requires an intimate knowledge of what a location has to offer and what creative variety is available there. It doesn't make sense to shoot a jungle series in New York, no matter how competitive the incentive. So, what do we need creatively to film the series, and what locations offer what we need for what cost? Oftentimes we can do more creatively—get more bang for our buck—if we look at locations outside Los Angeles.

How do you determine that bang for your buck? Is it all about the incentives?

First I look closely at the script to determine what it needs creatively. It doesn't mean the production isn't mobile, but I want to make sure I'm not considering a location that simply doesn't work creatively. Remember, too, I'm not dealing with features where you have the luxury of prep time. I'm doing series television where I'm often prepping a production without final scripts.
    Then I'll look more closely at the incentives. Everything changes so quickly. It's practically a full-time job to keep tabs on who is offering what at any given time.

But this is also why it's important to know what's happening: it keeps the world at our disposal. We can go anywhere. Is it more cost effective to re-create Chicago in Atlanta? Or do we just film in Chicago? If there are lots of toys, I'll start pushing for a competitive location. Does it have it to be Los Angeles? Why can't it be New York or Philadelphia? We're still early enough in the development process that these pitches are very similar to dating. Everyone is very receptive to my ideas because they want their show to get made. If you're dating someone you fancy, you're willing to do anything to get their attention. I used to go to flower shows all the time with my wife. I don't go to flower shows anymore. My point: it's easy for the creatives to agree with me while we're still in the romance stage; it's more difficult once the show is picked up.

So creative variety, incentives, and . . . ?

If a location has a competitive incentive, it's critical to also offer a solid physical infrastructure, crew depth [referring to the size and skill of the labor pool], and, for international locations, a competitive exchange rate. A successful television series will need a permanent home for a long time. It's nearly impossible to do a television series in a location without a studio or necessary equipment, like your cranes and other rigs. Given the budget and time constraints in television, it's equally important to have a highly skilled crew ready to jump into the trenches with us.

If you don't have an infrastructure or crew base, then we have to bring our own. We're bringing in more individuals, paying for more car rentals, accommodations, and per diem, and shipping the equipment we need to get the job done. You lose the tax credit.

Each factor can impact a production's degree of mobility, its costs, and its creative possibilities.

Absolutely. There are also the more intangible factors, like convincing talent and crew that spending eight months in Budapest away from their friends and families is a necessary adventure for the creative and financial well-being of a series. It's fun, but I'm sure not everyone enjoys it to the same degree.

Does it ever get to a point where you have to say to the showrunner, "Look, the numbers aren't working. We can't go forward with this show"?

At the end of the day, you can do any show for any price if you're willing to live with the outcome. My perspective is that it doesn't do anyone any good to run a show cheaply and efficiently if the final product sucks. You'll never hear me say, "I can do this cheaper, but it's going to look like shit." I'm at the table pitching reasons to my counterparts on the creative side why we can't do X or Y but can do Z to achieve the same effect.

I'm likewise there to prevent any financial surprises after filming starts. I'll read the script, then tell the showrunner that his or her series will cost X. The showrunner will start removing all this extraneous stuff and ask, "Okay. What about now?" I'll say, "It's still X because I already removed all the fluff when I read it the first time." I'm always budgeting things in my mind. I'm always removing what I know will make it an impossible project. I'm not as close to the project as the showrunner. It's sometimes easier for someone with some distance to identify what a viewer will or will not miss.

Sometimes I win battles. Sometimes I lose them. But the studio has limits. We have to have limits. We're in the business of making quality television, and my job is to figure out how we can do that realistically without compromising an idea's creative integrity.

So you're focused on numbers, but your job has some creative elements to it as well.

Don't tell anybody that!

We won't characterize you as a creative if you don't want us to.

I'm teasing. I like to think my counterparts at other studios are all doing various iterations of my job. I don't know. I've looked at my job, thinking it's very easy to say no *or* it's very easy to say yes. My challenge is how to serve both masters: the creative master and the financial master. I can simply dismiss an idea because it's too expensive. But what's the fun in that? The more exciting part for me is to figure out how I can help make sure that this idea, which might be initially too costly on paper, actually gets on television. I don't want to say no. I want to make it happen.

Do you work a lot with local film commissions when you're planning a production?

You always use the film commissions or film offices. They will hook you up with the local crew base. They will point me to the people I need to do the production there. We're a big company and at home in L.A., we don't need anyone else to do what we do. But if you're venturing into less familiar locations, the film commissions are critical. They help us secure permits and navigate local bureaucracies. They provide lists of available workers. They help us navigate the logistics of ensuring a smooth transition from here to there.

When we try to explain this process to our students, they immediately think about travel costs, lodging costs, shipping costs—all the expanded logistics. They wonder if the incentives actually compensate for what you're spending.

You can tell them the math works. If we're going to the right locations, we only have to take the key people with us. Department heads and key crew members will travel with the production. We make sure they're very well accommodated no matter where they go—they're treated well when they travel. There's little resistance there. Talent is a little more difficult. You have to figure out who they are and how best to appeal to them. If it's an established individual, I'll go to hell and back to get them to agree to go to Hawaii. Cable television was easier in its infancy because we were dealing with less-established talent, or the big names were doing passion projects on cable and were willing to do whatever was necessary to get it made. It's not so anymore. Today cable is a big game. And the reality is simple: if you do this series in Los Angeles, you're going to have $200,000 less to do your show. And that pays for a lot.

In all fairness, we are asking for an eight-month commitment. And if the show works, it's five, eight, ten years of your life. No matter how great the place is or how great we're treating them, they're away from family, friends, and significant others.

Who else finds themselves increasingly mobile? Talent, for sure. Writers? Directors?

Staff writers for television drama don't travel. They can be based in one place while the series films in another. Comedy, because of the hectic schedule, requires the writers to stay close to the product. So if it's filming in Los Angeles, they're in Los Angeles. If it's filming in New York, they're in New York. Showrunners must stay in touch with what's happening on set. They don't have to be there all the time, so they'll fly back and forth between their home base and the filming location.

Who are the key intermediaries, then, between the financial and creative managers in Los Angeles and the folks working on the shoot in Atlanta or Budapest or wherever?

On the creative side, the key intermediaries are the director who is there on the set and, to a lesser extent, the showrunner, just because he or she spends time on location. There's also an executive producer on the creative side who spends a lot of time flying back and forth.

On the financial side, I always have an executive producer who reports back to me. I also am very close to the line producer, who helps me keep tabs on what's happening on the ground. I'll spend some time flying back and forth, but I really rely on those key positions to keep me in the loop. There's too much money on the line not to keep an eye on how the production is unfolding.

Which locations are getting the most work these days?

We have L.A. Chicago. We'll do the United States first. Portland. New York. Then we have Budapest. We have Australia. We have some cable in Canada. We have some first-run in Connecticut.

Are those the most competitive locations?

Clearly New York is. Australia is a great place to shoot abroad. So are Budapest and Prague.

What does it take to turn a location into a production hub? We often hear: at least one TV drama series with a long-term commitment.

No, it takes more. It takes consistency. As you do more in a location, you build more capacity. People move there. Skills grow stronger. Services develop. If you're relying on one series, everything goes away when that series ends.

You mentioned earlier that tracking incentives is practically a full-time job. How do you do it?

One, I'm a workaholic, which is to the detriment of my family, but it has helped me greatly. I'm usually in the office by five in the morning. I usually leave somewhere around midnight. Sometimes it feels like twenty-four hours a day, seven days a week.

15

David Minkowski, service producer

David Minkowski is the head of production for Stillking Films in Prague, where he has worked on projects like *The Bourne Identity* (2002) and *Casino Royale* (2006). The company, founded more than two decades ago, played an early and integral role in attracting large-scale feature film and television productions to the region. Minkowski describes how the increased competition among different territories to attract foreign producers has increased the complexities of his job, while also affecting the fortunes of Prague as a production hub.

At the height of the production craze in the late 1990s and early 2000s, Stillking was a major player. Tell us about those early years when you found yourself servicing back-to-back features.

It was amazing. This was before incentives; producers were attracted to Prague because it was gorgeous and cheap. They were interested in it for its creative potential, for the looks it provided, and they were writing scripts *for* Prague. From 2000 to 2008, it was nonstop work; the industry just exploded here. Then Budapest got an incentive. London got an incentive. Berlin got an incentive. We saw other locations start to emerge, and work in Prague started to decline.

What was the nature of your job in the early years?

Our objective was to help people in a foreign land that was alien to them. In the 1990s, this place was more alien, more foreign, to Americans. Fewer people spoke English. Fewer services existed. You had to be much more clever about what vendors you used. It wasn't just a phone call to get this or that crane or camera. You had to have your wits about you.

It was such a wild ride then. Suddenly the big names were coming to Prague. The amount of talent we hosted here! Away from home and the prying eyes of the studio, they were so much more open and accessible. You could sit down with Jerry Bruckheimer or Matt Damon or Barbara Broccoli. You could take them out to dinner. You could hang out with them. You could learn from them. It was a really, really great time.

As we started amassing more credits, making more relationships, and establishing our reputation, our role also evolved—we became the line producers, essentially overseeing all below-the-line aspects. We hire crew. We manage crew. We supervise locations. We navigate local bureaucracy, like explaining labor laws, child work permits, that kind of stuff. Even though the industry has evolved, it's still different working in Eastern Europe than in the States.

What sorts of issues did you have to manage?

A lot of clarification, whether it was language or different assumptions lost in translation. A producer friend of mine is fond of saying, "It doesn't matter where you shoot. It's all about the concept of time. What does 'I need it now' mean?" And that can vary across cultures. For example, there's this great story from a TV movie shoot my friend did in the early 1990s in Lithuania. It's the day before the first day of the shoot. The producer wants to make sure they have the right film stock on the camera truck to start filming the next day. The camera assistant says, "No problem! It's all covered!" The producer isn't convinced, so he says, "Okay. Show me. Let's go to the truck so you can show me the film stock that you think is enough for the day." They walk over to the truck and there's only one roll of film there! One thousand feet! Because for them [the crew], in the Soviet days, they would never shoot more than a thousand feet in a single day. A single roll might last for days. They would film a single shot and then say, "That's a wrap. We'll come back tomorrow." They had all the time in the world. Our job was to make sure those misunderstandings don't happen.

When we did *Bad Company* (2002) with Anthony Hopkins, I had probably seven or eight translators. A translator at camera. A translator at grip. Three translators at makeup. You had to have them. Today, we don't have any. Zero. Everybody speaks English, even the electricians. It's just the common language of film production now.

Name one of the most critical services you provide.

Finding locations remains an integral function of what we do. It's the first thing that happens when producers are considering Prague. They need a location scout.

They also ask lots of questions: "Can we do this? Can we do that? Can we put snow down on the street?"

Our location managers are responsible for facilitating these requests. They'll advise the producer: yes, this is possible, or no, that's impossible. Oftentimes they'll think something is impossible simply because it's inconceivable to them that the authorities would ever grant permission for whatever request. Of course, producers don't take no for an answer. They'll come to me and say, "You need to make this happen. We need to get snow on the ground!"

The Bourne Identity is a great example. We filmed all the Zurich winter scenes in Prague when there wasn't snow on the ground. We had to fake it. There was this huge shoot in the center of Prague. We had to rent trams and paint them to look like Zurich trams. We needed to get snow on these parapets that were two stories high, which you can only do with cherry pickers [elevated work platforms]. We had cherry pickers running up and down the street blowing snow all over the place, and then when we were finished shooting, it all had to get cleaned up. That whole process is inconceivable for a location manager who hasn't done it before.

A similar issue popped up with the film we're doing now, Ridley Scott's *Child 44* (2015). The film is set in Moscow in the 1950s. We needed a metro station, and of course the only one that worked for our needs also happened to be the busiest metro station in Prague. No one had ever shot there before unless it was a quick scene they could schedule between midnight and three in the morning when the station is closed. Our schedule called for two twelve-hour days of shooting in a metro station. The location manager said, no, it's impossible. We can't do it. Why? Because we've never done it before! They'll never let us! So I got involved. I called the mayor of Prague and explained what we needed. By the end of the day, we received this great letter from the mayor saying Ridley Scott is a great producer and the city wants to help. They closed the station for two full days and rerouted the metro traffic on city buses. Of course we had to pay for it, but the cost was relatively low compared to doing something similar in London or New York.

This is why it's important for me to keep my crews together and work with the same people. It helps them realize what's possible—that anything is possible, really. Let's say "yes" and then figure out how to get it done.

With respect to the key positions on a production, describe the breakdown between local versus foreign crew.

It varies from movie to movie. Television brings fewer people because there are more budget constraints. The more money you have, the more people you bring with you. Forget about above-the-line; they always come with the production, and they pick up local extras. In terms of crew, they always bring the DP [director of photography]. They always bring the first assistant director. They always bring a costume designer. They almost always bring a production designer. They almost always bring their own makeup and hair. After that, it's about the budget. If they have money, they'll bring a set decorator and a prop master. They'll bring a camera operator. They'll always bring their own accountant.

We are very strong in technical areas. Grip. Electric. Sound. The production office also is strong.

How has the local crew base changed during your time in the business?

When I started working here in 1995, I was working with two different generations. There was the older generation that had been working on movies for ten or twenty years, mostly during Communist times. They were thirty, forty, and fifty years old and very difficult to work with. They didn't speak English. They had bad habits—they'd go get drunk at lunch. They weren't trained to work in the American style. But you needed them because they had the experience. Then there was the younger generation; the people I brought in. They didn't have any experience but they spoke English and they were young and eager. They were willing to work sixteen- to eighteen-hour days and learn as they went.

In 1995, they were in their early twenties. I've watched them grow up. I've watched them get married, have kids, and pay mortgages. I've watched their whole lives transform from this process; they had no clue what they were getting into when they started. The industry transformed them. Now we're reaching a point where they're in their late thirties and forties and they don't want to do it anymore. They'll be fifty soon. They'll want to retire. I have to start the process all over again. I'm constantly looking out for new young people who want to get into the business.

How often do you interface with public authorities?

All the time. We did a string of action pictures in the 2000s. That's what we became known for. I negotiated a lot of permits to shoot car chases and shootouts in the center of Prague. Filmmakers wanted all of this intense action against the beautiful backdrop of the city. I was rerouting trams, closing traffic, and getting permission for gunfire in the middle of the night. Each film we do always presents a new challenge, something bigger and more complicated than the last shoot. In the early days, that actually worked to our advantage. Public authorities were always a little bit dumbfounded by the things we wanted to do. You want to close down traffic on the river to film a scene that's supposed to take place on the Thames in front of the British Parliament? Um, sure? Maybe they just wanted to see if we could actually do it.

Today, they care more about the residents. They are much more concerned about the neighborhood and what disruptions we'll cause, so they're more cautious. Of course, if there's a chance to associate the city with a very big movie, things are much easier. *Casino Royale* (2006) is a perfect example. Everybody knows James Bond. Everybody loves James Bond. The series had always been filmed in London. They would do some second-unit location shooting in these exotic locales to make it look like they were there, but 85 percent of what you saw on screen had always been done in London. However, *Casino Royale* was the first Bond movie based primarily outside of London—we shot about 60 percent of the movie here. Remember the big airport sequence toward the beginning when a terrorist is going to blow up an airplane? We called up [Prague's Vaclav Havel Airport] and explained what we wanted to do and we were able to shoot on the tarmac, airside, throughout the whole airport, gunfire, fire trucks, police, everything! We had phenomenal cooperation and it was because they wanted to be involved with a James Bond movie. If I had wanted to close down the main airport for a sequence in a movie with no famous names? It may have been possible, but it would have been much more difficult.

How do you secure work?

Producers will send you a script. They want to see locations and a budget. You send them to a website with pictures you've loaded based on the script. It's important for them to visualize the locations. You want them to see their movie here. If they say, "Yes, this works," then you do a budget and they compare it to other locations they're considering.

If you're dealing with an A-list director, where does he or she really want to go? John Moore scouted four or five cities for *A Good Day to Die Hard* (2013). At the end of the day, he wanted to make the film in Budapest. The same holds true for big-name actors. I wanted to make *The Monuments Men* (2014) here; they were interested for a while. But they selected Berlin pretty early in the process. I don't think it was rebate-related. I think they had George Clooney and Matt Damon and other major actors, and they wanted somewhere comfy and cozy.

How do producers compare location costs?

It's the Big Mac test. How much is a Big Mac in Budapest? How much is a Big Mac in London? I can tell you what a grip costs in Prague, and what a grip costs in London. A grip in Prague is 100 euro a day. In London it's closer to 300 euro a day, plus a 35 percent fringe [taxes and additional employer fees]. Right there, you can multiply that by 150 crew positions. For Prague, you'll likely have more travel and lodging costs because you bring more people with you. You compare big chunks, like extras. Extras are always a major part of a budget. Are you building sets? Construction is another easy category. A carpenter in Prague will cost you about 75 percent less than it does in London. Your materials, however, are about the same. A piece of wood costs the same here as it does in London because it all comes from Sweden.

Line producers will often do comparisons for a project. They'll literally call five different cities to ask for budgets. The line producer will call me and ask, "Can I get a budget for Prague?" I know they're calling the same bloody places: Vancouver, Budapest, London. There's so much game playing that happens. Good executives know if the line producer is comparing apples to apples. Not-so-good ones get fooled. There's a lot of speculation involved that goes into creating and delivering a budget. Line producers can make the numbers do whatever they want.

Explain the speculation.

There are so many unknown variables when you're budgeting a movie, especially at the point when you're doing a budget just based on the script. Are we building that set or is it a location shoot? When the script says, "They walk into a bar," what is the size of that bar? Is it a little bar? A big bar? I can put $1 million in the construction budget, and get a lot with that in Prague and Budapest. Can I keep the budget the same if I'm the line producer who is comparing Vancouver? Sure, but it won't go nearly as far. You can goose each of those items to hit the overall budget number you want.

You can do it in other ways, too. How many foreign crew do you need to bring? I always argue that you don't have to bring many people with you if you shoot in Prague, but if a line producer decides to ignore my advice and budget for ten more people in Prague than, say, Berlin because he or she simply wants to go to Berlin, then that will cost you salaries, hotels, per diem, drivers, and assistants. Prague suddenly costs more. There are so many variables.

But if a line producer pitches Berlin at, say, $47 million, isn't there a risk that it will end up costing $55 million?

Yes, and that happens. I'm conservative because I don't want to get egg on my face. I don't want to keep dropping costs and dropping costs to get the job only to discover that it can't be done for what I've quoted. Look, if you do ten budgets, you're lucky to get one movie. What if you get the one with the unrealistic budget? Then you're screwed because you faked the numbers.

How has business changed in the last five years?

Prague went from more than $1 billion per year in film spend—just from larger Hollywood and British features, excluding smaller, foreign coproductions—to less than $200 million. We started pressing in earnest for incentives around 2006 and 2007. I remember taking the producer Mark Johnson and Andrew Adamson, who directed the first two *Shrek* movies (2001, 2004) and the first two *The Chronicles of Narnia* movies (2005, 2008), to meet with a government minister about incentives. Adamson is responsible for earning the studios billions in revenues with those films alone. Johnson has won an Oscar and an Emmy. I introduce Johnson and Adamson, including the films they've done, and the minister says to Andrew in the most condescending tone you can imagine, "So—you make fairy tales." Meanwhile, in London, the prime minister sends an RAF helicopter to fly Steven Spielberg from the airport to 10 Downing Street for lunch.

How do you account for the difference in perspective?

It's different cultural histories. England has always had a relationship, a love affair, with Hollywood. There are some obvious affinities there, language and culture being the most obvious, but also a serious appreciation of the economic impact of filmmaking. Sure, there's a rich history of Czech filmmaking, but Hollywood is more of a secondhand culture; it's just not Czech. Sure, they love Spielberg. Sure, they love Ridley Scott. But the whole creative industries rhetoric hasn't taken a firm hold here yet, especially when you compare it to places like England where there's a real determination to value the economic and cultural impact of information technology, knowledge workers, and cultural production. It's valued more than industrial production. The history here is very different.

What's your pitch in those meetings with government ministers?

We pitch economic multipliers, direct and indirect employment opportunities, growth in the service sector, and so on. But the problem here is that the politicians don't care about the public. They care about themselves. They want to know what's in it for them. It's a corrupt, narcissistic system—such an old, antiquated style of government and accountability. Unless you can explain what's in it for them, they don't appreciate it. Sure, in America and England there's corruption and selfish politicians, but the implicit rules are different. They know they are still held accountable for helping to grease the economic engine, and jobs are hugely important. That's how you get reelected. Jobs. "I created jobs." And that simply doesn't exist here. It's hard to make that pitch and have it stick. Politicians here don't believe the data. They don't believe the argument that for every dollar you spend, you get two or three dollars back in tax benefits down the road.

But we were persistent. We made those arguments over and over again and eventually, in 2010, we finally got a very, very modest incentive approved.

It was announced with great fanfare.

Of course, but it ultimately has had a disastrous effect on production over the past three years.

Tell us more.

Our intention from the start was to establish an incentive that would support major features. If you're shooting a $2 million Polish, Czech, Italian coproduction, you're not creating substantial economic impact. However, if you're shooting a $100 million blockbuster, you will create value for the city. From day one, our objective was to get those movies that generate lots of money. Perversely, the incentive program has done the exact opposite of what it was intended to do. It doesn't bring big movies at all. It brings the small European coproductions.

Why? Because it's been a flawed, poorly structured program from the very start. There's simply not enough money in the program—it's capped—and until very recently, it was distributed on a first-come, first-served basis.

Can you elaborate on those flaws?

Originally, I'm sure first-come, first-served seemed like the fairest approach, but the process wasn't structured correctly. Producers applied for the incentive before their movies were even green-lit for production. There was no mechanism to protect against that, and when the projects never materialized, there was no mechanism to release the funds back into the program until it was too late. The process tied up the fund's resources and reduced what was available to other producers, especially if they were shooting anything bigger than a $5 or $10 million movie.

Damn.

Exactly. It's been highly effective at alienating Hollywood and pissing off producers. We invite them to the city, they make the trip, and we show them around, and when it comes time to make the decision, it's, "Oh, the fund's depleted." There also was a real risk of people getting screwed. There was money in the program when they applied, if they were lucky, and maybe it was still there when their application came up for review. What if they were betting on that incentive? It never happened, fortunately. But we used to make four or five movies a year and now we're happy when we make two, and usually we're making only one. So the program has driven away the very business it was intended to attract.

Can you describe the effects of the most recent change to the incentive program?

It's made it even worse. Instead of being first-come, first-served, they open up a window during which they accept applications for the incentive. Everyone applies within this window. Then the government reviews the projects and prorates the approved applications against the available funds. So, while we advertise a 20 percent incentive program, you can end up with a rebate worth 7 percent because you applied in a year with too many projects. If you're expecting 20 percent, and you receive 7 percent, you get pissed off.

But that's the new reality this year and, in theory, going forward, unless we successfully lobby for more money. Really, that's my job these days. I now spend more than half my time dealing with rebate-related issues. It's no longer just about film production. I've become more of a lawyer and an accountant and a lobbyist. I spend so much time trying to understand how this whole process works from a legal perspective, from a financial perspective, from a policy perspective, and from a bureaucratic perspective. I spend time trying to figure out how to game it and goose it to secure work from foreign producers. I need to convince the government to support the film business. I need to figure out how to keep from losing business to other countries. All of this, instead of focusing on the production itself.

This is interesting. It clearly shows that no two incentives are the same, and that navigating them around the world can feel a bit like working your way through a labyrinth. It also illustrates how incentives structure production. In this case, the changes to the incentive affected the types of productions coming to town and the nature of your work.

We used to be the number one company in Prague. If you look at the Hollywood films made here before 2010, we handled most of them. Now? Those movies are going away. Instead we have small European movies, like the Danish film *A Royal Affair* (2012), or low-budget television series like *The Musketeers* (2014–ongoing). I'm American, so all of my contacts and relationships are in Hollywood with the networks and studios and their related partners in London. I put all my cookies in that basket. The way Prague business works—and this is true in most countries in the service business—is that you have a Russian guy who has a company here and services all the Russian movies, and a French guy services the French movies, because it's cultural. They speak the same language.

I did a movie with a French group once and I didn't understand the rules. It was a completely different system. I tried to do a Bollywood movie that came here once and it was like: no, thank you. I did not want to be involved in that crazy process. It was just so alien!

The companies here with their toes in the European coproduction world or the Danish production world have seen their business improve, because they can service three or four projects in a year that need a few hundred thousand dollars in rebate money. I need $10 million. A few years ago, *World War Z* (2013) and *Hercules* (2014) would have filmed in Prague, but instead they filmed in Budapest. It's hurt our business disproportionately when compared to the smaller companies here, or to similar companies in other cities with more competitive incentives. When you see articles here in the paper, you see people like me and others, whose business depends on Hollywood, bitching and moaning, but you don't see anybody bitching and moaning from those other companies. That's just how it is.

How has this affected your pitch to producers?

It's a dangerous game. My business is based on my reputation, and that's exactly what's at stake here. If you listened to the Ministry of Culture when they announced the incentive changes at Cannes this year, you'd think heaven had arrived in Prague. There were a bunch of interviews and press releases, blah, blah, blah. But I'm the one who deals directly with those studio executives. I'm the one they get pissed at. I get screwed, not some idiot in the government. I just have to be honest, more honest than people in the government or the Film Commission.

The main way we've responded to the situation is that we've opened an office in Budapest. Now I spend a good deal of my time selling Budapest and going to Budapest and working in Budapest. That's an easy sell. There's more competition in Budapest, more firms, and we weren't the first firm there. But there's so much production going to the city that there is enough work for everybody.

Ten years ago, I would do a budget for three or four movies and get one of them. Now, I do budgets for ten or fifteen movies, and get one of them. It's much more research and development and comparison work than it used to be.

How is Budapest different from Prague?

Budapest is more logistically challenging. It's a bigger city. It's busier, more crowded, harder to park. There are greater distances between locations. Yet there are more location choices because it is bigger. So creatively it can be more interesting. It also has more studios. A good tax credit brings investment, so they have built a lot of stages. It's become a major destination.

What other locations have potential to emerge as competitive production hubs?

I don't anticipate much change in the go-to locations in Europe. London is the first stop for big movies. Berlin has good incentives, studios, and locations. Prague and Budapest will remain strong as long as the incentives stay. They have the infrastructure, locations, and skill base.

Beyond that, I think Serbia is a place to watch. It has the lowest labor costs in Europe right now. It's also very welcoming. It's mainly because of one lady who left Serbia years ago to work in Los Angeles and then went back to open a service company. She took her knowledge of the business and started building up a really user-friendly base there. It just lacks location variation because it's been bombed and destroyed over the years. But there's a new studio. They're even getting an incentive. It'll never become Budapest or Prague. It's not big enough. Still, I'd rather go to Serbia than Bulgaria.

Why is that?

Bulgaria is a weird place. It's not just that it's corrupt. It's also this strange mash-up that results from out-of-control Western capitalism descending on a former Communist country full of a very poor, screwed-over population. And there are no good production partners there to help you navigate it. And then there's Romania. It should be a preeminent place that steals work from Budapest and Prague. The crew there is great. But it needs an incentive. And it needs new service companies that work in a transparent, cooperative way instead of ripping off their supposed partners.

Croatia is also great, but it will never be anything more than the place you go for two weeks when you need that beautiful location on the seaside. There's no reason to be based in Croatia. It's more expensive, and there's not much infrastructure. Instead, productions keep their bases in Budapest or Prague.

I don't expect anything from Ukraine or Poland. It's also too late for Slovakia. France has an incentive but it's not going to suddenly bring tons of work to France. People only go to France if the script requires it. It's the same with Italy.

Fifteen years ago it was a different story. There was some urgency to the question, "What location is next?" Not anymore. Now the globe is small. Everybody knows everywhere. The map is set, so to speak.

What about outside of Europe?

It's the same. It's already easier somewhere else. I don't expect a mad rush to Brazil, for example, even if they offered an incentive. Or Africa. If you go to Africa, you go to South Africa. Nowhere else. Dubai and Abu Dhabi want to get in the game. They're investing millions and millions of dollars. They will get the one or two odd movies that need the Middle East visual backdrop. Still, a lot of international television or regional films are shooting there because the finance is there. There is a massive film and TV industry in the region with nothing to do with Hollywood, and that is important business if you can meet their needs.

Asia is more interesting because the locations are more diverse. China is eager to invest money into production. But service-wise, the map is pretty established. It's China and Thailand. Malaysia hopes to siphon some of that interest. Maybe they will. Japan is too expensive—no one shoots there. I think South Korea is interesting. It's so cheap. It has amazing locations. It's untapped right now. If I started over, I'd look at South Korea.

What about Los Angeles?

It's still the center of film and television production, but the career opportunities are not there anymore. Maybe new tax incentives will change that. I graduated from film school in 1989. I could do whatever I wanted. It was an open-door policy for anyone who was eager and willing to work hard. I started in Portland before it unionized. I did fifteen movies there in less than three years. It was a TV movie factory—just one after another. I moved to L.A., and there was a ton of production happening there, too. It's not like that anymore. I wouldn't recommend this business to any young person in the States. It's not secure. There's just a general unease about the number of movies being made today, how long that trajectory will continue, and what kinds of movies Hollywood will make in the future. Right now, everyone seems to think we will end up with a dozen $300 million blockbuster movies each year and the rest will end up on your cable box or iTunes. You won't go to the cinema anymore. And that affects labor. What are they going to pay you to work on a film that ends up on a cable box? Not what they pay you to work on *Mission Impossible*. And those movies aren't being made in Los Angeles.

Maybe in New Orleans or Atlanta it feels like glory days. It certainly does in Budapest. But not in Los Angeles.

16

Adam Goodman, service producer

Adam Goodman is a producer and co-owner of Mid Atlantic Films in Budapest, Hungary. He has contributed to numerous projects over the past twenty years, most recently *A Good Day to Die Hard* (2013), *World War Z* (2013), and *The Martian* (2015). Reflecting on Budapest's emergence as a leading production locale in Eastern Europe, Goodman explains the challenges of managing transnational production logistics and up-skilling his core network of contract employees.

You operate one of the premier service firms in Budapest, but you've said you're still anxious about securing contracts. Why?

It's an anxiety that comes from a lifelong freelance mentality—you're only as good as your last job. And you only know that you did a good job when you're called for the next project. I was talking about this very thing the other day to my business partner Howard Ellis. I said, "The same buzz, the same high I got when I got a phone call asking, 'Are you available to get on a plane?' is the high I get now when someone asks, 'Are you available to service our film?'" But I'm a managing director now, which gives me even more anxiety. As a freelance line producer [before starting Mid Atlantic in Budapest] I had the flexibility to follow the work, which expanded my opportunities. I was only responsible for myself. As a service producer, I'm responsible for our company and the livelihoods of those who work with us. And our success is contingent upon producers wanting to come to Hungary.

It's turned out okay for us. In our early days, we never knew what we were doing in an upcoming year until just before Christmas, or more likely in the first quarter of the new year. Now we're working on budgets for shows that may or may not happen more than a year in advance.

What do you think is driving this change?

It's like running a good restaurant—the more people come here, the more buzz it generates, the more business we receive. We're now an established location. Since Hungary got its new tax rebate in 2004, which was instrumental in putting us on the production map, we've continued to draw business away from Prague. As business continued to develop here, so too did producers' confidence and comfort. And the fact that we established our reputation as part of that momentum means we've successfully positioned ourselves as a key partner in the region.

But as you say, your success is contingent on other factors outside of your direct control, especially the incentive.

We're actively involved in lobbying the Hungarian government to preserve and improve the incentive. It involves a lot of meetings with politicians, lawyers, accountants, film commissioners, and other producers. For instance, when the incentive was last up for review by the EU commission, we—the proverbial "we" being tax advisors from Ernst & Young—put together a proposal to increase the value of the incentive. We didn't simply ask to have what we had before. We thought, let's get creative. Let's do something unique. E&Y agreed. We added a foreign spend element to the tax rebate. Production companies get a rebate not only on what they spend here but also on what they spend outside of Hungary on Hungarian labor. So you now can take your Hungarian crew to Jamaica for a few weeks of location shooting, and you'll get a rebate on those labor costs.

It's been incredible for business here. But I know it really hurt Prague. It's symptomatic of any economy, not just the film business: when there isn't enough business to enable people to pay their mortgages and feed their families, they go and do other things. There was some fallout along those lines in Prague. It reduced the crew base—not the skill base—but a lot of crew had to find something else to do to pay their bills.

How quickly?

Quite frankly, almost immediately after the Hungarian tax rebate kicked in. Prague is marginally more expensive before rebates—but only marginally—and now with our rebate, we're cheaper. Once the Czechs got their tax rebate, we expected to see a significant reduction in our cycle of shows. But we didn't, largely because the Czech rebate isn't as competitive.

Ironically, Prague did so much to establish Central Europe as a viable location. There's greater awareness of and interest in shooting here. But when producers start comparing the rebates, they notice two things: one, the Hungarian rebate allows you to maximize spend; and two, the Czech rebate is capped by the national government.

Can you walk us through the steps it takes to put a project together?

When we first set up Mid Atlantic, our plan was to fly to Los Angeles, knock on the doors of all the people with whom we had ever worked, and start pitching for projects. We had intended to build upon those relationships. But we've never gotten around to taking that flight. We've just been too busy.

The key to our success is based on two very clear criteria: Adam and Howard. It's our address books. It's our reputations as honest, transparent, clear-thinking producers—the same traits that made us good line producers have made us good service producers. Given that people are traveling so far to make a film with so much money at stake, trust is a fundamental aspect of our business and key to our success. It sounds pompous, but you can argue that no one would consider coming here if it wasn't for us.

Of course, it *is* pompous because we couldn't do anything without the crew base here, which is second to none. We've developed four of the best teams in Hungary since we first started in 2005.

Are they exclusive to you? How much does their fate depend on your company?

People seem to think we have some kind of mafioso control over the local crew base, but that's not the case. They don't work for us exclusively. Of course, we want them to stay with us, but we always tell them to take the first job that's guaranteed. So if we lose out on a contract, then they're free to find work elsewhere.

Do you find yourself working consistently with the same people? Do you try to keep your crew together as a team?

Absolutely. I know whom I can trust, and I want to work with them. When you hire a production manager, they want their production coordinator. They will have a preference for a particular accountant. When you hire certain heads of departments, they will want to work with certain assistants. Is it particularly clubby, cliquey, and cartel-like? Yes. We work with the top four production managers in the city. Each has their preferences. We've encouraged them to harmonize a bit more, but they are pretty committed to their own opinions. And that's the frustration of a lot of new people trying to break into this industry. It's the same anywhere but particularly here because of the scale. It's a smaller, tighter labor pool, so there are fewer ways into the inner circle. It's fiercely guarded.

I get two or three emails each week from young people who say this is the only thing they want to do in the world. And trying to get our group to give them the benefit of a meeting is hard, but I'm very passionate about meeting as many people as I can. I think it's to the benefit of our industry. We need new blood. We already struggle to find crew when there are multiple productions in town. My job is easier when I can say yes to producers' requests. Having more crew allows me to say yes more often.

You can go to film school in Hungary for five years and spend two million forints [approximately US $7,000] on tuition but end up unemployed for five years after graduation because I can't integrate you into my crews. I can give you a job as a PA [production assistant] that pays 25,000 forints [approximately US $85] per day. In Hungary, that's a very good entry-level salary. Plus, it gives you the first credit on your résumé. You start to climb the ladder. So when I recognize completely capable people who could step into these entry-level professions and start to train for more advanced jobs down the road, it drives me absolutely crazy that it's so difficult to integrate them. It makes me so angry. What a waste!

What's causing this? Are the crews too exclusive? Or perhaps the film schools in Budapest and Prague—impressive as they are—have yet to reimagine themselves for a new era of film production. They're training auteurs, not working professionals or craftspeople.

I think there's truth to both explanations. Hungarian crews are very protective. They don't want to dilute the crew base to the point where somebody might get offered the job before them. It's not arrogance or selfishness, but they worry about new blood. They worry about someone shining on set and then replacing them. It's a fundamental insecurity that the nature of this work breeds in the crew. You never want your current job to be your last.

We also struggle with the film schools. I'll often ask my production manager to call the film school when we need additional support—like a camera trainee. You would think that someone who dreams, sleeps, and eats being a director of photography would jump at the chance to work as a trainee under Oscar-winning DPs. In fact, this opportunity to rub shoulders with the best of the best is unique to locations like Budapest. You won't find the same opportunity in Los Angeles so early in your career.

But we can't get them to work. They won't do it for the education. They won't do it for the art. They won't do it for the money. Call it arrogance. Call it snob factor. Call it naïveté. They would get rates that most people in this country don't even earn as a bank manager. It's dumbfounding. When I meet someone as a production assistant, I ask, "What do you want to do in this business?" And they say, "I want to be a director." Fantastic! But they want to be a director *now*. They don't want to train as an assistant director. They don't want to train as an editor. They've got their degree. They've been rubber stamped as knowing everything. But they don't. They don't know what it's like on a set. In fact, I'd rather meet people who don't know exactly what they want to do. They're more willing to jump into the trenches and do whatever work is offered for the chance to learn and hone their craft.

What does the typical crew member look like?

Demographically? We may have a film student or two, but the biggest issue we face here is that there is not enough regeneration of our crew base. The answer to your question is "mostly older men." Camera operators. Electricians. Construction. We're generally not talking about people in their early twenties or thirties.

It sounds like there isn't a career apprenticeship system or a structured process for advancement.

You're correct. We try to introduce trainees into our budgets when we're calculating costs. On bigger films we'll always put in a camera trainee. We'll aim to include additional grips and electricians and production assistants. Honestly, trainees are cost-effective ways to increase your labor, so it's a win-win. But as I've described to you, it's a problem in Budapest.

I am most concerned about the hair and makeup and costume departments. It's a very old club that's particularly unwelcoming to new faces. It's to their own disadvantage. The current regime can't work forever. Who is going to replace them? I've had to intervene a lot to make sure we're bringing in more entry-level workers in those departments.

Let's talk about on-set dynamics. You have American and British crews alongside Hungarian crews for sixteen-hour days. What sorts of issues does that create?

Certain foreign crew members are very much like good wine. They don't travel well. They're great in L.A., in London, or in Rome. But put them on a plane and bring them to the "evil dark empire" of Eastern Europe? They arrive with expectations for a certain comfort level so out of sync with the reality that they struggle to work here. We call it "casting" the crew. We advise producers that knowing who to hire means knowing who travels best and who doesn't travel well at all. Who has to bring their aunts, uncles, mother-in-law, two sisters, and three brothers? And that happens! You hire a very highly respected gaffer, and they say, "Great, I'd love to do the job but just so you know, here's who I'm bringing." A best boy and electrician and suddenly ten names. In those instances, we say to the producer, "This person doesn't need ten people. They need one or two." It's an unrealistic expectation and an unnecessary cost to bring any more than that with you to Budapest, especially in the electrical department. It's one of our key strengths.

It requires the producer to make the decision. Either give the department head what they want, or encourage them to embrace the peculiarities of working in a country that doesn't speak English. "If you want this job, you can only bring one or two people." Problems start to happen when you have foreign crew bringing in coachloads of people. When the balance of power is weighted more toward the foreign hires, then the Hungarians get sidelined and become nothing more than hired hands. There's simply no chemistry. The best composition is a few foreign hires who travel lightly and work with a majority-Hungarian crew.

At the same time, I always remind my local crew that they are not equal to their US or UK counterparts. The foreign department head is the boss. End of story. Deal with it. It's never going to change. They have more responsibility and more authority.

Does that pose challenges?

Communication is our biggest challenge. Different people from different parts of the world communicate in very particular ways: what words they choose, the tone in which they say them, how they use body language. An electrician from Pinewood doesn't enunciate, and suddenly there's a complete clusterfuck because a scaffold is here when it needs to be there. I've been doing this long enough now that I can actually see it happening: a department head is communicating something to the crew, and the crew is nodding along but not understanding. That's when I need to intervene to preempt any problems.

It seems to involve more than just language competency, though.

Right. There's a different division of labor, too. For example, in America, a key grip sets your flags and your stands but the unions won't allow that person to touch a light. In Hungary, our grips handle camera rigs but they are very happy to move a lamp. Our electricians will handle anything that's connected to a lamp, including hanging them from the ceiling, which in America and the UK would be a rigger. When you enforce those job categories, it causes the crew to grow bigger than what you'd find on a Hungarian film. It looks wasteful and unnecessary to local crew. I think sometimes it is!

We had coachloads of foreign crew when we did *47 Ronin* (2013). The movie was here only for a short while before returning to the UK, so they wanted continuity in their crew, which is a fair expectation. At one point during the shoot, the Hungarian electricians came to me confused. They needed to run some cables between two stages, and the UK electricians wanted to build a waterfall, which is a really large scaffolding structure. My guys just wanted to put the cables on the floor and run a ramp over them. But the Brits wouldn't have it. UK health and safety regulations required it done a certain way, and that's how they had to do it. So, my guys helped build this monstrous tower with lights and ballasts. It looked like a low-flying aircraft, and cost an extraordinary sum. My guys thought it was hysterical. Why go to all this effort and money when the other way is so much easier?

You mentioned electrical as one of Budapest's strengths. What are others?

I would say electrical, grip, costume, production management, transportation, and construction. Construction is very, very good here. Fantastic. We are weak in special effects. It's more a question of crew depth. We can represent four really strong teams in pretty much every area. But if one of those teams or a part of those teams is on another show, then you start to feel the pressure. Who do we find now?

Are there creative opportunities for local crew members?

It's rare. Most of the shows we do here are such high-end productions. They are going to bring their department heads with them. I can think of only one exception: Judit Varga was the set decorator on *The Borgias* (2011–13). She did a magnificent job, and now has the credits to replace a foreign hire. But there aren't many people like her. There are more opportunities on some of the smaller European coproductions we do, but that's 5 million euro compared to US $125 million. Let's face it: those are very different budget parameters. If you want to get your 5 million euro movie made, hiring locally helps you do it. Creatively, local people are very capable, but you're not going to do it on a high-end movie.

So what are the key local positions?

I think the production office is a key space for those positions. Production manager. Production coordinator. Service producers often act like line producers. Location managers are an essential local position. We have two of the best location managers in the country, and they thankfully work almost exclusively for us at this point. We have been able to keep them busy over the past eight years. It's also an area where I've seen the most opportunities for regeneration. They're open to new blood. It's developing at a slightly faster speed than other areas.

Are foreign producers interested in exteriors or in infrastructure?

It's a question asked in tandem. Shows come here not because Budapest is the best place creatively to shoot but because the numbers work. When Showtime asked us if Budapest was the best place to make *The Borgias*, we were honest. We said, "No. You aren't going to find a lot of great exteriors to match Renaissance-era Rome. Budapest is nineteenth-century Austro-Hungarian Europe." But the numbers worked. I told them, "There's not a doubt in my mind that we can build whatever you need to shoot here." Conversations with producers are much more productive when you're honest about what you can do. Budapest has a distinct look that isn't going to work for every movie creatively, but we have the skill base here to build what we lack when the numbers work.

Studios have someone whose only job is to chase tax rebates and incentives. There are very few movies over US $25 million in which anybody cares too much about the location's creative "fit," apart from the director. Producers want it to make money.

*But then there's something like **Dracula** (2013–14), in which there's some creative resonance between the narrative and the location.*

Let me put it this way: if there was a cheaper place to make *Dracula*, they'd be there.

*What's more difficult: a blockbuster production like **Hercules** (2014) or a television series like **Dracula**?*

Hercules.

You didn't hesitate.

It goes back to what I was saying about the right balance between the foreign and the local. It's much easier for the scales of control to spin out of balance on those behemoth Hollywood productions. It's a machine: a fucked-up machine with lots of money, big personalities, and even bigger egos on the line. If the person leading the charge on something like that is a monster, it can throw the whole machine out of sync. It trickles down. It can affect everyone on the set, from the top to the bottom. It can feel like you're riding on the back of a headless chicken.

Television is a different budget and a different timeline. Certainly you have obstacles—a lot them have to do with making sure talent is here when you need them to be here because you're putting together an episode each week. But because of the lack of time and money, you don't have the luxury of things spinning out of control. You're much more dependent upon everyone pulling together and collaborating to get this thing done on time and under budget.

Hollywood blockbusters are known for their excesses, not their limitations.

And you're on the front line when those excesses spin out of control.

The best comical example of this—comical now, not then—is the day that I'm standing in the city's tenth district on the set of *World War Z*. I receive a call that the weapons we need for the shoot three or four days away have been impounded by the Hungarian Counter-Terrorism Unit after a SWAT team raided the airport. We're talking pistols, machine guns, sniper rifles, and grenade launchers. I need to report to the National Bureau of Investigation for questioning. It was one of the most intense experiences I've ever had.

Here's the long and short of it: British Airways refused to transport the weapons for us. We had all the permits in place, but for whatever reason, they wouldn't do it. The only way we could get the guns here on time was to charter a private jet. So we chartered a private jet. Unfortunately, the problems began when the chartered jet arrived at three in the morning at a smaller airport in the region. Someone called a tip in to national security and here we are with what looks like a chartered plane with a weapons cache arriving in the middle of the night under cover of darkness. It also happened less than two weeks before October 23, which is a very politically charged public holiday in Hungary [marking the start in 1956 of what was a failed rebellion against Soviet-imposed policies]. The plane lands. The tactical team swarms. They're wearing balaclavas with machine guns ready to go. Elsewhere in the city our Hungarian weapons supervisor was marshaled out of his home in his boxers at three in the morning while they raided his residence. I get the call the next day, informing me that I'm under suspicion of arms smuggling because my name was on the permit. So I go in for questioning.

Eventually we were cleared of all charges, but the problem for us—and this goes back to your question about the nuances of this job—was that Hungarian law requires permanent deactivation of all ammunitions used on a film set. Yet in the US and UK, you're only required to put a screw through the barrel to prevent the bullet from exiting. Removing that screw makes the gun a functional weapon and thus not sufficiently modified under Hungarian law. So, it looked like I was smuggling a fully functional arsenal. Obviously we weren't the first production to bring in weapons.

Productions have been bringing them into the country illegally, probably unknowingly, for years. We just got caught. And we got caught—I think but I can't prove it—because a local ammunitions company that wanted the business turned us in.

As a result of all this, I started a lobbying campaign before the production of *A Good Day to Die Hard*. I said to Parliament, "Look, you can change the laws or you can lose US $40 million in local spend and income when these movies choose another location." It wasn't easy to convince them, but they changed the law—it was a massive legislative change.

It was such a process, and you know what? The scene [that we originally needed the weapons for] didn't even make it into the final cut of *World War Z*.

It's interesting to note that the most successful service firms in Prague and Budapest are run by American or British expats.

The cultural connection establishes a level of comfort and sense of confidence. A studio doesn't want to spend the level of money they're spending here without working with a known entity. We are the known entity. And we know the value of 1,000 forints. We know what that will buy you. A foreign producer does not. And that makes them vulnerable. Working with us ensures you're not spending 1,000 forints when you could be spending 500 forints. We ensure the studio is maximizing their spend. We ensure they aren't wasting it.

Does the studio's desire to "maximize their spend" ever pose problems? Do you find yourself having to educate producers about production costs in Budapest? Do they sometimes have unreasonable expectations about, for example, labor costs?

I don't know why it's such a challenge to explain this to people, but I often encounter this impression that I can just adjust the crew rate to better fit the budget. Rates don't fluctuate in Budapest. The same rates apply whether you're shooting something at US $125 million or US $20 million. Hotels don't adjust their rates. Crews don't adjust their rates. I know it's slightly different in the United States and the UK because of the various union contracts that adjust rates according to budgets. But that doesn't happen here. When I do a budget for a foreign producer, I know what a grip costs. I know what an electrician costs. I know what a hotel room costs and what building materials cost. Yet because they're filming here, they think they can tell me what costs *they* think are fair. It doesn't work that way—I'm not performing magic. It requires the foreign producer to adopt a different mindset. If your budget is $20 million—which is low compared to the productions we normally do here—then you need to decide how much you're able to spend on construction. Producers send us a script and expect a budget the following week, but the process is far more complicated than that. What do you want, and how much can you spend? You can spend $100 or $100,000. I can tell you what each will get you. But you can't tell me the budget line for construction is $100 because you think that's appropriate for Budapest when what you want to build will cost $100,000.

It *is* cheaper here. Budapest is generally 25 percent less than Los Angeles. So you will save money, but you can't ask me to price a piece of string without first telling me how long it is.

It sounds like there's a lot of back and forth with producers.

Always. And they're always seeking the best deal. I don't blame them. But I tell them, "Unless you give our budget to a competitor or give a competitor's budget to us, you will never ever hear a true apples-to-apples comparison." Budget lines are easily manipulated. Even when it's not intentional, how information looks on paper is different than how it turns out in practice. For instance, Romania always looks cheaper on paper but you encounter so many problems there that you end up having to bring more people with you than you anticipated, or incur so many unexpected or indirect expenses. How much are you actually saving?

Part of our success is attributed to our honesty. I don't play around with budget numbers. I'll show you what it will cost even if you don't like what you hear. I'll tell a producer that I can't match whatever competitor they're quoting. I'll say, "We can't do it for that cost." If it's an honest budget—and sometimes that's a big "if"— the producer is better off going somewhere else.

You're not just protecting your company and your reputation. You're also protecting your crew.

I think we're one of the few companies that operate that way. Others are much more willing to say, "I guarantee that it's cheaper to do it here. Come! Come! Come!" It's such a risky game to play. No one ends up happy when what was promised isn't delivered.

17

Stephen Burt, production manager

During his twenty-year career, Stephen Burt has worked on such projects as *The Borgias* (2011–13) and *Penny Dreadful* (2014–16). Although he has a flat in Glasgow, he travels extensively for work, shuttling off to places like Sweden, Germany, Belgium, and Hungary. Here he discusses the rewards and challenges of this mobile lifestyle and reflects on the obstacles his native Scotland faces when competing for foreign productions.

What kinds of jobs are there in the production office?

We're the administrative hub of the production, so the size of the office will vary depending on the size of the production. You'll have your line producer, assistant director, and production manager. You'll have your location manager and his or her assistants. You'll have script coordinators, and a variety of coordinators and administrative assistants for accommodations and travel and office management. We are also responsible for production assistants.

What's a typical workweek like for you?

It depends on the producer and what's customary in different places. A normal production workday in Ireland is twelve hours. But we've been very lucky on *Penny Dreadful*. We've implemented a ten-hour continuous day and a five-day workweek. We start at eight and end at six. I work with a very unusual group of producers who care about the crew. We're incredibly fortunate. But it is a new thing here, so it has required some adjustments. For instance, the whole crew has to eat on the run. There's no time to sit down for a lunch hour, which made it necessary to speak with catering to adjust how they serve meals. We needed something the crew can eat with a fork out of the box while they're working. I think it's been a successful change. People are getting home a few hours earlier than they would on other productions. There's still a bit of light outside. They have some time to enjoy the evening with their families, which is extremely rare in the production world. We're no longer getting home late at night and waking up a few hours later to return to the set. We're also not losing momentum on the set. We're simply working more efficiently.

How so?

It never fails that after lunch on a really long workday everyone loses momentum. Your talent has left the set. Your crew has left the set. It takes time to get everyone revved up and back in tune with the production after we break for lunch. It causes this incredible lag. Shortening the workday has proven to us that when everyone's energy level is high, you can get just as much done in a ten-hour day as you can get done in a twelve-hour day. You're more focused. I've worked eleven-day fortnights and sixty-hour weeks, and I won't do that again. It's just too hard on the crew. There are better ways to get the work done.

Crew members in the United States often tell us that they love the overtime, but the hours are grueling and excessive. They wish the producers were better organized, but if the days were shorter and contained, they would lose the overtime. So nobody speaks out against the system even though they think it's screwy.

I've done American feature film productions. They *are* grueling, particularly because of the "freaky Friday" phenomenon caused by the SAG-AFTRA agreements. Productions are required to give talent a twelve-hour turnaround between shooting days. So, when you run over your call sheet for the day, it pushes back your start time the following day to allow for that twelve-hour turnaround. You inevitably run over the next day, too, and so on. It's a snowball effect. Then you find yourself on Friday working a nineteen-hour day to complete your shot list for the week. It's simply horrendous. I don't know why anyone does it. It doesn't allow for any quality of life at all. For me, quality of life is more important than money.

Those producers don't understand that the crew is completely exhausted. They don't get the same quality of work in the nineteenth hour as they do in the ninth hour. On our set, we have a built-in safety net already scheduled into our ten-hour workday that keeps us from running into issues with talent and turnaround time. If we're scheduled to end at six in the evening but end up running over for whatever reasons, we have a two-hour window in which we can catch up before it affects the next day's start time. So if we end the day at eight in the evening, we aren't cutting into our turnaround time. We can give the actors the twelve-hour break stipulated in their contracts and still start on time the next day. But if you're starting with a twelve- or fourteen-hour day and you don't make your schedule, it immediately pushes back the start time the following day. The delays each day then start to pile up until you're working around the clock on Friday to meet that week's schedule.

As production manager, does your workday differ from the crew's?

I'm usually here an hour before the crew arrives. I start at seven in the morning unless it's a particularly tough day. If I anticipate a rough day, I'll come earlier. And I usually leave an hour later than the crew. So I'm working a twelve-hour day, five days a week. I have my weekends to recover. I know it sounds like you're talking to somebody in a different industry. *Penny Dreadful* is a compelling case study—it's the most humane job I've ever worked, and that's to the credit of the individual producers.

What are some places where you've recently crewed up?

In the past three years, I've worked in Gothenburg, Sweden; Hamburg, Germany; Ostend, Belgium; Budapest, Hungary; and Dublin, Ireland. In each country, it's imperative for me to liaise with local production managers. They advise me on who's available and who's qualified and what those locations can provide—and, more often, what they can't provide. You simply won't find the same skill levels in other countries as you do in more established filming destinations, like the United Kingdom or Ireland. So my relationship with these local production managers is crucial, but depending on where you're filming, you may end up finding crews from anywhere in Europe to bring to the production.

That's an astounding list—a little daunting, even. Do you find hopscotching around Europe to be challenging?

I think it's fantastic. I love to go to different places. Every country does production work slightly differently. I find it incredibly valuable to learn different systems. It's a great education. It allows me to take the best of what I learn in each location and integrate that knowledge into my own practices. Maybe they're doing something a little better than how I'm accustomed to doing it. I think it makes me much better at my own job.

Of course, it's not without its challenges. There are different union rules. There are different working practices. Standard workdays are different. Are we doing ten-hour, eleven-hour, twelve-hour, or fourteen-hour days? Job categories and functions are different. You may have a production coordinator and expect that person to do one thing because that's what he or she did on the last production, but now the production secretary does it and the coordinator does something totally different on this production. A classic example: on European productions, grips work with the camera department; on American productions, grips work with the electrical department.

But this is what keeps it exciting for me. I change jobs every six months. If I had to show up to an office every day for thirty years and work with the same people in the same place, I would go crazy. I find it much more interesting to shuffle around to different places, work with a new group of people, and learn from them.

Professionally, you find it exciting. What about on a personal level? Does it take a particular type of person to do this job?

You can't have a family. You have to be a single man. I don't know anyone who does my job who manages to hold down a relationship. Your lifelong friends also become Facebook friends. I see my mates very rarely. I'm always on the move, in a different place. It doesn't bode well for any sort of commitment. I do keep a flat in Glasgow. I think it's important to have a place to call a home. But it just sits there empty. I think I've been back in Scotland for a total of six weeks in the last three years.

*You said "single man." Do you mean a single **person**? Or is there a gendered dynamic to this line of work?*

I think the production office is one of the most inclusive spaces on a film set. There are plenty of women who do this job, and they're fantastic at it. Absolutely. In fact, some of my best mentors have been women. I don't know exact percentages. I'm not even sure they exist. But I'd estimate 50 percent of my contemporaries are women.

Do you find some locations easier than others?

Some locations work like a dream. Some locations are a nightmare. I find crewing up a production in Germany very difficult. They have a very different system. When you're looking for crew in Germany, you'll see people advertise themselves as trained in the "Berlin system" or the "international system" or both. The Berlin system is a unique system of working, with roles that don't appear anywhere else. For example, they have a position that is a cross between a production assistant, an assistant director, and a location manager. Part of the reason the lines are so blurred in the system is because it came about after the war when they had no money for the arts or to make films. Everyone had to muck in in order to get the work done. The system involved really compact crews. Different jobs became the responsibility of a single person. I've had to work with this system in other countries outside Germany, including Scotland, and it just doesn't work. You spend so much of your time resolving conflicts. People are always clashing on set: "He shouldn't be doing that. I should be doing that." Or, "He should be doing that. Why isn't he doing that?" Then "Me? It's not my job. Why are you looking at me?" It's a mess.

I love Budapest. It's such a vibrant location—the most fantastic place I've ever worked. I love the weather in the summer. It's affordable, so your per diems give you a nice quality of life while you're there. It offers an incredibly high-caliber crew. It has amazing studios. They have a well-earned reputation as a top-notch production service center right now. Blockbuster film productions and big television series are their bread and butter. What's not to like? They've replaced Prague. I think Romania is on the rise because of its currency rates, but Budapest is simply fantastic.

You raise an interesting point. We hear about locations investing in infrastructure and human capital only to see Hollywood's interest dissipate as the next location emerges. Are these places just the flavor of the month? Does it seem sad to you?

I feel for the crews when that happens, and it does happen. But I don't think it necessarily plays out the way you describe. I think that growth requires a genuine commitment from governments to create a *stable* incentive system. Look at the notable incentives in the United Kingdom and Ireland. I would include Hungary, too, though its incentive isn't limitless. Hungary's incentive has a cap, so there's always the chance of it running out in a given year. I suspect we'll see that change soon because all it takes for producers to run somewhere else is the perception of a little wobble in the system. You won't lose producers' interest if the incentive program is stable.

But that's taxpayer money going into the producer's pocket. They already have deep pockets. Doesn't that seem like a system that works against the locations?

I don't see it that way. I've worked in enough locations to see the massive spending that productions bring with them. I'm convinced that there's a direct benefit to local economies and local crews. It's absolutely worthwhile. Keep in mind that I don't think there's a need to cut each other's throats in a competition to offer the best incentives, though. It doesn't take a huge incentive to make it worthwhile to producers as long as the location has the necessary physical infrastructure, crew depth, and exchange rate that makes costs like labor and accommodation advantageous.

You have to look at the bigger picture of what a location offers. A tax incentive is part of a larger package to build upon and sustain existing strengths.

What about a place like Scotland?

Scotland is a disaster. It makes me incredibly sad. There's no film studio, no dedicated screen agency. The skills base is moving south because the government is embarrassingly apathetic. There's absolutely no support. There's no sense of a genuine interest from the authorities that this is a sector worth saving. When people can't work because there are no jobs, they're going to leave to find work elsewhere. It's certainly a reason why I'm not in Scotland right now.

I can't tell you how many Hollywood producers have visited Scotland because they're interested in our gorgeous mountains and lochs. They love it. Then they ask to see the film studio. When they hear we don't have one, they have no choice but to look somewhere else. We had a chance to host *Game of Thrones* (2011–ongoing) but it went to Belfast because that location had both a studio facility and local incentives.

Scotland is the only country in Western Europe without a film studio. Local crews have been extremely vocal about it. We actively lobby the government. I've met with the culture minister and other public officials. I've done so much work to convince them of the value of a studio facility. But they pat us on the head. They think they know what's best but refuse to acknowledge what's happening in all these other places. They clearly have no clue.

Let's say Scotland gets the film studio it deserves. Do you think there's space on the global map for one more production hub?

Absolutely. I know from personal experience that you cannot book a stage in London. There's nothing available. We toured the entire United Kingdom looking for a space to film *Penny Dreadful*. We couldn't find anywhere to shoot it—nowhere! It ended up being quite the embarrassment for the UK. *Penny Dreadful* was earmarked as the first major production to take advantage of the new television tax incentive in the UK, but when we couldn't find a soundstage, we ended up in Dublin.

Glasgow benefits from the same incentive as London. Yet labor rates are much cheaper because the cost of living is lower. Accommodations, transportation, and other services are far more affordable than you'll find in central London. Glasgow also has an indigenous workforce. It has production and postproduction service companies. It has a variety of urban locations. You can reach the countryside in forty-five minutes. The only thing the city is missing is a studio. If the government doesn't act soon, it's facing a future in which a lot of the creative resources that the city has to offer won't exist anymore, especially the crew. Glasgow's crew is leaving.

The best people are working, but they're not working in Glasgow. They're working in London, Dublin, Budapest, and Belfast. They're following the work.

What's your message to the Scottish government?

Build a state-of-the-art studio. And offer a local incentive to complement the UK incentive. The government simply needs to be more proactive. Scotland needs to be seen from the outside as being proactive. You can't take six months to research the implications of a job that only lasts for four months. The government doesn't have the drive and doesn't have the brains. Look at Wales. Look at Northern Ireland. Look at Ireland. It's all around them, and they are oblivious.

How do you describe the value of production to a location?

I think there are economic arguments to make about the value of film and television production, but for me, there's also a real value to the local crew base that is a critically important factor to consider. You're building a sustainable workforce. You're establishing opportunities for local crew to learn and train among some of the best practitioners in the world. You're establishing opportunities for professional advancement. You're creating opportunities in a context where very few already exist. Scotland makes less than ten high-quality feature films every year. International productions will create more opportunities to learn skills and use equipment that indigenous productions don't offer. This, for me, is a big plus.

You have been a very vocal proponent of increasing government support for Scotland's local crew base. In fact, the country's motion picture workforce is quite active in lobbying for improved conditions.

I'm not as active as I was a few years ago. It's hard to organize when you're away from home for such long stretches of time. But I did help cofound an organization in 2009 called the Association of Film and Television Practitioners Scotland (AFTPS). At the time, I was introduced to Willy Wands through a mutual friend who thought we would have a lot in common. Willy also has an international career that keeps him away from Scotland most of the year. He's also become quite outspoken about the embarrassing lack of support for film and television production. So, the idea for an association of practitioners originated out of that initial meeting with Willy, which was a long moaning session at a local pub.

I just couldn't shake the sense of frustration we discussed that night. It stuck with me for about two weeks after that first meeting. I rang him up to say, "I'm absolutely sick of this feeling. I'm going to call a meeting of the entire industry.

Something needs to be done. We can't just sit here and watch it die." So, thanks to Willy's reputation and my crazy persistence, we managed to fill the room with more than three hundred freelancers, a vast majority of the industry in Scotland. We decided then that the association would work as a lobby group that would pressure key stakeholders to do a better job for film and television workers in Scotland. We targeted public bodies. We targeted individual members of the Scottish Parliament. We targeted the BBC. We targeted STV.

We had the press on our side. We got a lot of visibility, and they championed our cause. We ended up scheduling meetings with key individuals within those organizations. We saw some real, tangible outcomes from the broadcasters, with some commissioning a few more productions in Scotland. We had less success with the government—just more false promises about what it hoped to do.

I'm less involved today, but the group is still active. It's continued to evolve as a meaningful forum for local crew to raise questions and concerns about job opportunities, working conditions, and so forth. It's also been an active voice in the efforts to secure a studio space. It's a slow process. It's hard to prompt the government to act, but the group is a persistent voice for change.

It's a fascinating example of workers taking it upon themselves to organize in place of more traditional institutions, like the union.

BECTU is a useless organization. Its representative in Scotland is worse than a chocolate teapot. In fact, someone who picks up a weekly wage is not the best advocate for freelancers. He has no concept of precariousness. He has no genuine investment in the fate of local film and television practitioners. He attended that initial meeting of AFTPS. I think the fact that no one knew who he was when he showed up to the meeting speaks for itself. He got a bit of a fright from the amount of anger in the room targeting the union's lack of support. It prompted some tangible change as well. For instance, as a consequence of that meeting, BECTU now offers training schemes in Scotland—seminars on budgets, production scheduling, special technology, how to handle firearms on sets, and so forth. You can't qualify for certain jobs without having the right training modules. Previously, workers always had to trek down to London to attend sessions. It's a small step, but it is a product of the AFTPS's efforts. And these efforts take so much time and so much labor. It's sometimes so much effort to keep your chin up when you're constantly disappointed. Honestly, it's grueling work.

Are we at a point where production hubs are interchangeable, or do you still film in certain locations because of the distinctive topography?

There are moments when geographical considerations come into play, but if a location has a skilled labor pool and physical infrastructure in place, anything is possible. For example, *Penny Dreadful* takes place in the 1890s. In Dublin, we can find streets that pass for Victorian London. We wouldn't find those exteriors in Budapest, but the crew is so great that they would have no problem building it for us on a studio back lot. Now, could we film *Penny Dreadful* in Spain? No. We would have no use for the bright, sunny weather or architecture in our gothic drama. And Spain doesn't offer the same physical or human resources as Budapest. But this is an occasional exception to what has become a global market. Film and television production can take place in any of the established hubs.

Productions also base themselves in a location for the duration of filming but shuttle off for a few weeks of shooting here or there as necessary. You may set up a production office in Budapest but spend a few weeks in Croatia to get seaside exteriors, correct?

True, but people don't realize how much that adds to your budget. Even if you're only there for two weeks, it takes time to plan and prepare the logistics for moving between territories. You have to establish some sort of home base there, which requires duplicating some of your production staff and crew. Plus, you have to move your talent and key department positions. Everything comes to a halt in one location as you pick up and move to another. It causes a lot of inefficiencies and logistical nightmares. It's much easier to stay in one place.

*How does a production like **Game of Thrones** manage so many locations?*

Game of Thrones films across five or six territories simultaneously, and each location operates completely distinctly from the others. Other than key department heads, there's no need to shuffle cast and crew across multiple locations. It's a different production model rooted in this particular script: dragons film here, this kingdom films there, and so on. These characters only appear in this world, those characters only appear in that world. It's the only way to make a show like that logistically possible. As soon as there's too much crossover between narrative worlds, it won't work.

How do you get jobs?

You build a reputation. In Scotland, I'm very well known. It's easy for me to work there; there's just no work. I secure jobs through word of mouth. I've been fortunate enough to work on some high-profile productions. Producers remember your name, and they'll offer it to whomever asks for a recommendation. Or that producer will keep you on for his or her next production. I have some successful friends who always recommend me when they have the opportunity to do so—I make sure they get very nice Christmas gifts from me each year.

It's about becoming part of a mobile production network. We're constantly in contact with one another. We know who is available when and where. It's a good time to work in Europe right now. It's a booming job market. Studios are booked eight months in advance.

If someone gave you an opportunity to work in Los Angeles, would you? How would you feel if you had the chance to move to L.A. for a stable job over the next ten years?

I could do with a little beach and a little sun. [Laughter] Honestly, I am willing to work anywhere for a few months. But any longer than that? I don't know. I actually enjoy a new job in a new place every six to nine months. I worry I would feel a bit trapped working in the same job in the same place for ten years.

You're certainly the right person with the right mindset at the right moment for the industry.

That's kind of you to say. I may be the wrong person tomorrow. You're only as good as your last job.

18

Belle Doyle, location manager

Belle Doyle was the premier location manager in Scotland for nearly a decade, with appointments at both Scottish Screen and Creative Scotland, where she worked on a range of local and international productions, including *Red Road* (2006), *Doomsday* (2008), *The Dark Knight Rises* (2012), and *World War Z* (2013). Throughout her career she has been active in mobilizing resources for the Scottish motion picture industry. Here she reflects on the country's place in the greater UK production economy, with particular attention given to the plight of local film and television practitioners.

You left Glasgow for the southwest of Scotland. Why did you leave your post at Creative Scotland?

I was working too many hours a day. Tons of travel every few weeks. I was always on some transatlantic or European flight. I was going to Los Angeles, Cannes, Toronto, Hong Kong. I also was very involved with the Association of Film Commissioners International [AFCI]. I attended a number of AFCI board meetings, conferences, and meet-ups with counterparts in other countries. I was visiting film studios as well to see how they worked and what the model could potentially be for Scotland. It was never-ending. I started having health issues. My blood pressure was high, and I had gained loads of weight. It got to a point—you know, I'm fifty—where my body was telling me I was working too much. It's all glamorous and lovely for a while, but then there's a moment of realization when you say to yourself, I'd rather be home watching telly with a cup of tea than attending another party at Cannes.

The southwest is a beautiful part of the country. It's rural and laid back with a big arts community. I still do bits of scouting work, but because I'm so involved in the arts scene here, I don't have time for much else.

You've spoken openly about your frustrations with Creative Scotland.

It was certainly part of the problem for me. We lost our dedicated film agency [Scottish Screen] when it was dissolved to form this much larger arts agency [Creative Scotland]. As a result, film became just another art form. No one recognized or understood it as an industry and a business. And that became very frustrating to me. I had enjoyed working with and on behalf of the industry, and I wasn't able to do that working for Creative Scotland. The agency's unwillingness to engage the film community in that way made my job feel very unproductive and limited. I remember thinking: I don't have to do this anymore. In fact, I can have a bit more free time as a freelancer. I will no longer have to speak on behalf of the government. I can step outside the party line to say what I really think.

So what can you tell us now that you couldn't tell us then?

The bodies! Where the bodies are buried! [Laughter]
There was a party line for even the most basic things, like, does Scotland need a film studio? The official answer was, "No. People come here to film on location. We don't need any infrastructure. We don't need an incentive. Everything's fine." No! Everything is *not* fine. We need a studio *and* an incentive. Again, the agency believed film was an art form and there was no need to discuss how to develop it as a business. I couldn't even have conversations with my counterparts at Scottish Enterprise and Scottish Development International [business development agencies]. It didn't make sense within the institutional culture of the agencies or their funding strategies. SE and SDI support business development and research but don't recognize film or television. Then you have the arts agency where I worked that supports the creative aspects of film and television but didn't see the business side as its concern. So film and television ended up in this massive black hole with no one trying to nurture it into a sustainable and viable national industry. There's been some recent acknowledgment from the government that this is an oversight that needs to be fixed, but it remains frustrating.

There is a specific Scottish way of doing things in the public sector: we schedule meetings, discuss the issues, write reports, and hire consultants. It takes an incredibly lengthy amount of time and often produces little in the way of results. We've been debating a film studio for three decades! I became very uncomfortable justifying the slowness of the agency's decision making—their decisions and overall lack of support for the sector. It wasn't really my responsibility to justify it, but I was a public servant working for the agency; I had lots of relationships with the film community, so I frequently found myself having to explain their logic. I'm not someone who can shut down her computer at five every day and then go home and not worry about things.

What were some of the things that worried you?

Right now the local film sector survives as a gift economy. For instance, we have excellent postproduction service companies in Glasgow, like the Savalas sound studio, but they can't operate with sustainable business models by relying on local productions alone. They are offering their state-of-the-art facilities at reduced rates for local producers simply because they [local producers] can't pay the company's standard fees. So, we have a renowned company accepting lower rates or doing favors for local producers in order to help out the indigenous film sector. It's a recurring and persistent problem across the sector as a whole. It's no way to run a single business, and it's no way for an entire sector to thrive.

Why do service providers do it?

Because producers haven't raised the finances or simply can't afford it. Or the service provider will think about it realistically: I'll just accept the lower rate because it's unlikely I'll see any money from the producer anyway.

Do they do it because they have a noneconomic—call it a moral, ethical, or nationalist—investment in seeing Scottish film flourish despite the sector's limited resources?

I think so. There is a palpable desire among those of us who live and work here to see the sector thrive.

More so than other locations?

Absolutely. Service providers won't do massive amounts of work for local producers. They are more willing to help micro-budgeted projects or emerging filmmakers, which is great and should be encouraged. In fact, all local facilities and service providers go out of their way to do that. That's great. That's how people make their first films. But on your third film, you shouldn't still be asking for favors. You made a promise. You said, "I'm on my way up. When I'm successful, I'll pay you properly."

A gift economy is not a very reassuring long-term business strategy. How does a company like Savalas survive?

Because Scotland is part of the UK, local facilities and service providers bid for larger UK-level projects. Companies here are members of the UK Screen

Association. They can bid for work coming to SoHo [in London]. It's the only way they can survive, but competition for that work is fierce, too. Yet this is the sort of big-picture thinking that a local film industry needs to survive. We need to think beyond our borders to help what happens within our borders.

Where's the breakdown, then?

We don't have any sales agents or distributors. I can name one company here, but they only distribute old films, not new material. When you don't have direct access to the market, you are working with firms that you don't know and that don't know you. We're left with so few options that we have very little negotiating power. Producers are eager to sign all of their rights away just to make the film. When you do that, you don't see any returns. You're left with nothing to invest in your next project. I think Sigma Film's Gillian Berrie is probably the only local producer in a position to make some money to reinvest in subsequent films. I can name one! Again, this isn't a realistic business model. But when you're trying to make films in a country with so little support, you're left with few choices.

Let's make sure we understand what you're saying: producers are selling any and all rights they have to their intellectual property to finance the production up front, and then it's completely out of their hands when (or if) it's released. Nothing comes back to their coffers.

Like I said, it's a completely unsustainable model that requires everyone to do favors for everyone else. I have traveled to Los Angeles and London quite a bit. You meet people there who want to get into the industry to make money. You don't hear people say that in Scotland.

It sounds like a film-school mentality on a national scale.

I couldn't have said it better myself. People are working for free. People are maxing out credit cards. And these aren't students but producers and production companies. There's still this film-school mentality: I have this vision, and this is how I want to realize this vision. No one looks at it in black-and-white terms. What can I actually do with the resources I have? What can I afford? How long might it take me to develop the project to ensure I can afford it? Can I pay people?

Let's switch gears from the creative process and financial decisions to talk more about the crew. They have been one of the most vocal contingents advocating for a studio. What are working conditions like on indigenous films?

[Laughter]

That's not reassuring! Let's talk specifics. Black Camel's **Outpost** *(2008) was a relatively successful genre picture. It played in the United States. It sparked a small horror franchise. Aren't there three films now?*

They financed the first installment with their credit cards and by mortgaging their home. I don't know what distribution deal they had with Sony, but I've heard it wasn't great.

But working on that film?

One of the things they did on the film that upset a lot of folks was hire local art students to paint sets for nothing. They worked twenty-hour days for no pay. But they thought, "Glamour! Film!" They reported to a well-respected production designer who made sure the production values were outstanding—and the film looks fantastic! People want to do their best here. They care about the art and the craft. It's why outsiders are always impressed with local crew—the professionalism, commitment, and standards of work you find here are second to none.

How can you get away with twenty-hour workdays with students? Where was the union?

BECTU is largely ineffectual in Scotland. It essentially ignores the film sector. The union rep here is not sharp enough to run around and police all of the violations, likely because the projects are so under-resourced and underfunded that he couldn't keep up. But this leads to other problems: a production culture that makes certain things "okay," even on sets that can afford to (and should) do better. Unfortunately, union membership in Scotland is quite low as a consequence, because people don't see the value in it: Why pay dues for something that won't protect you?

Right now it's a bit of a free-for-all. We don't adhere to the working time directives enforced in other European countries, so sixteen-hour days on set are standard here. I also think there's an implicit threat on film sets: This is what you wanted to do. You're lucky to be doing it. Why complain?

You'll also often hear from producers, "Here are the BECTU rates, but what are your rates? What will you work for?" Crew constantly undercut each other's rates. You're supposed to place a value on your labor during negotiations, but because work is scarce, you never want to push too hard. If they don't like your rate, they don't have to hire you. Likewise, if you really want to work on a particular film, you can value your labor at a point you know is lower than other people up for the job. This process ultimately drives down everyone's wages, especially women.

You'll find the heads of departments have negotiated rates, but if she is a woman, it's always oddly lower than her male counterparts.

It's even worse when you're dealing with visiting producers from Hollywood or London. They will want to hire someone to location scout in Scotland but not pay him or her the official rate for doing so. You wouldn't ask somebody in London to work for a lower rate. Why us? For some reason, when production companies come here, they immediately think everybody in Scotland should be cheaper, which irritates people here. We're performing the same roles. We're highly trained and highly skilled. Why are we less valued?

A local location manager was so tired of it happening that he started rallying location scouts in the area, asking them not to accept anything lower than the standard rate. It was exciting to see people become extremely vocal about it, but it's a difficult proposition. People need to work. People need to eat. It's another way crew undercut each other. A producer will call for a scout and say, "I know I'm supposed to pay you 250 pounds a day, but we can only afford 200." How can you blame people for accepting the offer when they know the next person the producer calls will say yes?

But the producer is thinking that Glasgow must be cheaper than London.

I agree. You'll save some money on accommodations, and on catering. Permits and logistics are less costly. You won't pay local government the same thing here as you do in London. You can shoot something in the middle of the city, and it won't cost you what it would cost you to shut down the center of London. I get it. But people aren't cheaper. Skilled labor isn't cheaper. Why should your camera hire in Glasgow—who is performing the same tasks as any other camera hire—be cheaper than a camera hire in London? We're the same country. Labor doesn't magically become cheaper just because you cross the border from England to Scotland.

You've mentioned pay rates, long hours, and an impotent union. Are those the three biggest concerns?

I would add access to work. Is it too much to expect that people can find work where they live? Isn't it a fair expectation for someone who lives in Glasgow to work in Glasgow? Right now the UK incentive allows productions to take on crew from anywhere in the UK. So, they'll crew up in London. It creates this vicious cycle: anyone from Glasgow who wants to work ends up traveling to London to look for a production job. It's an even crueler irony when they get hired in London to return for a location shoot in Scotland.

Ultimately, anyone who is any good in Scotland ends up leaving. People are going everywhere; there's so much moving around. There are lots of people working in Belfast on *Game of Thrones* (2011–ongoing). There are huge staffing shortages in Manchester right now, so people are rushing there to get work. Cardiff. Dublin. There is a huge Scottish contingent filming a Channel 4 series called *Indian Summers* (2015–16) in Malaysia. They are happy—it's beautiful and they're not working in the pouring rain. They're enjoying the sunshine. It's a bit of a novelty for them! But how long does that last before you tire of it? How do you settle down and have a family? You eventually reach a point where you don't want to do it anymore. Or you reach a point where your mind or body won't let you.

Are there job categories where people can expect to work regularly in Scotland?

I knew you were going to ask me this question. I've given it a lot of thought. I think location managers are the one group of film professionals here who possess such unique skills and talent and knowledge that they are absolutely key local hires. They don't chase work elsewhere as much as other people in Scotland. They aren't going to London. Look, we lack a studio. Everything filmed here is filmed on location. It's not impossible for someone who isn't from here to manage locations, but he or she will still need a local hire to help navigate a set of relationships and issues that are very unique to Scotland. So location managers always are in demand.

Actually, I think Scotland is a unique case because of the peculiar demands on the location department here. I don't think a local hire is as necessary in other places, but here location managers will read the script, break down the script, scout locations, make suggestions, and manage those locations. They are 100 percent responsible for the locations—sometimes they are managing twenty different locations! I know in the States the individuals who manage locations aren't necessarily scouting them. But here we do everything. We have to do everything.

Why?

We wear so many hats. We are mediators. We are facilitators. We hold the keys to the city. We know the right questions to ask the right people. What location best matches your needs? How do you get access to this space? What permissions do you need to do what you want to do? What rental car companies or hotels are best? We are a vast resource of local knowledge, and that helps ensure the production is not only spending their money locally but also happy with their experience filming here. It lowers the chances of missteps when you work with someone who has local knowledge.

Like I said, I think Scotland is an especially important place for the location department. Without a studio, it's the primary—the only—reason productions come here. So many of the requests involve very specific period details. If a producer needs a street for a nineteenth-century drama, we know where to look. We also know there isn't just one street for nineteenth-century drama. Do you want urban or rural? What social class are the characters? Do you want an upper-middle-class street? It's a very specific process here because we can find that variety. It's even more detailed when it comes to castles. Preservation is so much better here than in England or other countries. Castles are immaculately maintained. So we can find a lot of variety, but we also know how tricky it is to get permission to film in these precious historical sites. We know the rules. We know what you can or cannot do. We gain access to key historical sites and then are responsible for protecting them during filming. All of this makes locations a very specialized skill set in Scotland.

Are good location managers proactive or reactive?

Reactive, always. It's the nature of the job. They're always responding to someone saying, "I need this." Even if they're reading the script, they're responding to what they think it requires, and then negotiating with other members of the production team to match their vision of the right location with other ideas. In fact, that's a key strength: you have to be very good with people. You have to be an excellent communicator and collaborator.

What types of individuals make the best location managers?

The very best are the ones who stick with it. They are professional. They are committed to training up younger people. But it's a hellish job. People often don't do it for very long.

What makes it such an immense responsibility?

Lots of people view the location department as an avenue through which to become a production manager. Nobody in London wants to be a location manager. It means getting up early, going home late. It means running around, sometimes miles and miles at a time, between different locations. Everyone's gunning for you. You are responsible for everything, and the logistics of the job are so difficult, especially in Scotland, where we often negotiate for access to historic buildings and castles. First there are so many legal hoops to maneuver, and then you're responsible for protecting that space from damages. You need a special person who can charm the public agencies or private landowners and assure them that nothing horrible will happen in order to get the keys to their castle.

If we gave you a magic wand, what would you change in Scotland?

We need an incentive that is linked to local crew and location spend. It needs to be in addition to the UK incentive. We also need to increase the film fund to give producers with decent scripts enough money to make their films.

What about a facility?

We need a studio. Imagine a little village shop with very few items. Someone gives you 50,000 pounds to spend in that shop. You would struggle to spend it. I see the need for a studio in the same way. What money can productions spend if we don't offer anything for them to spend it on? It's a serious impediment. We don't need to build another Pinewood. But there is such a tiny amount of dedicated production space here, especially if you need a facility with blackout capabilities and sound insulation. Nearly all filming done here at the moment is shot on location or in converted warehouses and makeshift soundstages.

What crew positions are increasingly critical for locations that want to attract the attention of international producers?

Location managers, production managers, and line producers. Any location that wants to host global productions needs to make sure they have hometown men and women in these positions. They are the individuals who can convince producers that yes, the project can be done here or there.

What's the holdup with the film studio?

The Scottish government is still figuring out what it wants. They were starstruck when Brad Pitt was here. They were obsessed with tourism in the wake of Disney's *Brave* (2012). They spent 7 million pounds on a tourism campaign. Can you imagine how the film sector would have benefited from that support? *Brave* had nothing to do with the film industry here! At other times, they seem to want local filmmakers winning prizes at Cannes for art films.

It's also the same arts-versus-business divide that's stunted support for the sector. We have to think of film and television as an industry that requires investment. Yes, it's creative. Yes, it's cultural. But it's also an industry that creates jobs and ensures livelihoods. And it requires infrastructure and incentives to grow.

Right now local producers and crew are frustrated with the lack of any real progress. There's so much interest in filming in the UK, especially after the launch of the high-end television incentive. It's increased demand; studios are bursting at the seams! I think that only adds to the anger—they're tired of jumping up and down for someone to take notice that Scotland can benefit in the same way England, Wales, and Northern Ireland benefit from those productions. We could easily be working here, but opportunities keep passing us by because we have nowhere to host them. I know we lose productions and we lose work because we can't offer producers a local incentive and permanent studio. *Game of Thrones* is the most recent and visible example. It's just so competitive right now that we can't afford not to invest.

But that's taxpayer money.

Incentives require strategy. We need local incentives to complement the UK incentive, but we also need to include stipulations that we can police. You need to hire so many crew. You need to have at least one local department head. An incentive requires accounting and accountability, which would help us ensure that those criteria are met. Ironically, without an incentive, we can't police anything. It's hard to track down accurate figures on employment and spend because they aren't accountable to anyone in Scotland. And without a studio, productions are here for six weeks, not six months. It's absolutely frantic.

I think a film studio with the right incentive structure will change the situation. Right now international productions will pick up a local location team and local extras for second-unit shoots. They'll hire some local services—hotels and catering and restaurants—and facilities. Of course, they're paying the city for permits and security. It helps in terms of tourism and some local spend from the production while they're here. But for the most part, they're bringing all crew and equipment with them. If they are able to establish a production base here for a length of time, there's more development and prep. There's more money being spent. There's a greater need for local hires. It just seems like a no-brainer to me.

So despite the celebratory headlines about filming a key scene from **World War Z** *(2013) in Glasgow . . .*

There are reasons to be excited about it. In addition to what I just outlined, it proves the city is capable of hosting a production of that size—that we're film friendly. But it didn't employ a lot of local crew except for locations and extras.

I'm not suggesting that we think exclusively about Hollywood production. I'm leery of chasing the Hollywood dollar because it's becoming harder and harder to grab it from other locations that are chasing the same dollar. I'm arguing for a slightly different approach. I think a smarter strategy is to offer more support for European coproductions. Right now the current incentive in the UK isn't designed to support smaller coproductions. That creates a feasible opportunity for us. Target smaller, more interesting productions. Build a studio. Implement a local incentive to ensure that those productions use our facilities and our crews. It doesn't have to be a huge incentive. But if Scotland is ever going to make better films, we need to ensure that people get opportunities to train and learn.

I think an occasional blockbuster is great. It brings international investment into Scottish service providers and facilitates, which makes them even stronger because they're actually making real money. It raises our international profile. It also ensures continuity of employment. It helps train them and increase their skills. You see how things are supposed to be done. But other types of productions also offer great experiences. You're less marginalized. You have more authority, more opportunities to advance professionally. Let's put our effort and resources into films with proper financing so they can create appropriate working conditions and pay their crew and operate on a realistic budget without asking for favors. It may not be a Hollywood film but it's no less global. It's a broader perspective on the industry that the government doesn't seem to understand.

Really, my dream would be for us to cultivate productions here that are culturally and economically compelling. Films people take seriously. Films people want to see in the cinema. How can we use a studio and an incentive to develop a global audience for these sorts of films?

19

Wesley Hagan, location manager

Wesley Hagan has worked as a location manager for number of Hollywood studios over his twenty-year career, most recently on the feature films *Hidden Figures* (2016) and *Selma* (2014). In this conversation, Hagan breaks down the responsibilities of a location manager, the shift in productions from Hollywood to Atlanta, and the increasing importance of location managers in a mobile production environment.

What does a location manager do?

Location managers are one of the first people to see a script. We work very closely with the production designer in both film and television. Producers are also key collaborators in television. In features, it's the director.

Location managers break down a script into different locations based on what the narrative requires, and then we start thinking about what's realistically possible. Do we find it or build it on a stage? It's a little more complicated with features because you're likely to cover a more expansive geography. In those instances, I'm the first person on the ground to see if it's even possible to shoot where they might want to shoot. I could end up anywhere in the United States; rebates are driving that process now. It has really narrowed the options.

Early in the process we have lots of creative discussions with our collaborators. We need to know how the key players are envisioning the look of the series or feature. I start picking locations, lots and lots of locations, based on those conversations. Options are absolutely necessary when you're trying to mesh your creative vision with that of the producer or director and production designer. Oftentimes

I'm working with the production designer on a feature before the director is even hired. I provide him or her with thousands and thousands of photos, which they help to narrow down so we can present a short list to the director. It's a process of weeding out what does and doesn't work until we finally have a manageable list from which we can start choosing final locations.

It is at this point where the creative process really needs to consider logistical concerns. It's always schedule driven, of course. We want a location, but is it available when we need it? We have to consider the weather at the time of year we're scheduled to film. Is it going to be winter when we need it to be spring? When are the actors available? It's an intense, detail-oriented process of collaboration and negotiation—the goal is to strike the perfect balance between creative vision and logistical realities.

Once we get a schedule tentatively finalized, we have a tech scout with the department heads to make sure the locations work for their needs. They'll tell me things like, "I want to mount a light on that corner of the building. It's a night shot, and I want an interior light on in that particular window of this skyscraper and this window in that skyscraper but all other windows dark. I want a car to come speeding around the corner to crash into another car in front of this building." We also need to make sure the location is accessible and safe. Can we access the location with our lighting rigs? Can we find spaces to park our trucks? Where are we going to house the extras? Are there overhead electrical wires that will get in the way? I keep track of it all to make sure we can do it—that's where permits, contracts, and permissions come into play.

In television, this whole process happens in a matter of weeks. Sometimes a producer will hand you a script and say, "We need this tomorrow!" You have to be on your toes and have an idea of what's available at a moment's notice. In features, we have three to six months to prep. So, time pressures are a big difference between the two.

I start to put together my department once I have my list of locations. This is when you start making deals with private homeowners, business merchants, and municipal or state authorities. It's an arduous task that requires a great deal of support, especially for features. They have become so massive, and we're no longer making them in our own backyard [Los Angeles]. You can't handle them without a really solid team behind you. You need people who have done it before, who can think on their feet, and who can think three steps ahead to preempt any potential problems. It's absolutely critical for me because I'm only as good as the people I hire.

Can you sketch out the department for us?

It depends on the size of the project, but typically the location department will have a location manager and a couple of key assistant location managers. On larger shows you'll have a supervising location manager. You'll then find two location managers and each will have a key assistant if the show warrants it. These positions are all filled by seasoned veterans. Additionally you'll have assistant location managers. This is an entry-level position. Their duties include, but are not limited to, helping with crowd control during filming. They'll take care of the dog barking in the background. They'll help secure signatures from residents for their approval to film in their neighborhoods.

In Los Angeles, the union [Local 399] keeps the department's job categories distinct with a very clear process for advancement. You have to work so many days as an assistant before you can become a key assistant and then so many days as a key assistant before you can become a location manager. Likewise, if you're a location manager but want to take a job as a key assistant because you can't find work, then you can't accept another location manager job for a whole year. You're committing to your decision to step down a rank. It's a very smart process. It forces you to think about your career and guarantees a certain skill level as you advance professionally.

That's not the case in Atlanta, where there is a different local [Local 728] that doesn't have the same rules governing job distinctions and advancement. You can go from being a production assistant on one feature to a location manager on the next. Location managers are highly dependent on their assistants' skills and experience. Without a strong team, you run the risk of pitfalls that could have been avoided during prep.

Sometimes people are smart enough to figure it out and build a successful career. But more often it just confuses a process that was designed to help us develop our craft in a logical, linear fashion.

So it's the wild, wild East?

I wouldn't describe it that way. It is just so busy here that the supply doesn't meet the demand. We're pulling people from everywhere just to keep up with the work. They will hire someone as a manager who has only been an assistant and then two weeks later that person makes a mistake. Then they'll realize, "Okay, we need to call somebody else in who is qualified."

We've read that staffing is a major issue in Georgia, with one out of every two productions suffering shortages, and that the location department is one of the weakest in the region.

Managing locations involves so much work. It's not only a creative process but also a logistical one. It's so demanding to preserve a creative vision while you're balancing logistics, scheduling, and a budget. I'm responsible for anything from

$1 to $2 million on the type of features I do. There are so many different facets to the job that you can't just "step into it" without some training. They're hungry for location managers in Atlanta right now because the field is so thin. I was fortunate enough to have the experience in Los Angeles. You can throw me into the mix in any city, and I'll figure it out. But, again, it is paramount that I surround myself with the right people.

The "right people" assumes some knowledge of the actual location. You have to surround yourself with people who can help you navigate a terrain with which you are less familiar.

Correct. I understand how to creatively put the project together. I understand how to manage the department. I understand how to budget the department. I understand how to negotiate logistics and schedules. But I may not know the region's geography. But it doesn't take long for a good location manager to figure it out. Once you've done two or three projects in an area, you get comfortable. But I still hire one or two local location scouts who know their way around the city really well.

So you've got your team together and you start negotiating with local residents and businesses. Now you focus on permissions?

Once we've finished the tech scout, it becomes a contract and permit issue. If we're filming in a corporate office building, we need a contract with them to ensure they will let us do the stuff we need to do, like keeping the lights on overnight. We also negotiate payment. Then we approach the city to propose what we want to do. It helps to say we have permission from the building; now we're asking permission from you. We also need the city's help to ensure we get the proper permits to close streets and reroute traffic. We work with the roads and transportation departments and the police department. I'll often hire an independent security officer who has their own team of security professionals, and we discuss our road plans, street closures, sidewalk closures, and so on. We have to close down most of the surrounding area for safety reasons. We need to be able to control the environment we're filming in, and that's often a difficult task once you leave the soundstage. People live and work in these areas! Having that security expertise is helpful when we submit our plans to the city for approval.

This is a very extensive, lengthy process. Contracts often get held up because of negotiations over money, sometimes liability. Permits always are about liability. The city wants to make sure we're safe, and we're not causing unnecessary disruption to traffic, residents, and local businesses. If residents or merchants are unhappy, the city will hear about it, and that makes our jobs that much more difficult. I was on a film once that needed to shut down Hollywood Boulevard for a length of time. I had to speak with every single merchant on that street, and make individual deals based on what it was we were doing that affected that particular business. Maybe we just needed people walking in and out of the store while we filmed in front of it. Maybe we needed to dress the windows to make it look like a different business. All of these contingencies affect your negotiation, and the price. It requires a particular skill: you have to be able to communicate with everyone. You meet all kinds of people who have all kinds of different perceptions of what we are and what we want, and a lot of people think that the movie companies are an endless bank account that can just hand out money, which is not necessarily the case. I have limited funds.

But I love it. It's always different. I've seen places nobody else gets to see. I think I've been on the rooftop of most every building in downtown Los Angeles and Atlanta. I meet so many interesting people, residents and business owners. I have to talk to them. I learn about their lives. It's a fascinating education.

I've had to negotiate with gangs before. I was the location manager on a Danny Cannon and Jerry Bruckheimer production a few years ago—a cop show for Warner Bros. We were filming a gunfight scene in East L.A. Of course we picked one of the toughest, grittiest neighborhoods in the area. Gunfire is something you hear there on a regular basis. But we still had to knock on doors. We still had to talk to everybody. You need those permissions and signatures no matter where you shoot. Yet, in those neighborhoods, they're even more reluctant to speak with you. Yards are fenced with dogs ready to bite you if you pass the gate! I ended up hiring a guy who worked with the gangs. He was well known in the neighborhood and was instrumental in making it okay for us to be there. He would let me know, "That house there? You'll need to pay them $1,000." Absolutely, whatever you say. He made sure the residents knew we were just making a movie, which helped prevent us from having our equipment stolen or our trucks tagged. In those cases, it's worth every penny to have someone like that help you navigate. Otherwise you end up spending more to solve much bigger problems.

Right now I'm filming *The Accountant* (2016) in Atlanta. I'm in an entirely different neighborhood, similar to Bel Air or Hancock Park [in Los Angeles]. Yet we just spent three nights in a row from six at night to seven in the morning shooting .50 caliber and automatic weapons. I start with the city, explaining what we hope to accomplish. They'll nod their heads at me and say, "Well, we need to talk more about this." You better start that conversation well in advance of when you need to film those scenes because you can expect a number of follow-up meetings with the city, the police, and neighborhood organizations. We start posting flyers all over the neighborhood. We write letters to each of the residents with as much information as possible: who we are, what we're doing, when we're doing it, and for how long. Cities require signatures from 90 to 100 percent of the residents in areas being affected by filming. In this case, Atlanta wanted a signature from every single resident within a 250-square-foot radius from the house where the filming was happening. My assistants were working around the clock just to catch people at home.

What happens when the cameras start to roll?

Once filming starts, you're on a nonstop, high-speed train with the potential for all hell to break loose. Your job is to keep that train on track. Ideas are constantly changing or evolving. A director will say, "I was thinking last night. I know we talked about this location for the last three months, but now I have a new idea!" You're up at two in the morning to set up base camp. You are there to make sure crew can park and find the shuttle to the location. You are there to make sure craft services are ready to go. Do they have a space to set up? I'm in charge of everyone's comfort. Do they have a place to eat? Do they have shelter in case it rains? Do they need heat or air conditioning? Did the port-a-potties arrive? You're praying that everything you've prepped and planned for over the past four months proceeds accordingly.

Are you an on-set problem solver?

Locations are the first to arrive and last to leave. Morning is the most crucial part of the day. If I've done my job well, the crew will get its first shot off with no incidents related to the location. I'll leave that location six or eight hours later in the hands of a key assistant to resolve problems and ensure it's properly shut down at the end of the day. It's time for me to move on to the next day's location to make sure it'll be ready first thing in the morning. We're constantly dealing with the past, present, and future all at once: open, maintain, clean up, close down, and then what's happening tomorrow?

Do you generally find that the location budgets cover what you need? Or do you often feel squeezed?

As I mentioned, I'm usually dealing with a $1 or $2 million budget on features. When you work episodic television, you're responsible for roughly $200,000 per episode. I think the biggest challenges in location budgets are the constant unknowns. You never really know your incidental costs until the film is happening. Overages arise in aspects of security, police, fire, and permit costs. You must pad those line items to ensure you're covered. I find producers don't worry too much about individual line items. They're most concerned with the overall costs—what you've estimated for the whole project. So as long as you don't overspend your bottom line, you're in good shape. But, damn, things *always* change, especially schedules and weather. In those situations, you rob Peter to pay Paul.

We just had to deal with a major schedule change on *The Accountant*. It was a very difficult negotiation to obtain permission to film in a high-end hotel lobby. They finally gave us a small window on a Monday morning from two to six. It's the *only* time they would allow us to film. I don't blame them. They're a business, and we're in the middle of their lobby. We were all set until Ben Affleck was invited to present the Oscar for Best Director at the Academy Awards ceremony, which of course coincided with the night shoot at the hotel. There was no way he would make it back to Atlanta in time. I call the hotel to explain. They don't care. It's a hotel. They're not in the movie business. They're not interested in working with me to find a new date. My producers are telling me to figure it out. Make it work. I do everything I can to negotiate a new schedule, but the hotel won't budge. I finally tell the producers we need help from someone more powerful than me. Sure enough, someone from the Warner Bros. top echelon makes a phone call to the hotel's owner. He agrees. We end up paying an additional $25,000 to shoot the scene there. There was no way I could absorb that in my budget. It was too much. But the producers wanted it, and when the producers want it, they can always figure out a way to make it happen. They adjusted some other part of the budget and found the money.

Why are you working in Atlanta so much?

I'm not getting calls for L.A. Hollywood is in Atlanta now.

You're saying, "I'm so busy that I have to turn down jobs," whereas a lot of people in L.A. seem to be struggling with the opposite problem. Do you think it's because you've been willing to pick up and go?

I think so. I was willing to follow the work very early in the process. I don't think a lot of people shared that willingness for whatever reason—maybe they thought it was a temporary fad. But now they're realizing that it's not coming back anytime soon. More and more people are willing to pack up for work.

Why do you keep doing it?

I absolutely love Atlanta. It's a great city. And it's fun to learn a new place. I don't have any kids. My wife also travels for work. So, it fits our lifestyle.

There are no features in Los Angeles at all?

There are, but not many, and the budgets are small. It's hard to do anything in this town without money. People know the industry here. They know to ask for a certain amount of money when you're negotiating with them to use their house or business. Yet on low-budget features, you're trying to get as much as possible for as little as possible. I've done plenty of features on that level, but it was a long time ago. It was a great education for a twenty-eight-year-old. It's also much easier to rebound from all the running and gunning when you're young. It is too physically demanding for me. I would rather work on $25 to $100 million movies. You have more creative input and a little more leeway with time and money. Moreover, you don't end up burning bridges by constantly asking for favors; you don't "owe" anyone anything because you have the money to do the negotiations properly.

I know the California incentive has just changed. Maybe it will bring back some big-budget work. Maybe features actually written for L.A. will film in L.A. Will Ferrell and Kevin Hart's new comedy *Get Hard* (2015) takes place in Century City, South Central, Hollywood, and downtown Los Angeles. They filmed the whole thing in Louisiana.

Do you miss Los Angeles?

I do miss the city. I miss the weather, my friends, and my house. I would love to work here again on a more permanent basis. But this is the first time I've been back to L.A. in eight months. I have an empty house that just sits here. So, I feel like a gypsy. I've been doing this for four years already, and it does start to take a toll.

Why has Georgia emerged as a production hub?

They have weather that allows you to shoot year-round. You have a growing crew base. Right now there are more features than the city can staff, but they're working hard to catch up. They are establishing schools to help train crew. They are establishing postproduction facilities. They have excellent soundstages, and are building more. They have the equipment you need. You can make your entire film there. Today it's not much different than Los Angeles.

I remember when the area was relatively new to the industry. It was a lot cheaper. I was securing locations for half the price I would pay in Los Angeles because no one knew what to ask for. But that seemed to change overnight. Now everyone knows what we're willing to pay for a location. I find myself paying the same price to film in Atlanta homes that I would pay to film in Malibu homes. Of course, the incentive in Georgia helps offset those costs.

You say Atlanta is actually building capacity. But if the incentive disappears, does the capacity disappear, too?

There's so much momentum there. Pinewood Studios has built an outstanding facility. Disney and Marvel are there for a number of pictures in a row. If the incentive disappears, producers and studios might hesitate to return, but there's enough capacity being built that Atlanta will remain a hub. In fact, I work with at least ten service companies that have packed up from Hollywood and moved to Atlanta because they feel that it's a strategic business move. There's confidence that production is there to stay.

Can you talk more about the city's evolution? Staffing shortages exist, but the situation is improving. It's getting costlier to shoot there. What else do we need to know?

It was a logistically difficult place when we first started filming there. It didn't have an established film office until this year, 2015. Previously it was a woman who had a small desk with stacks and stacks of paper. You couldn't even see her behind them. She was responsible for all transportation projects around the city, not just film. It made permit approvals extremely difficult because it would take her forever to weed through her regular job before she even found your request. Now with the Atlanta Film Office, everything is so much more efficient. They'll help you navigate local bureaucracies. They'll help mediate problems with local businesses. They're happy to get involved. It's still a young organization with a learning curve, but already I can tell a difference in the city. They've been very receptive to feedback from location managers.

Do you think the value and status of location managers has risen as productions have become more mobile?

Absolutely. Studios are making huge features, and they're making them in a number of different hubs. It's a much more difficult process, both creatively and logistically. When I first started in the industry, location managers were on the outskirts of the production. But in the last ten years, I've noticed we have so many more responsibilities. We also garner much more respect thanks to organizations like the LMGA [Location Managers Guild of America]. We are looked to for creative and logistical answers. We are expected to have a certain expertise about how the production can do what it needs to get done in whatever location we're filming. It's a tough job.

Producers often talk about the competition to put the money on the screen. Locations are a big part of that. Yet we're in the era of computer-generated graphics. How has that affected your work?

Selma was the hardest project I've ever done. I was responsible for forty-six locations over a thirty-two-day shoot. We used CGI only when we needed to increase the number of extras; we sometimes had five hundred but needed ten thousand.

We didn't use it for set extensions like we're doing with *The Accountant*. You definitely have to take CGI into consideration when you're selecting locations. Does this location give us the space to digitally insert the Chicago skyline into the background? In Atlanta, I've done Tikrit, Kuwait, London, and Tokyo. We've found it or created it but always with the help of CGI. Next week we're filming Lake Shore Drive in Atlanta. It's insane! You want me to find what? Why don't we just go to Lake Shore Drive?

Selma was a different set of problems. I had to consider the story's history; these events happened in actual locations. I also had to contend with a budget that didn't allow us to spend a lot of time outside of Atlanta. So, while most of the story takes place in Alabama, I was forced to find a lot of Selma, Alabama, in Atlanta, Georgia. Mark Friedberg, the production designer, was an amazing collaborator. We did so many side-by-side comparisons of the Selma locations and Atlanta locations. We had probably thirty different options for each location, then we would compare them until we found the best match. It was a great challenge. Because we were dealing with real locations, you didn't want someone in the audience who was part of that history to recognize the location as false: "Oh, that's not it!"

We've reached a point, I think, where certain places have emerged as reliable hubs. They have the soundstages and the crew and the incentive. There's no reason to go to Tikrit, I guess, when you can find it in Atlanta.

Can you identify the top five to ten hubs?

Atlanta. Louisiana. New Mexico. New York. London. Vancouver. Toronto. Australia. Cleveland has had some success lately; they're very film friendly. For *Captain America: The Winter Soldier* (2014) they shut down one of the city's major freeway arteries for weeks. They just opened their doors to the production and asked, "What can we do for you?"

Los Angeles is still the best place to shoot.

You just ticked off a map of global hubs but said L.A. is still number one. What do you mean?

You've got it all in Hollywood, and you can cheat to get different looks, depending on what you're shooting. It's hard to beat this city, but right now it just can't compete with the incentives that other places are offering.

20

Fringe City

Editors' Introduction

Our third section focuses on visual effects workers, the wizards behind many of the most popular films worldwide. It may seem odd to characterize VFX as a fringe activity given the current ubiquity of computer-generated imagery in explosive action flicks and franchise films featuring favorite comic book characters. Indeed, visual effects now account for one third of an average studio production budget, and three out of four shots in an award-winning feature like *Life of Pi* (2012) are computer generated. Still, the sector remains on the margins in numerous ways.

Historically, visual effects came of age on the cusp of the tech bubble in the 1990s, giving it an origin story disconnected from the old studio system in Hollywood. Its work routines and organizational cultures owe much more to the entrepreneurial ethos of the digital start-up firm than to the creative and technical hierarchies of screen media production. After all, tech jobs in the 1990s represented the future at a time when workers, especially fresh college graduates, placed a premium on individual autonomy, flexible workplaces, and portfolio careers. Youthful, enthusiastic, and eager, the confident VFX worker (who also was predominantly white and male) was laser focused on his own professional passions, and with good reason. He had access to top-line technology, worked in a cutting-edge industry, and produced highly sophisticated screen-media imagery. By comparison, the industrial mode of production and rigid division of labor that defines film and television production must have looked like the work his parents did, and union membership like a relic of a bygone era.

Although Los Angeles VFX shops thrived during the early years of computer-generated imagery, global competition began to escalate after the turn of the century. National and local policies that aimed to refashion human creativity and innovation into mechanisms of economic regeneration and urban renewal focused their attention on service and information industries. Economists, politicians, and other thought leaders approached the visual effects sector as part of this broader strategy. By cultivating the sector through tax incentives and other subsidies, they wanted to link their cities' fortunes to the global knowledge economy. These developments gave rise to new creative centers and circuits of production, which then made it possible for producers to leverage one hub against another through a fiercely competitive bidding process. Moreover, the end product of visual effects work makes it especially prone to outsourcing, since digital files can travel long distances at great speed. It doesn't matter if the work is done in Los Angeles, Vancouver, or Bangalore.

The precarious conditions for visual effects artists are a product of intense competition among firms and unrelenting demand from studios. With more than five hundred visual effects firms worldwide serving six major clients, the power imbalance is astounding, and the toll it takes on workers excruciating. Producers use the competition to their advantage by demanding lower costs and threatening to take the work elsewhere. Firms bid for work with fixed prices, meaning they enter into a contractual agreement with producers to deliver the required imagery on a fixed deadline at a guaranteed price. There are no allowances for the additional time or resources a firm may require because of production delays or requested changes.

Decision makers, like directors, often misunderstand the complexity of visual effects labor, a likely consequence of those artists being so far removed from the site of physical production. It's not uncommon for an anonymous director, producer, or studio executive to dismiss a finished graphic—sometimes months in the making—or request changes without realizing that even the slightest tweak may take days to complete. As our interviewees elaborate, many of these decision makers assume that visual effects artists are simply button pushers or geeked-out fanboys happy to work into the wee hours of the morning for free pizza.

The reality is much more stark. Given the fixed-price bidding, visual effects artists face tremendous productivity pressures to deliver perfect imagery under intense deadlines. Many do so with no overtime pay, health care benefits, or other protections such as sick days or vacation leave. They often work in isolation for long hours in a small cubicle or toil away at long worktables that are reminiscent of piecework stations in sweatshops. Some of the more egregious incidents our interlocutors share include reports about digital surveillance and abusive bosses. But job security remains the paramount concern. The vast majority work as freelancers, hired by a firm for a particular project and then terminated when the project ends. To make matters worse, the sector is characterized by constant bankruptcies, with some firms closing shop before the artists are fully paid. Those at the top of their game face an endless cycle of displacement, bouncing from one firm to another, and often one city to another. Less-fortunate artists are trapped in low-wage positions, hoping there is enough incoming work to at least ensure some continuity of employment before the firm goes bust.

Recall the fresh-faced techie in the 1990s who was swept up in the excitement of the dot-com boom. Like many of his colleagues, the VFX worker still speaks about his craftwork (notably, most refer to it as an art) with significant passion. Yet today he is in his thirties or forties with a family and bills to pay. Employment gaps are more difficult to straddle, and the prospect of moving abroad to the latest visual effects hub wreaks havoc on one's personal life. The scenario is even worse for women. Much as we have heard from other workers in this collection, structural factors make it difficult for women to accommodate the demands of the job alongside the additional domestic burdens they are disproportionately expected to shoulder. They furthermore must cope with a culture of chauvinism among colleagues and dismissive line managers, all of whom operate under the assumption that women are out of place in the tech industry. Maternity leave, we learned from one interviewee, was a privilege rarely granted and seldom requested.

Sadly, there is little recourse for either firms or workers. Employers at VFX shops are at the mercy of studios and producers. With such a small client pool, firms worry that organized labor would jeopardize their chances at securing more contracts. It's simply too easy to take the project to another provider. Meanwhile, visual effects artists often suffer in silence. Workplaces are defined by a culture of fear that prohibits speaking out against violations lest it jeopardize an individual's chances at finding or keeping a job. Tellingly, most of the individuals who talked with us are no longer in the business. They still speak about their art with tremendous enthusiasm and in great detail, but have turned their attention to other jobs while still remaining part of growing movement for reform, one that is actively debating ways to alleviate the sector's downward spiral. Options such as trade associations, unionization, and legal action are described in this section. But any productive solution must be global in scope in order to fully intervene in the structural conditions wreaking havoc on the visual effects business. Fortunately, the digital savvy of these artists and activists has opened the door to transnational deliberations about the state of the industry. It's a tentative but necessary starting point for serious reform.

Today, visual effects work is arguably the most geographically dispersed aspect of film and television production. Los Angeles was once the world's leading VFX hub, but has been completely hollowed out by the migration of firms and artists to a growing number of worldwide locations. Once a metaphorical fringe city of Hollywood, the business has now scattered to literal fringe cities around the globe. Always at the margins of the production process and at a distance from studio decision makers, workers struggle to develop a nascent labor consciousness to address the abuses common to the industry. The workaday experiences that our interviewees share reveal the extremes to which visual effects artists have been pushed, both personally and professionally. Although in many ways they labor at the fringes of the motion picture industry, their experiences represent the most severe manifestation of nearly every issue raised in this collection. In fact, listening to their voices feels very much like carrying a canary into the coal mine. We can learn a lot from those on the fringes.

21

Scott Ross, VFX manager

Scott Ross started his career in 1988 as a general manager at Industrial Light & Magic (ILM), one of the pioneers of computer-generated visual effects. In 1993 he cofounded Digital Domain, another industry leader, with James Cameron and Stan Winston. These days Ross produces films, teaches, and advocates for the creation of a VFX trade association. Here he recounts the origins of Digital Domain, the challenges that confront VFX shops, and the prospects for industry reform.

How did you get started in the industry?

I happened to arrive at ILM when digital was just emerging, and we ended up reorganizing the company. It was sort of a perfect storm. I was coming out of video postproduction, where so many things were digital already: film-to-tape transfers, flying spot scanners, and paint boxes. But when I got to ILM, everything was still optical, and because it was optical, things were very slow. I was shocked at how *dumb* everything was. For example, you had to send film to the lab and wait three days before you got it back and *then* you'd look at it? And then maybe you had to shoot it all over again? Really?! So it was the perfect storm of me being there and connecting with guys who were incredibly bright, like John Knoll, Dennis Muren, and Scott Squires. We embraced this new technology that allowed us to manipulate images in the digital realm.

Tell us about the evolution of Digital Domain.

The Bay Area in the early 1990s was entrepreneurial heaven. Everybody who was anybody was starting a company. I was running ILM and had a team around me with some of the greatest creative people and winners of multiple Academy Awards. And yet our owner was basically not there. He was an absentee landlord. In the five or so years that I ran the company, I only met George Lucas three or four times.

At that point, ILM was carrying the rest of Lucasfilm. We had turned a company that was unprofitable into a company that was mildly profitable. We turned a company that was lost in the doldrums of technology to a leading-edge company. The guys (and they were all men) who were working with me at the time were all about my age. They all thought, "Why are we working for George? He's never here. It's not like he's making movies anymore. It's not like we're here for *Star Wars*. So what are we doing?" And I said, "Let's have a leveraged buyout, a management buyout. George always talks about how he hates all of these services and that the overhead on Skywalker Ranch is too expensive. Let's put together a financial package and make George an offer he can't refuse."

Unfortunately, he refused it. And then I was out because from George's perspective I had gone behind his back to buy his company. I was persona non grata. It was unbearable. So I decided to start my own company, and that's how Digital Domain came about.

I had written a business plan, and then out of the blue I got a phone call from James Cameron, with whom I had worked on *The Abyss* (1989) and *Terminator 2: Judgment Day* (1991). Jim had heard that I was starting this company and asked if he could be part of it. I went to my then-wife and asked, "What do you think?" The concept of bringing in another powerful director, having just left George, didn't sit real well with me. She said, "If you start this company and it is just you, you're going to have a difficult time of it. But if you start the company with Jim Cameron's name attached, everybody's going to want to come work for you, because if you work on a Jim Cameron movie, you win an Academy Award." I thought long and hard about it and realized she was right. I always felt that Jim looked up to George. If George had ILM, then Jim needed his own version of ILM, right? And Jim was very excited about it. I said, "Let's have a meeting," and flew down to Burbank, where his company was at the time.

Unexpectedly, Stan Winston, the most celebrated makeup effects guy in the world, showed up at the meeting. It turned out that Jim and Stan were very close friends, so Jim felt that Stan should be part of the company as well. So I flew down to Burbank thinking, "I'm not sure," and I left thinking, "Okay, I've got two partners, Jim and Stan." And that's how Digital Domain was born.

What were the projects that helped to build Digital Domain's reputation?

In 1994 we got *True Lies*, which was Cameron's movie, and that put us on the map. We were even nominated for an Academy Award for it. We also won the Golden Lion Gran Prix Award for a Budweiser commercial. We even won an MTV Music

Video Award for "Love Is Strong" with the Rolling Stones. That was a big year, and we became the most talked-about VFX studio in L.A.

*Then **Titanic** (1997) came along, which was a great project but a financial nightmare for you. Can you walk us through that story? It seems to encapsulate the challenges facing the VFX industry.*

Let's leave the *Titanic* realm for a second and establish a few things. The production of visual effects is as amorphous and strange as you can get. Even the people in it don't fully understand it. It's more an art than a science. It changes and morphs. To be a production person, or a director, and truly understand how visual effects work is almost impossible. It's sort of like going to a brain surgeon if you're a podiatrist and saying, "So, we're both doctors. Let's talk!" It's very, very different. It's very complicated and has a ton of moving parts.

This means that when you budget visual effects, it's a best-guess scenario. In Hollywood, with almost everything that is budgeted, the people in charge of making the decisions are always interested in the deal, less so the actual price. It's a hard thing to get your head around, but if you don't know what something costs and I tell you it costs $100 but I'm going to give it to you for $75, you will want it for $60. That's how pricing in Hollywood works. The answer to any bid is, "It's too much!" Now, do they know? No. No idea. But it's always too much.

That became the case even with my partner, Jim, because he put together an agreement with Digital Domain that basically said that he doesn't have control over where the VFX work on his movies gets done. He can *suggest* to the film studio he's working with that they choose Digital Domain. He can *strongly* suggest it. But at the end of the day, it's not his money. It's 20th Century Fox's money. So 20th Century Fox ultimately makes the determination on where the work is going to go. So while Digital Domain was saying, "We're going to enter into an agreement with you, a services agreement. You've *got* to bring the work to us," his response was, "I can't guarantee it. I'll do the best I can."

In return for "best efforts," he got a significant discount off of what our normal price would be. Going into *True Lies*, it was a brand-new company, and we're pulling in people from all over the world, and at times running around like chickens with our heads cut off. It was a disparate group of people coming together to work on very high-profile projects. It was like the all-star team figuring out how to play together.

So we're working on *True Lies* with Jim, but we're getting the typical response one expects from a producer or director: "I don't trust my effects company; I want a better deal; you're not doing it right. We're not gonna pay you." On several occasions Digital Domain was almost forced to miss payroll because we were depending on cash flow coming from 20th Century Fox. But the producer and the director, who's also the chairman of the board of the company, is saying, "We're not paying you because the work's not done!" I said, "You have to trust me. The work is going to get done. We'll get there." And, lo and behold, the work gets done and in the end we were nominated for an Academy Award. But it was a brutal process.

Fast forward to *Titanic*. The studio, 20th Century Fox, already had some difficult experiences with Cameron, in that every time he does a movie he goes well over budget, so they were very pleased that Jon Landau, their head of production, took the project because he knew more than anyone at the studio about how movies are actually made. Jim and Jon put together a budget for *Titanic* somewhere in the low hundred-million-dollar range and unbeknownst to me, they put together a visual effects budget of around $18 million. But when we took a look at the project, our budget ended up around $27 million. So I went back to Jim and said, "We can't do it for $18 million." And the response from Jim was, "If you don't do it, I'll take it to ILM. They'll do it for that amount." Remember, he was not obliged to bring the work to us.

At the time, ILM's biggest competitor was Digital Domain. ILM's general manager thinks, "The guy who once ran my company is now running my competition and if I can do a movie with Jim Cameron and Jim Cameron can't afford his own company, then I can put a nail in the coffin of my major competitor." How much is that worth? And if ILM can *manage* the process so that maybe the budget starts off at $18 million dollars, but finishes up around $25 million, then ILM only loses $2 million. For $2 million he can put his only significant competitor out of business.

It's one of these things. If I don't take the work, I'm out of business. And if I do take the work, I might be out of business. So I go to my board of directors and tell them what's going on and they say, "You're between a rock and a hard place. You have to take the work." And I said, "Okay, as long as you know it." So we took the work and then in typical Jim fashion, he had a reality distortion problem. I'd ask him, "Where's your film? Where's the stuff?" He'd reply, "I'm still shooting," which was a big problem for us because it was crimping our production schedule. Finally I went to Jim and said, "Listen, we're not going to make your July release date." His response: "Well, I'm taking some of the work to ILM and to VIFX." I said, "You have to do what you have to do, but we're not going to make the release date. And it's your problem." And he says, "Just get it done!"

This forces us into major overtime and we're burning through cash like crazy. Normally in an overtime situation I would have the ability to go back to the studio and say, "Guys, your director has put us into overtime. He did *not* deliver his footage on the date he said he was going to deliver it. Here's a change order." But Jim, the director-producer of *Titanic and* the chairman of the board of Digital Domain, says, "I won't let you do that. We have an operating committee comprised of me, Stan, and you, and we make those decisions." The decision by a two-to-one vote of the operating committee was that Digital Domain cannot go back to the studio for change orders! Needless to say, we were screwed, and quickly moving toward insolvency.

Of course we miss the delivery date, which makes us look like fools because Jim's saying the reason we missed it is because Digital Domain fucked up. In fact, the reason we're missing the delivery date is because he hasn't delivered the footage, but I can't go to the studio and tell them that's what's going on. So I'm just sitting there, powerless, watching us burn through cash. On top of that, we lose part of the work to ILM and VIFX, which means it's no longer solely our movie.

In the end, it worked out great for Jim. Had he delivered on July 2, *Titanic* would've been up against some other major movies. We delivered in October. The film gets released in November and therefore has clear sailing all the way until next summer, which drives the movie to the number one box office hit of all time. Missing the original date benefited him and 20th Century Fox, but it didn't benefit us. We wound up hurt financially, and our reputation suffered as well.

On the heels of *Titanic* Cameron decided Digital Domain needed a new CEO. He didn't feel that I was capable of running the company, so he wanted to turn our operating committee into the CEO: he would be the C, Stan would be the E, and I would be the O. He also wanted us to hire a president, so I started a worldwide search and interviewed half a dozen possible candidates. While this worldwide search is under way, a board meeting is scheduled at which we review the financials, which were terrible because of *Titanic*, and then I tell the board, "By the way, the operating committee is searching for a president."

The Cox and IBM directors are shocked. They ask Jim, chairman of the board, to explain why the company needs to hire a new president. Jim says, "We don't think Scott is capable." And the board responds, "Bullshit! Not only do we back Scott as the CEO, but your services agreement is done and we want you to resign. Scott's the chairman, Scott's the CEO, and that's the way it's going to be." At which point Jim grabs his jacket, throws it over his shoulder, and as he's leaving, he turns around to quote a line from *Titanic*: "Gentlemen, it's indeed been an honor and privilege playing with you." Then walks out and I don't see him again until Stan Winston's funeral, many years later.

The story explains so much about the extraordinary challenges confronting VFX shops.

The VFX business model has never worked. People start to say, "In the good old days," and my response is, "No, there were never any 'good old' days." The good old days are the bad old days. And today is just as bad. It was never good. You barely eked out a profit or a loss and you never showed a return on equity to your investors. It was never an environment that was profitable. You worked really hard and for really long hours to create some of the greatest images known to humankind and you got nothing for it, from a financial point of view. Those were the old days. Now today, when you add the subsidies to the picture, it's disastrous.

At the time, did you have any premonition as to where things were headed?

Yes, without a doubt. Around 1994 I tried to start a trade association. I called it AVEC, the French word for "with," the Association of Visual Effects Creators. I wanted to get the major players in the visual effects industry together to form a trade association and change the business model. It didn't work.

Why?

The folks who run these companies are not businesspeople, and because they're not businesspeople, they're all scared to death. It goes back to that line that George Lucas has about the crews who worked on *Star Wars*, which was, "If you give 'em enough beer and pizza, they'll do anything!" And so you have these fanboys (and now fangirls) who are prepared to offer whatever it takes because they get to see their names in the credits of *Star Wars*.

But wouldn't it be in their interest to form a trade association?

Think about Pepsi and Coke. They're selling sugar water that sort of tastes the same and looks exactly alike. Talk about rivalry! And yet they have a trade association. Automakers. General Motors versus Ford. Again, rivalry! But they have a trade association. The motion picture industry: Paramount versus Disney! They have a trade association. So if you approach business like business, you understand, "Okay, guys. We all know that we are incredibly competitive and frankly don't trust each other at all—but the problem is not us. The problem is the clients and the business model. We're starving and doing all the work and they're making billions of dollars. They're the fat cats. Let's get together here and stop this stuff!" But to date, there still isn't a trade association. Given that six major Hollywood studios control the biggest feature films, all the VFX companies are too afraid.

You mentioned the artists who are willing to work for beer and pizza, but are you also saying that the people who are running the shops lack an industrial mentality? Would that include John Hughes, for example, of Rhythm & Hues?

John Hughes is not much of a businessman. He is an incredible human being and cares about his people and works really hard and is very, very smart. But he has a serf mentality, which is, "I am not worthy! Okay, we'll do it for $1.98, please don't hit me!" He's scared to death of the major studios. Even near the end, when his company was on the verge of bankruptcy, his response to me was, "I'll consider a trade association, but only if everybody else joins. And don't use my name."

And that's the common response?

Well, things have changed now. John Hughes and Scott Ross were the last of a dying breed of owner-operators. Nowadays the people who run the major facilities are not the owners. They are salaried. From their perspective, why would they want to rock the boat? They're figuring they're going to be fired in a couple of years anyway because they couldn't make the company profitable. Why should they be mavericks and try to do something that involves a long-term plan? They're thinking: "I should make as much money as I can in the shortest period of time."

What is the root of their fear?

The fear is that there is only so much food brought to the table and if I don't kiss the ass of the person who is bringing the food, I won't get my share and I'll starve to death. Remember, there are only six clients!

This sounds like a nightmare for VFX companies. What's left in Los Angeles? Rhythm & Hues went bankrupt; so did Digital Domain and dozens of others.

Look, subsidies don't talk, they scream. From a studio's perspective, they're going to go wherever the subsidies are the highest. From a visual effects facility's perspective, they're scared to do anything but follow the subsidies. So if the studio tells me, "I'll give you the job if you move to Vancouver," I'm moving to Vancouver. And then when all of a sudden Montreal offers a better deal than Vancouver and the studio says, "I'd love to give you the work because we have a relationship, but . . . " the studio knows full well that you're going to Montreal. There's no doubt about it. From a studio's perspective, everything works perfectly.

By the way, the interesting thing is that about five years ago people were saying China and India were going to eat our shorts. That hasn't happened, and the reason why is because I can go to London and get better prices [due to government subsidies] than I can in Mumbai.

It sounds like an ideal world from a producer's perspective. But doesn't it undermine a VFX company's ability to bring together talent? Or are people so mobile at this point that you can pull together talent regardless of location?

VFX companies need to hold onto their core talent. The teams that make major motion pictures today are comprised of about five hundred people. Of that team, maybe a hundred and fifty are critical. So you want to hold onto those, but the rest you just hire. It's like, "Would you like to spend the next two years working on *Star Wars* and living in London?" The people who are starving to death because there's no work in Los Angeles say, "I'd rather not, but sure! Let's go! I'll pack some clothes and some toothpaste and I'll be okay."

How about the shops in Canada or the United Kingdom, where they benefit from subsidies?

When the subsidies happen, the visual effects company sees none of it. The good news is that if you're in London and you qualify for the subsidies, you get the job. The bad news is, you get the job. It's not like the studios are giving a portion of the subsidy back to the visual effects company—they're keeping the subsidy and still using their leverage to lower the rates they pay to the VFX shops.

Visual effects companies are not making do. They're losing money. So how do they survive? Volume! Nobody's making any money, but if you manage your cash flow correctly and keep your labor costs under control, you can keep going. Why do all of these issues fall on the shoulders of the artists? Because that's the biggest cost of your show. If I'm a facilities general manager, where am I going to cut corners? I could stop serving donuts, but, really, what does that do? Instead they say, "Let's not pay them overtime. How about their medical? Let's cut back on their medical. Let's do everything we can to cut corners." Meanwhile the artists are under the false impression that managers are doing it to make a fortune. Not true! They're doing it so they can stay in business. There's only one group that's making a fortune, and that's the motion picture studios.

Do you think the subsidy game will end up hurting the studios in the long run?

No. Listen, when the sun shines, the sun shines and you take it as you can. I think the studios are run by extremely good businesspeople and they're going to let this run as long and as hard and as fast as it possibly can. They'll take the subsidies while they last and they'll develop contingency plans.

If I were a studio executive, I would do everything I possibly could to make the major VFX companies open up shops in places like India and China. I know that today I can't do *Avatar* (2009) in India, but if Weta opens up a shop in India, or if Weta hires and trains enough Indian workers, you take a couple of cranks of the wheel and all of a sudden you have what you need in India. And then you don't need subsidies, because the cost of living there is considerably less.

If I were a VFX artist, the first thing I'd do is look for work elsewhere. I'd look for work outside of the motion picture industry. Or if I'm really creative, I would start making my own product. And if I'm both, I would work outside of the movie industry *and* I'd try making my own product.

Is there anything that can be done to put an end to the subsidy game?

In the best of all worlds, an international guild would be great. You take all the people who are working as digital artists or digital manufacturers in the visual effects, animation, television, and gaming industries, and you form a guild that operates as a negotiating platform against and *with* producers. But there are so many reasons why it doesn't work and why it might not work. The people in the subsidized locales are as happy as pigs in shit—today, at least. They don't see what the future looks like. They're only focused on what's happening today. Therefore, anybody who speaks out against subsidies is their enemy. If you're a working professional in Vancouver and somebody says, "Subsidies are terrible," you're up on your heels and ready for fisticuffs. "Subsidies aren't terrible. My kid goes to school because of subsidies. I'm going to do whatever I can to fight for them." The distrust and warfare among digital artists is such that I don't see hope for a guild, particularly not on an international level. As for the traditional unions like IATSE and the IBEW [International Brotherhood of Electrical Workers], they have the wrong profile for these men and women, so they're immediately mistrusted.

Why do they have the wrong profile?

First of all, most of the people working in the digital, visual effects, and animation world have advanced degrees and are stereotypical nerds. The people who run IATSE look and feel a whole lot more like the teamsters. They don't look like the sorts of folks who might represent these white-collar, advanced-degree, pseudo-intellectual artists who are twenty-five to thirty-five years old, listening to Sublime, and have tattoos all over their bodies. It's a cultural disconnect between your father's union and you. It's an uphill battle.

No hope at all?

Let me tell you why I think a union wouldn't work. Unions are not international, by their very nature. So let's assume that IATSE could get enough workers to sign cards here in Los Angeles and that those cards allowed certain jobs to become unionized. Most of those shops already have international locations where most of their work is now going.

The cost of working with a union shop is higher than the cost of working with a nonunion shop. I don't care what anybody in the union says, it is! I sat on the board of trustees of a union, and I've run a nonunion company. Running a union company costs more money than running a nonunion company. And if it costs more money, who is going to pay that? The studios' sole interest is to keep costs down. So if I run a union company, I'm going to come in with a higher bid, which gives more impetus for the studio to contract with a facility in India or the Philippines where there isn't a union, or in Vancouver or London, where unions offer more concessions and benefit from subsidies.

If you had an international association of workers, and all the workers in all of the major shops agreed on it, now that's a possibility. But the reality of organizing that sounds overwhelming to me. We don't even have a union here, and the artists in Vancouver are arguing with the artists in Montreal, who are arguing with the artists in London. They're all at each other's throats. Why? You'll hear, "Why should I rock the boat, I work in Vancouver. I get subsidies, why should I go against subsidies?"

The only reason you're in Vancouver now is because that's where the work is. So if you want to become a gypsy, migrant, digital-labor worker, yeah, then be in favor of subsidies. You'll spend nine months in Mumbai, nine months in Shanghai, nine months in Beijing. Wherever you have to go. And maybe at age twenty-five that's not so bad. But at age forty-five, it sucks. Still, they're not interested in unions.

Do you think they would be if times were different? For example, the reason guilds and unions emerged in Hollywood was in part because of a New Deal consciousness.

Yes, it was the zeitgeist of the 1930s and 1940s that allowed unions to come into play.

Do you think we're headed for another moment like that?

No, I don't. I wish we were, but no. And the reason is, it's a different world. It's now globalized. It's no longer about protecting the workers of Detroit or protecting the migrant farmworker. Now it's, "How do you deal with China?"

Artists are getting screwed in China, too.

Maybe over time we'll see it, but not as long as there's fear among the workers and not enough rice on the table. I don't see it as an immediate fix. Can you imagine what would happen if even four of the top VFX companies told the studios, "We're no longer going to work under the current business model of fixed-price bids. The new business model is going to be time and materials. We're going to charge you cost plus markup. And we want to participate in the back-end royalties. And it's going to save you money! Here are all of the reasons why." What would the studios do? It would be a different world.

By the way, that's how other parts of the production process work. There's a producer and an assistant director, and you know that if you put in ten hours on the set and then decide you need three more hours on that set, at the end of the day the accountants are going, "Jesus, that ran $130,000 dollars over budget. We have to make that up." Not with visual effects! It's not the studios' problem, it's the visual effects company's problem.

If a trade association won't work and a union won't work, are there any other possibilities?

There's one other pipe dream that could be interesting. All of the companies that we're talking about, those in the top ten, none of them are making any money. They're all in the shitter. Well, if four of us got together and we put together a half-billion dollars, we could do a roll-up and buy another five or six. At that point we'd control the movie industry. "New Co." is now setting the prices. You want your stuff done? You've got to go through us. It would make the days of Michael Ovitz and CAA look like a walk in the park because every major movie—I think it's forty-nine of the top fifty movies of all time—are visual effects movies. Talk about power.

Why doesn't anybody do that?

Nobody has the guts.

What are the top ten facilities right now?

ILM, Sony Pictures Imageworks, Digital Domain, Weta, Method, Double Negative, Framestore, Pixomondo, and Prime Focus World. A few years ago I would've put Rhythm & Hues on there, too.

Walk us through this. How would this scenario work?

Step one, you do a roll-up. You buy up the companies and lock in the top talent. Once you're consolidated, you have economies of scale. Then you install good management, because a lot of these companies don't have good management. With really good management and economies of scale, you bring your costs down. Then you go back and renegotiate your deals with the studios. Now you've become a major broker in Hollywood. It's all about negotiating leverage and controlling the available pool of talent, because in the end, the very biggest studio feature films depend on world-class visual effects.

22

Dave Rand, VFX artist

Dave Rand is a visual effects artist and activist with stints at some of the best-recognized firms in the business, including Disney, Rhythm & Hues, Sony Pictures Imageworks, and Digital Domain. His film credits include *Frozen* (2013) and *Life of Pi* (2012), among others. Here Rand describes the precarious and mobile lifestyle of a VFX artist and recounts what it was like for employees at Rhythm & Hues when the celebrated firm filed for bankruptcy in 2013.

You've worked for a lot of different companies in a lot of different places. Your longest stretch with one company was four years, correct?

Yes, and it's not because I wanted to leave that particular company. I've fallen in love with at least six visual effects companies and never would have left if it weren't for other things that happened. Five of them went bankrupt; the other I left for creative reasons. But I've never been asked to leave, you know? They always wanted to keep me on.

Even when you were working on big, successful feature films, it didn't mean the VFX company benefited. For example, you worked on **The Matrix Reloaded** *(2003), a blockbuster at the box office, but the VFX company went bankrupt.*

It happened like this: I was working at Centropolis and they called everyone in for an unscheduled meeting. I have never been in a last-minute Friday meeting that's been anything but, "Your paychecks are going to stop," or, "We're going fucking bankrupt." This was my first one. I'd already been prewarned that if we went into dailies on Friday and the lights were on, it meant that the place was closing. As I'm walking out of the meeting, I noticed one guy's cell phone rang, and then another guy's cell phone rang, and I knew they were key players in the movie. And then mine rang. It was the head of recruiting at Sony Pictures Imageworks saying, "Come on over!" So I went over to Sony to finish *The Matrix*.

What Sony didn't tell me is that they were starting over from scratch. I thought I was just going there to finish up some shots. No, they were starting over. They had ninety days until the release date, and so they hired everybody in Los Angeles. We had to be at dailies every morning at eight and work until we dropped dead. There wasn't a day off. We were fed rows of Fatburgers and fries and pizza and Chinese food. It was tough. It was *The Matrix*, so it was fun. But it was rugged.

When it was over, all I wanted was to go to Belize for a break. I had a little place down there. And they're like, "You can't leave." They were going to do a Will Smith movie. "We've got to have you on *Bad Boys II*." But my deal had already expired. So I'm like, "Nah, I'm going to Belize. When I get back if you guys want to hire me, it'd be great." They threatened me! They thought I'd signed a contract. I'm not that stupid; I had an expired deal memo. So I left.

When I got back three weeks later they were apologetic. I said, "You ruined my vacation for a while." They said, "Oh, don't worry! We've got all this work for you!" So I sat for two weeks, and there was nothing to do. Something was on hold. That's the thing with VFX companies: their clients always put stuff on hold. That's how the major studios killed Rhythm & Hues. How is the shop supposed to pay seven hundred people until you decide to put your movie back on line?

Then I get offered a job on *The Chronicles of Riddick* (2004) from an outfit called Hammerhead. I checked it out and I loved the show. I told Sony, "I'm outta here. Two weeks' notice, whatever you want to do. You guys haven't been giving me anything to do anyway; everything is on hold." I hadn't signed the contract yet. They were pissed.

Riddick was a cool experience in the beginning. Hammerhead wasn't geared up to do a big 3D show. They made some decisions that were not, I think, the best decisions. I tried to offer my opinion based on my experience. It didn't go down well with them. So I left Hammerhead, and I think I went to Meteor Studios after that, a Canadian company.

Meteor was an incentive-based company. The tax incentives weren't as dramatic as they are today. It proved to be a nightmare, and that's where my story starts, as far as becoming way more active in the politics, business decisions, and business models that visual effects uses. It's because of what happened at Meteor Studios.

I was a supervisor and we began work on *Journey to the Center of the Earth* (2008). Big movie. Brendan Fraser. A lot of water effects, which has become my favorite thing to do. And right away there were issues with the director. Things were changing a lot, and I'm thinking, "I can't imagine they bid enough to cover all these changes." And then I heard that when Meteor submitted change orders to the studio, they were rejected. Meanwhile, I'd be in meetings with all the supervisors each morning. These things would come up and our producer would say, "Don't worry about it. Just keep working."

All of a sudden there was this Friday meeting. It started with an email because our paychecks didn't hit that week. I thought, "That's weird," because I had put in a lot of overtime. Then this email went around that said, "Payroll will be a day or two late at the most." It was a glitch or whatever. Oh, okay, but I've never not been paid in my life. And then two days later, no direct deposit. Three days later, no direct deposit.

Now it's Friday and there's a meeting. So we go to the meeting and the head guy gets up and says, "This is what's going on. The movie's in the hole, big time. They actually don't have any money. But there's a big check coming and our parent company is worth $8 billion." They even put *me* in front of the group to convince them that there's no way this parent company, which was Discovery Holding Company, is not going to pay people—if just from a PR standpoint—because the holidays were coming up and we were working on a big, giant, multi-million-dollar movie. "The company will make hundreds of millions of dollars!" That's what we were told.

In my mind, I'm thinking they're going to pay us because they promised us these completion bonus deals: if you work until delivery without being paid, you are promised your money, all your overtime, and a completion bonus. At the time, delivery was not far off. People were working to finish the show without pay because we had these guaranteed deals. I found out later that they only gave you the deal if you asked for it in writing. It was only a handshake deal for a lot of people, which is amazing to me. But it didn't matter. When you go bankrupt, all those contracts are worth their weight in paper. So, boom. We deliver the last shot, everything is final, and then there's no money.

One guy got angry and they had to call the cops. He was the quietest guy, too, but he just flipped his lid. He's got kids, a house, they owed him something like $22,000. Christmas is coming. I remember him saying, "I can't even buy Christmas presents for my children." Also, I found out later that they didn't pay the Canadian staff as much as the American staff. The Canadians earned less than half of what the Americans did.

I was owed a lot of money and couldn't believe this was happening. I went to Maine for the holidays. I was sitting at my mom's kitchen table with my laptop and I started writing emails—to *Variety*, to the Canadian film commission, to the Canadian Ministry of Labour. At one point I called Brendan Fraser's manager, just to make people aware. David Cohen at *Variety* wrote back, saying, "We're going to write about this. This is news. What's going on? The company owes its artists $1.3 million? Can you get anyone else to talk?" It was hard getting other people to talk, but we managed to get a few.

We're going with a major Hollywood publication because the writer wants the exclusive. And then one day I get this email that says—and I know it by heart because it hit me so fucking hard—it says, "The paper has decided that another visual effects company closing and artists not getting paid, however sad, is happening frequently enough that it's not that newsworthy anymore."

I was like, what?! Just because it's happening more often it's suddenly *not* newsworthy? As in, people are tired of reading about this? This is huge! So I copy and pasted that into a Word document that eventually became a press release that I did myself. It's still on my website.

Off goes the press release. Right away the writer calls me and he is furious that I took what he called a "private" email and put it in a press release. I said, "It was a rejection letter; there's nothing private about that. It's not from you. The paper told you to write that. It's not you deciding." He got back to me later, after everyone calmed down, and said, "The paper will write something but you have to rerelease your press release without that quote in there." So I put it to our group, saying, "What do you want me to do?" They go, "Take it out! We need coverage." I took it out. But the paper still didn't write anything.

About a week and a half later I get a call from a woman with the *New York Post*. Yes, finally! She's a fast-talking New York gal and she says, "We're running your story! Is it true Brendan Fraser never called you back?" I say, "Yes, but there's a whole lot more to our story." "But that's the angle!" I say, "I don't think Brendan Fraser ever got the message." She asks me a few more questions and I think she's going to write this big comprehensive article, but it ends up being on page 6 of the *Post*. It has a picture of Brendan Fraser holding a camera and simply says that we didn't get paid and we called him and he's not helping us.

I'm reading it and my cell phone rings. "Dave Rand?" "Yes." "This is Brendan Fraser. What the fuck is going on?!" That is exactly what he said. And I thought, "My god!" And then I thought some of my friends might be playing a prank on me so I asked, "Where were you born and where were you raised?" I had read about him and he answered it directly.

I'll tell you that Brendan went to bat for us. Of all the actors who have benefited from visual effects movies, he's the only one who got concerned about the way we were treated. He was not only the star of this movie, but also the executive producer. So, given those two roles, of course he should be concerned that there's a whole bunch of people not getting paid!

He started poking around. He would call me back every couple of days. He'd call me! And he'd say, "I called this guy at Discovery. They didn't believe it was me, either. No one believes it's me! I've hardly ever done anything like this on my own!" Then at one point I get a call from one of his agents in Florida, who says, "You are no longer to call Brendan Fraser." I tell her, "You know what, *he* calls *me*." And she says, "We've already spoken to Brendan about that, so any numbers you have, delete them." I say, "You know what? I can't hear you over the sound of the wheels turning in your head."

And Brendan just keeps calling. He is really cool. That guy is on my A-list forever. The *Post* does another story that says he's helping us and then suddenly everyone wants to write about it. *Variety* calls: "Why did you talk to the *Post*? We were writing the story!"

Over the long haul, Dave Cohen at *Variety* became a huge heavy hitter for us. He's become a good friend. It was never his decision not to write the story; he's always been 1,000 percent behind us and now *Variety* is, too, and so is the *Hollywood Reporter*, the *Los Angeles Times*, everybody. Back in 2007, I couldn't get anyone to write about the fact that there were 130 visual effects professionals owed $1.3 million. It wasn't news. Now, I'll throw a pizza party for the union at Rhythm & Hues and it'll end up in the press.

What are the chances of the workers getting paid in a situation like that?

Good question. It's a lot better in the United States because the labor laws are tighter. After I became vocal at Meteor, Brendan Fraser helped me recover $750,000 of the $1.3 million, which is like a world record for visual effects right now. And that's just because of the media attention. So we recovered that money but usually what happens, especially in Canada, is that you get nothing. Or you get a tiny bit. In March the Canadian film commission said, "We have to do something or word is going to get out that this is a big problem." So they took some taxpayer money and now if you're a visual effects artist and your company goes bankrupt, you get $3,000. No matter what happens.

Can you tell us the Rhythm & Hues story, at least your side of it? As we understand it, that was one of the best shops to work for.

By far. That's why its bankruptcy caused such outrage in the visual effects community worldwide. Rhythm & Hues was like the Alamo of digital effects in Los Angeles. It was run by John Hughes, who was one of the best people I've ever worked for, just a super friendly guy. We became friends because my office was so close to his and he was an avid follower of all of these causes, both for the VFX studios and for the artists.

Anyway, after taking a break from work for a while, my friend called me from Rhythm, saying, "I heard you're in L.A. You have to come by and see this show! It's a giant water show!" As I said, I love doing water. So when I visited, they showed me stuff from *Life of Pi*. I thought, "Oh my god, this is awesome."

It was an amazing experience to work on *Life of Pi*, but they had to pack the joint, so it was kind of close quarters. I'm used to having maybe one other person in my office. In Vancouver, on *Transformers: Dark of the Moon* (2011), we were like an Indian call center. Fucking horrible. And the temperature soared because they couldn't keep up the air conditioning. They treated us like crap. They didn't care. It's like those guys down in the bilge, rowing the boat, "Throw 'em some more food and shut 'em up!" On *Life of Pi* the worst of it was it just the somewhat close quarters. They had to bring on such a huge staff to do that movie. It was great that they were employing so many people in the United States, but I could sense right away that some things weren't right.

Bill Westenhofer is absolutely one of the best visual effects supervisors I've ever worked for. He got an Academy Award for *Life of Pi*. Brilliant. I wished he was directing the whole movie. They say Ang Lee was there more than I perceived, but I never saw him in dailies. Dailies at Disney are called "director time." That's what it should be.

So Bill's doing a great job, but then there's a lot of studio stuff and tension with Ang Lee that I'm not privy to, and suddenly the whole operation goes on hold. And my mother's dying so I have to leave. And then my mom passes and I come back and *Life of Pi* is still on fucking hold. There was another show in-house that they put me on, *Seventh Son* (2014), but then after a while I'm doing nothing. It was a lot of us doing nothing. And they had to keep the whole staff there because when freaking Fox decides to put the movie back on line, we can't re-muster that talent.

Finally *Life of Pi* comes back on line, but the studio is ordering all these changes, a ton of them! So Rhythm & Hues is going to be bankrupted. You can sense it. John Hughes calls a special Friday meeting and I'm thinking, "I've been through too many of these. This is getting old." "Your paychecks are going to stop, but keep working on the movie. If you go home, we understand." There are no jobs in L.A. so where the hell are you going to go unless you want to move to Canada or New Zealand or London or Australia? Where are you going to go? People have leases and homes and stuff, so we're all just hoping for the best. That's why visual effects artists keep working when the money stops. Because you can take our money away but we actually feel married to our work. We start living inside of our shot work. "Take my money away, but don't take my shot away, too, and leave me with nothing." I know that's a weird way to think, but it's valid.

John Hughes was so transparent—he always was. Every Friday he opened the books and went through everything for us. The entire financials were in front of us on an overhead projector and he's there explaining them and answering questions until everyone's satisfied.

The entire staff?

Yes, everyone who wanted to go: the roto guy, the guy who's running the render queue, the guy who's parking the freaking cars, the guy who drives the van to bring us to our cars. Anyone can go to these meetings as long as you work for the company. Toward the end, John was having a lot of meetings. Every time he had something to say, we all had to march over to the biggest room in the facility that could hold five hundred, six hundred people. And he would spell it out and stand there and answer questions until everyone was satisfied. It was heartbreaking. There was a group that filmed all of this. Hughes gave them permission to do it, so there's a documentary coming out [called *Life After Pi*].

And then comes this Sunday night when my friend Bobby calls me. Bobby's in a panic because he's on a visa and he's being laid off. He's scared to death he's going to have to go back to Lebanon because there are no visual effects in Lebanon and he loves it in the US. He goes, "Did you get the call yet?" "What?" "Yes, they're calling people not to come in tomorrow, it's all going to shit. It's over."

At this point, I'm living in a hotel. I had surrendered to living in hotels because you can't sign apartment leases because you never know what country you have to go work in. And even though I'm considered a good visual effects artist and I've been on staff at five or six different companies, you never know how long it's going to last. So you can't buy a house. You can't even rent an apartment. It's just so flimsy. They've totally forgotten Maslow's hierarchy of needs for creativity. Somebody needs to rattle these film executives and say, "What are you *doing*? You have these prize racehorses and you're beating them to death."

After talking to Bobby, I drive in the next morning. I'm walking in from where we park, which is an eighth of a mile because Rhythm had expanded so much. Only the original staff got to park close. But John Hughes parked where we all had to park. He drove a little shitty car. He's the coolest guy ever. He's walking in with me, and says, "Oh, good, you're still here! I put a word in." I say, "Thanks! No one called me, but are you sure I'm still working here?" "If you didn't get a call, you're still here, I'm pretty sure." So I go to swipe my card to let us in the gate. My card doesn't work. He says, "Oh, let me get that." His works. I say, "I don't think I have a job." He says, "No, no, no, let's find out. Let's find out."

So we go in and walk up to the front desk. I'm not on the list of people laid off, but my card doesn't work. I go upstairs and am able to log in. This is what life had become: you didn't know what's going on. How can anyone be creative in this kind of world? They've turned California into a creative dust bowl.

In any event, I can log on to my shot, so that's a good sign! But I don't know what I'm supposed to do. So I just start working on what I was doing when I was there last. And then my line supervisor walks by and says, "You're still here, thank god!" He had to walk around to see which part of his staff was still there so he could put together the schedule for the day. He says, "Just keep working, I guess. I don't know." It was a nightmare. And to make matters worse, the studio was constantly asking for changes.

Recently I've been working at Disney, on *Frozen*. You meet with the director, the decision maker, who says, "I want water to splash up on here and it's going to be cool here," and then they have a guy come and storyboard it out. So you have a blueprint and then you go be creative within that structure. And you do version one, maybe version two, and it's final. You move on to the next thing. It's such a joy compared to dealing with version 120.

That was one of the major problems with *Life of Pi*. We had no contact with Ang Lee. For example, I am working on a sequence where the main character is petting the tiger on the boat. There are twelve shots and they ask me to add rain to the shots, which involves more than just having little dots go by in front of the screen: it's hitting the tiger, it's hitting the boat, it's leaving wet marks running down the sides, making a ripple in the water around it in little jet drops. So you have to come up with these systems that create this rain environment. And you have to do it in layers, and every shot's a different setup. Bill Westenhofer, our visual effects supervisor, is helping me fine tune the rain. We're playing with it together, we're color coding the foreground, middle-ground, and background rain. We make them red, green, and blue so we can see in the picture which rain is doing what. We're making it look cool. We're syncing it and it looks real! The tiger looks so real, so you feel obligated to make whatever you do as good as that tiger, because you'll ruin the shot otherwise.

We get the twelve shots done and they look great. They're ready to be in the movie, so they're going to show Ang Lee. That was right before my mother died and right before the whole show went on hold. When I come back, I'm on a different show because there's nothing to do for *Life of Pi*. It was almost done. But then I walk into this other artist's room one day to talk to him and see this girl I know next to him, working on my rain shots. I ask, "I thought those were final?" She says, "Oh, you didn't hear? Ang Lee saw the sequence and said, 'Why is it raining?'" So they took the rain out and then they showed the new version to Ang Lee and he said, 'Let's put half of it back in.'"

So there you go. That's three months of my time making that rain, fine tuning it, making it just right. And then two months of this girl's time taking it out. And I don't know how long it took to put half of it back in. I didn't work on it. And I'm sure they didn't understand my side because the software we use, Houdini, is like an erector set. I mean, you build stuff from scratch. Every time I've seen an artist pick up another artist's Houdini shot, they usually just go in and start over, because it's like, "I don't know what the fuck he was doing."

Toward the end of the Rhythm & Hues days, it was sad. Just sad. There's a shot in the documentary where John Hughes is being interviewed in his office. He's all choked up and saying, "You know, it was always about the people." That's the real nature of the guy. I would've worked for him forever. He's the reason I kept working when my paycheck stopped. Because I really wanted to see his company make it, one way or the other. A lot of people did.

*Ten days before **Life of Pi** won the Oscar for Best Visual Effects, Rhythm & Hues filed for bankruptcy. What was the impact of that?*

Scott Ross, former CEO of Digital Domain, tweeted, "I had a dream about 500 visual effects artists marching the Hollywood Walk of Fame, protesting the Oscars." I remember reading it, thinking, "Wouldn't that be great." And then I started thinking about it again on the Thursday night before the Oscars. I thought, "You know what? I'm not a sign-carrying guy. I've never pictured myself on strike. I'm an artist. I'm creative. Maybe there's something else I can do." And then I thought, "Let's see how much it costs to have the Goodyear Blimp fly over with a sign." So I went online and it's like $20,000 and it's booked already. But if you Google "Goodyear Blimp signs," right underneath it there's this company called Air Signs. It's a plane with a banner. I'm like, "Whoa, $1,100. Fuck. I can put that on my credit card right now."

So I tweet something like, "Hey I'm having a plane fly over the Oscars with a banner for visual effects. I need some help coming up with a slogan for the banner." A reporter for *Los Angeles Times*, Richard Verrier, calls me immediately, he's so excited. I hang up with him and the *Hollywood Reporter* calls. I hang up with them and *Variety* calls. Everybody was reading my tweets. And they're getting retweeted.

Then VFX Soldier sends me an email: "Heard about the plane. Don't you think that's a little over the top?" And he wasn't making a pun. A lot of people thought it was kind of wacky but it ended up being the spark. A lot of people started emailing me, "Hey, we should still rally." Then the girl who fixed my rain shots, she comes in and says, "I really admire what you're doing. How can I help? Are you doing a rally? I hear you're doing a rally." I wasn't doing a rally; I was going to fly a plane over! But I say, "Let's do a rally. You're good on Twitter, right?" I barely tweeted anything in my life. And she says, "Yes, we'll make up a Twitter thing for the rally and find out what people want to do."

I suggest we meet at Hollywood and Vine, the most famous intersection in the world, right? So I get in my car and drive over to talk to the local police. I say, "We're going to have a rally for the Oscars, is that legal? Do I have any permits to pull, or what?" They say, "No, as long as everyone stays on the sidewalk. And by the way, you can get closer than Hollywood and Vine." I ask, "Can you help us do that?" And I explain it's about jobs, and they say, "Sure, we'll help you." They assigned to us twelve officers practically in riot gear. They were like punctuation marks at the event; it was awesome. It made us look important to have the cops there like that.

We had five hundred artists show up, which was amazing considering there are hardly any artists left in L.A. And it was such short notice, from Thursday night until Sunday. Not only are there hardly any artists left, but there was real fear among those still in town. Back in 2007 I couldn't get anyone to talk to the press, even anonymously. Suddenly we had people willing to have their faces out in public with a sign. We had many issues but it boiled down to the same three things: it's subsidies, it's bidding, and it's a poor creative environment that does not even benefit the studios themselves. We're trying to show them that they are blowing it. Those issues were presented on posters and signs. Some people brought their kids and whatnot. It was a hugely successful rally.

We want to prove that the movies that are the most profitable are the ones where the director directs the visual effects with scrutiny and in real time, with the meter running, as they do on set. If you want to change the lighting setup on set, someone is there telling you how much that decision will cost you. Like *Frozen* or *The Lego Movie* (2014): the director was there, the production was treated like a movie set, you barely get past version two, you're done. You move on. Because everyone knows exactly what they're doing. And there's no bidding because it's an in-house creation.

Are you saying that independent shops should go away? That VFX crews should be internalized within the production structure itself?

That's a very viable model. That's how feature animation works, right? They move from one show to the next. They accumulate and nurture their talent. They keep it in house, under one roof; it's all human interaction. Disney Features, DreamWorks—no outsourcing for their work. They've both tried it, and it wasn't as great as they thought. Not that it won't work or they're not still trying it, but we didn't do *Frozen* that way. They didn't outsource anything on *The Lion King* (1994).

You've talked about living in hotels and you've mentioned mobility. Can you talk about the toll this takes on artists?

I'll tell you about my friend from Lebanon, the one who panicked when he got laid off from Rhythm & Hues. He paid something like $15,000 to get an American visa that could let him stay beyond an employer's visa, and that was inches away from going through when he got the news of his layoff from Rhythm. But the visa went through. Now he's got a life in Los Angeles. A longer-term visa, a car, a lease, a girlfriend. But there's no work. The only place he can go is Canada. So he finally gets his American visa, but he has to move to Canada to work.

At the rally we had at DreamWorks where Obama spoke, there was a woman with her three kids. The kids were holding a sign saying, "Mom, why are we moving to Canada?" It's hard to imagine. I don't have a wife and kids. I don't know how they do it, to be honest with you. I've got a friend in New Zealand. He transplanted the whole family there. They were in a panic. They had a home in Santa Barbara but had to sell it and move to New Zealand. He doesn't even know if he's going to be kept on because he's on an at-will contract. There's no obligation. So he doesn't want to buy a place in New Zealand. He's renting a place. His kids are in school and they make friends, but not too many because they don't know how long it's going to last. There's no stability. Ultimately you've got artists more concerned with their stability than their shot work. You can't do that. It's just a bad recipe for creativity.

Do you have a long-term contract with Disney?

Nobody in our business these days is on anything but an at-will contract. It's become an American standard. From the conversations I've had, I can tell Disney wants to keep me around. So I actually had the confidence to sign a lease for one full year on an apartment. *Frozen* did really well and I know I did great work for it, and I feel a hundred times more creative now than I have in years.

23

Mariana Acuña-Acosta, VFX artist

Mariana Acuña-Acosta has worked in the film industry for more than fifteen years, both in Mexico and the United States, contributing to such notable projects as *Lost* (2004–10) and *Green Lantern* (2011). Besides her VFX credits, she has also trained VFX artists in the latest technologies and served as a consultant to shop managers around the world. Here she discusses the tyranny of iterative VFX work, gender dynamics in the workplace, and the challenges confronting labor activists in the effects industry.

How did you get started in the business?

When I was little I saw the movie *Young Sherlock Holmes* (1985). It had a lot of visual effects and I loved it. One day, I actually went to see it five times. I knew that that was what I wanted to do. I just didn't know how. Then in college I wanted to study something artistic and a new major came up, a bachelor of fine arts in new media, which was 3D animation, video art, net art, programming, and scripting. I thought, wow, this is the future. This is where it's all going.

What school did you attend?

It's called Universidad de las Américas Puebla. Before, it used to be called the American College. It's in a town called Puebla, three hours away from Mexico City.

Why did they start the program?

Back then everyone was trying to make websites, and use email and the Internet in universities. They saw that this had a lot of potential. At the same time, there were exhibits of Internet art and digital art. They were very progressive at that school. I was the only woman in this major and there were only eight of us in total: seven guys and me. We started doing short films together and putting them in film festivals. We also saw that there was a market for it, so we put together a visual effects studio. We would make corporate videos and do digital effects for wedding videos.

After I graduate, a visual artist in New York hires me, so I move to New York and I'm super excited. I just graduated and I'm living in SoHo. I'm thinking, wow, this is a dream come true. I had these amazing computers and I would do all the visual and audio effects for this artist who was exhibiting at the Guggenheim and galleries in Chelsea or wherever. The only problem was that I didn't have any days off. I was working every day from ten in the morning to one in the morning. She didn't think I was allowed to have a day off because I was living in SoHo and that should be payment enough. She paid for all my living expenses in New York in exchange for my work, and that was it. After a year, I got tired of it. It was like living in a golden cage.

Is that even legal?

No, it's not legal. I didn't know. I was young. Obviously I was so excited to be living in New York with this visual artist that I didn't realize the position I had put myself in.

Did you get credit for your work?

No. She didn't want people to know that she didn't actually know how to do all of this. She was friends with one of my teachers in college, who introduced us. I don't regret it, because it was a great experience, but throughout my career I've seen the same sorts of behavior. People take advantage of your willingness to do whatever it takes to do something you love in the visual arts.

After New York you moved back to Mexico, but you decided to move to Mexico City instead of Puebla.

Puebla was great for going to college but work-wise there was nothing I could have done there. So I went to Mexico City and I kept doing my short films and putting them into film festivals. Then I got a job working in production on American films like *Troy* (2004), *The Day After Tomorrow* (2004), and *Nacho Libre* (2006). There were all these movies being shot in Mexico back then, so I started working on set as an assistant, which was awesome. The pay was good and we had per diems. All that was fantastic. I did that for a few years.

In one of the last movies on I worked on, which was *Troy*, I became very good friends with all the visual effects people. I thought, oh, wow, you can do this for a living. So I went to Spain and did a master's degree in new technologies and post-production. I was there for two years. I did film festivals and a lot of other things, like interactive design. Then I realized I needed something even more specialized, so when I won some money from one of my short animated films, I came to L.A. to study at the Gnomon School of Visual Effects. After that, I got my first job as a compositor, which is what I've been doing ever since. When I went back to Mexico, the day after I arrived, I went to the biggest movie studio and I had a job on Monday.

What was it like to work for the studio in Mexico City?

At the beginning, I thought it was really cool, because we had valet parking, free coffee, and good food, but realistically, the pay sucked and because we were hired as freelancers, we didn't get any of the staff benefits like health insurance, pension, or sick days. We had all the responsibilities of being a staff employee, but were hired as freelancers.

Was this a Mexico City studio or a division of a Hollywood studio?

It was a studio in Mexico City, but it handled a lot of overflow work from shops in Hollywood. Oddly enough, I thought it was because we did such fantastic work. Later I found out, no, it's because our studio would underbid all of the studios in L.A. Obviously when you're bidding in Mexican pesos you have an edge. The same was true with working conditions because there are no labor laws in Mexico. The owner could make so much money from one shot that at the end of the day, he could pay all our salaries. The overhead was not that high, so he could underbid everyone in the US. That's why we ended up getting all that overflow work.

How big was the shop?

The studio was pretty big, but the visual effects division was only five people.

What were the other parts of the studio?

They produced films, programs, and commercials. They also acted as an advertising agency. And they provided services for Hollywood productions—lab services like scanning the film and then turning it into data and then doing some of the data wrangling. They also did color conversions. And a lot of motion graphics for television commercials. That division generated a lot of work, but the people who worked there were treated like we were.

How many people were working at this studio?

I would say 150.

That's pretty big. And your group focused on VFX for feature films?

Yes. Between the five of us, we did one movie that had more than four hundred visual effects shots. We worked for three months straight and didn't have one day off.

There seems to be a pattern here.

Exactly.

What was a typical workday like?

It was probably ten in the morning to maybe midnight or one in the morning, seven days a week.

How long did you work there?

For two years. Until I got sick of the working conditions.

What were some of the other challenges when you were working there?

They started to eliminate the perks that we used to think were great. Suddenly we didn't have a valet service. Parking in Mexico City is a pain in the butt because it's so crowded, so basically there was nowhere to park, and they were like, yeah, we don't care. We're reducing costs. They fired all the valet parking people on Christmas Day, I remember that specifically. Then they stopped providing free coffee and closed the cafeteria. They wouldn't raise our salaries at all. Basically they didn't want to do anything for us. At the end, they roped us into a group health insurance plan that we all paid for, but that was so they could get a tax break for it. If you complained, they'd say, there are a lot of people who want to do this, so if you don't, there's the door.

Were you paid hourly or weekly?

Biweekly. A flat rate, no matter how many hours you worked.

Compared to other professions in Mexico City, was it a good wage?

No. I was making way more as a production assistant on Hollywood movies in Mexico.

How much more?

About 35 percent.

Was the studio in bad shape financially?

No, no, no. The owners had a lot of money. All this was just so they could make *more* money. They also pirated all their software. Nothing was legal. They didn't care. One of the owners was this super-privileged rich guy. His parents were European and owned hotels around the world. They didn't care about the human component at all. This shop could have been fantastic, outstanding. It had a great group of employees. It could have been an example of a good company, but they didn't care about the workers.

And it wasn't just the studio owners in Mexico; the Hollywood executives knew what was going on. They knew why they were getting a deal, and they knew about the pirated software. I can send you an article about this shop in Spain where everything is being done illegally, and all the studios know about it. As long as they make their money, they don't care what's going on at the other end. The same thing is going on right now in India, those poor guys are doing all this rotoscoping work under terrible conditions. But does anybody care? No.

What can you tell us about those conditions?

At some of the shops the worker has to pay the company a bonus because the employer says it is giving them a chance to work on a Hollywood movie. These are horrible places where people are working side by side, with bad equipment and terrible hours. VFX Soldier has posted a lot of detailed stories on the conditions for the Indian workers. VFX workers are not treated as artists. They have become human commodities.

Can you elaborate? Why human commodities?

Many films today will have 2,500 shots in them. That's a lot of work for a lot of people. At the end of the day, it doesn't matter what brand it is or who is producing it, as long as it gets produced.

Back to Mexico City . . .

In the spring of 2008, I realized the industry was not that strong in Mexico and I would never be able to expand my knowledge or learn more from the people around me. I knew more than post-producers and supervisors, so I thought to myself, okay, I need to move or I am never going to make any money. If I want better working conditions and a better salary, and if I want to make this a career, I need to move. So in January 2009, I moved to L.A.

How would you compare the working conditions in Los Angeles to those in Mexico City?

In Los Angeles, I started getting paid a reasonable hourly wage, even enough to save some money. And they actually will pay you, no shenanigans. And the more you know, the more you can earn. Still, it was a big surprise to me that there was no health insurance, you didn't have a 401k, and you still had crazy hours. I thought it would be a normal job, but it's the same crazy hours. The pay is definitely better. You can't even compare. Here you get paid hourly and you get overtime, and double overtime on the weekends or if you have to work on a holiday. That would have never happened in Mexico. The problem is that it's hard to keep a job. It's crazy to think that I moved here in 2009 and five of the places where I worked have gone under, bankrupt. I have been offered jobs in Vancouver and in London, but I don't want to move. I have already moved to a lot of places. But that's what many people feel they have to do.

We want to talk about the artistry of visual effects, so let's zero in on a scene you worked on from the very end of the film **Surrogates** *(2009), starring Bruce Willis. Most of the time when we think of visual effects we think of dinosaurs, space travel, or spectacular explosions, but this one is short and seemingly simple. In it, we see a soldier at a computer screen that flashes "Surrogate disabled." Then the shot widens to include Colonel Brendon striding into the command room, grabbing a clipboard, and turning to FBI agents Tom Greer, played by Bruce Willis, and Jennifer Peters, played by Radha Mitchell.*

The reason to talk about this shot is not because it was my most challenging work or my favorite shot or the shot that made me rich or anything like that. Instead, it's because this shot was given to me the first day I started working in L.A. It was also the last shot I worked on in that particular movie, even though I finished more than twenty shots overall. It was a nightmare because I ended up doing ninety-seven versions, but there was no extra compensation for all the work I did. The shot was just part of the workload that my company was responsible for once it signed a fixed-bid contract with Disney.

In this particular shot, all of Bruce Willis from the nose down is a 3D model. I had a production sheet from the studio that told me what to do to his head, like put more hair on it—that was because Bruce Willis decided during the filming to cut his wig, which didn't go over well. Then the nose: they didn't like the way his nose was shaped, so I had to reconfigure the nose. Then the forehead had to be reconfigured as well. Then I had to remove or soften his nasal labial fold. I had to make his cheekbones more pronounced so he could look more manly. That was actually on the notes: "make him more manly." I had to reshape the inside of his nose and reconfigure his nostrils. I also had to push back part of his mouth and make his lips plumper. Then I had to reconfigure his sideburns to make his earlobes prettier. Yes, prettier earlobes. Nothing that you see in the movies or in commercials is natural. Nothing is real. Nothing is real at all.

They also wanted me to change Jennifer's face. I kept saying, she looks pretty. They said no, make her look younger. They kept asking me to change her. I decided they're never going to look back at previous versions so I started telling them, yes, I softened up her cheekbones, or, I softened up her features. They said, "Oh, yes, she looks great." I actually did nothing on her.

Every time I got notes from the studio, I had to do another version. Ninety-seven versions of this shot, in total. It was relentless: add more hair, make less hair, put the hair up, put the hair down, make the cheekbones smaller, make the cheekbones more concave, make the cheekbones stand out, make him blush more, no that's too much blush, plump his lips more, now plump them less. Make his ear smaller, make his ear bigger, make it more manly—whatever that means. Jesus Christ, it was never-ending.

The managers in our office would do Friday cupcakes or throw a farewell party for someone, and everybody would gather together except me. "Ah, Mariana is busy doing version eighty-seven, eighty-eight." It was like a joke. Then at some point the studio people said, "It's not you. It's just that we don't like Bruce Willis's face."

Ninety-seven versions? Who in their right mind would order ninety-seven? If you were shooting principal photography and someone asked for ninety-seven shots, it would cost a bundle. The meter would be running.

Of course. I think that's one of the most unfortunate problems for the VFX industry. There is so much artistry going on behind the scenes after the filming is over. And it's invisible to the eye. Unfortunately, directors, producers, coordinators, people at the studios at the very top don't understand what VFX entails because—

—many of them won't even come into the shop.

Exactly. They think a computer does the work—that you just click a button and it's done. They don't know what it takes.

Once when I was working as a PA [production assistant] on set, it was a night shoot and one of the focus pullers was tired and didn't realize that the shot had gone out of focus. They finished up their work on that scene and then they broke down the set. The following day in dailies they realized that the whole scene was out of focus and it was a million-dollar mistake because they had to rebuild the set and reshoot the scene. It was just insanity and a very costly mistake, right?

Well, that happens with visual effects, but the directors and the studio executives don't realize it. If on a movie set, a director doesn't like the look of the set and says, "Let's change it, let's do Art Deco, everything is going to be orange and three stories higher, and we're just going to move the whole set over here and do a week of night shots," people will say, "You're crazy. That's not happening because it's going to cost too much money." This is what happens during principal photography because the meter is running.

And it's all unionized labor.

It's all unionized labor and you're on the clock. So if you're going to change the set, you have to rebuild the set. You've got a whole bunch of people working on it hour by hour and it's all costing you extra money.

Another reason the studios can make demands on VFX shops is because of the competition and the fixed bidding system. You're not just bidding against Digital Domain, Rhythm & Hues, and the other shops in L.A., but also against shops in other parts of the world. Some of those shops are very specialized with very low overhead. They will be doing wire removal or rotoscoping or whatever, each of which requires different levels of skill and craft. In a way, it's like the fashion industry where people in one shop are sewing on buttons and in another they're assembling pieces of garments and in another they're doing fashion design. All these people are spread around the globe now. Part of that has to do with government subsidies, but part has to do with the fact that you can communicate electronically and you can fly people around the world.

Let's look at this issue from a policy perspective. If we were government officials in Mexico City, it would be our responsibility to create new jobs, especially skilled jobs that pay well and don't pollute. We'd want to build capacity so that Mexico City's VFX companies could compete with others around the world. If subsidies help us do that, what's wrong with it?

From their perspective it seems to make sense, but there's also a lot of exploitation. There are so many people in Mexico City aspiring to these kinds of jobs that the schools can't keep up with demand. So some shops lure young people in with, "You're going to work in Hollywood someday, so work for us for free." You get a lot of students who are working for free in the shops in Mexico City. As for government subsidies, it's the owners who get these rebates. They do some deals with producers and of course for them it's great. I mean, why wouldn't they? It's free money.

Could you speak about your experience as a woman working in an industry largely dominated by men?

It's funny because in Mexico we were mostly women, so I assumed when I moved to L.A. that it was going to be the same. But in my first job, *Surrogates*, I was the only woman for quite a while, among twenty or so men. I was surprised.

You have an interesting perspective on this issue, since, as a software trainer at Foundry, you now travel around to a lot of different VFX facilities.

Yes, I've done training in places like Pixar and Rainmaker. At Pixar I was training forty men and I was the only woman in the room. This was in visual effects. In compositing you'll find a few more women; 3D animators, maybe a little bit more; but lighting and effects and cloth simulation, no.

There are two reasons why it's so male dominated. One is that it's our problem. We women think that men are more technical. I once read that until age four we're exactly the same and then from four on up, it changes: your parents and TV and all these things have an effect. Your parents may give you a little iron or a dress instead of a video game. They don't tell you that you can do computer programming, that's more for your brother. You're supposed to do other things. But not me, I actually loved video games and programming, and my mom was good with all that. I was lucky. Most women come to believe they're not as technical or as talented as men—that they can't, for example, do cloth simulation effects. I've noticed that more and more.

All the VFX tutorials that you see online are done by men. Whatever the software, it doesn't matter. I got pretty tired of that, so I said, "I'm going to do a YouTube channel. It's going to be called VFX Chicks and I'm going to grab matte painters and lighters; I'm going to put together a whole crew of women and I'm going to put them on screen." I actually raised the money for it. I had a camera and a crew. I had the list of the women I was going to approach: fifteen of them, aged twenty-four to fifty-five. We were going to post a tutorial every month: matte painting, compositing, lighting, et cetera. And I was going to pay them, so it wouldn't be for free. It was going to start with a two-minute interview, because you never see faces in the tutorials, but now people are going to see that they're cute, and they'll stay and watch the rest.

I was ready to go. How many of the fifteen women accepted? None. What answers did I get? "I'm going to look fat on camera. I'm going to look ugly." So I said, "Let's skip the two-minute interview at the beginning and go straight into the tutorial." "No, I'm not technical. I've never done a tutorial. I can't talk in front of a camera." "But you're not going to be looking at the camera. It's a recording of the software you use." Still, none of them accepted and they all gave me awful answers, not believing in themselves. Women lack confidence and men are overconfident. It's sad.

Another reason the industry is male dominated has to do with family responsibilities. Let's say you're in your twenties and you get into the industry because you've seen really talented young women between the ages twenty-one and thirty-two. Maybe they're driven and willing to do whatever it takes. But then, what happens? At thirty, you get the baby-craze hormones. You want to have a family and maybe you get married. Then you realize that you're working in an industry with no maternity leave and no one is going to pay your hospital bills. And then there's your work schedule. In every job I've had, you work six to seven days a week, twelve- to fourteen-hour days. If you tell them you're going to work part-time because you're having a baby, they're going to go find someone else. When I was pregnant, I worked in a shop that was very nice: they let me work eleven-hour days instead of twelve, and six-day weeks instead of seven. That's as good as it gets.

True story: One of my friends in Mexico City had a baby, and she brings her baby to the visual effects shop. The baby has a crib there and my friend says, "They're very nice because they let me bring the baby to work." And I'm like, are you insane? She says, "They let me breast-feed in the bathroom." Oh, how nice they let you do that!

A lot of women start in this industry when they're young. They're not thinking about a family or getting married or anything else. But then when you have a baby, you realize the working conditions are not making it easy. So you end up changing industries or becoming a stay-at-home mom and then going back to work later, because most shops are not going to make adjustments.

Do you see the same sorts of gender dynamics in the shops you visit outside the United States?

In the US it's white males between the ages of twenty-two and thirty-five. Obviously you will find producers and VFX supervisors who are in their forties, fifties, and sixties, but for the most part, the artists are going to be young white males. As for the shops I've seen around the world, in Vancouver there are lots of Mexicans and lots of Europeans because they can't find enough people locally. Australian shops also have a lot of Europeans, but again, they are all male and from a certain age group. You hardly see any African Americans. I've never seen an African American woman, for example, and maybe two African American guys. I've never seen an African American supervisor and there are hardly any women who are supervisors or leads. They will always go for a man and they will always go for a white man. Of course, when I started out, I thought there would be more women, but it's a boys' club. And obviously that creates a workplace dynamic that is not comfortable for women. But the same sort of thing happens whenever you work in a place where everyone comes from the same background. It's like a fraternity.

Tell us what you're doing now for Foundry.

I wear multiple hats. I create demo materials for trade shows like NAB and SIGRAPH. I create training videos. I also do customized trainings for studios like Pixar or Blizzard or Rainmaker. I reach out to universities and training facilities in multiple locations like San Francisco, Mexico, Brazil, Portland, Australia, and Vancouver. I talk about the industry and show them the tools, and also go to studios around the world showing them new features and new workloads, gathering feedback, doing technical talks. I also have to be on the forefront of what's going on with technology. For example, now I'm gathering feedback from all the shops about issues that are arising with virtual reality.

That's an amazing list of responsibilities. It sounds like you have the opportunity to peek into many different work environments. Do you think your perspective on the business has changed since you've been doing this job? Have you seen trends emerging that you think are remarkable?

I feel very privileged that I get to see all these different studios around the world and see what the working conditions are like, because it interests me a lot. At the same time, this whole gender issue stands out—whether you're in Australia, New Zealand, Canada, or London. It feels like a sexist and ageist industry. It burns people out. As you become older it's like, man, I'm tired of this. I need to have a job that is going to last more than three months. As you grow older, obviously you want a better pay rate and you're more concerned about benefits, especially health insurance. When you're younger you don't think about those things and you're willing to do whatever it takes to get your foot in the door, whether that's working for free or working seven days a week. Worldwide, it's very ageist and very sexist. I keep seeing the exact same dynamics over and over again. Women get passed over for leadership positions. Sure, they are great for marketing or coordinating or HR but not for the creative, technical, or decision-making positions. A woman would never even be sought for a position like that. That's the same across the globe.

Have you seen a shop that has done a good job of overcoming that gender dynamic? Are there shops where they have made it a priority to incorporate the creative energies of women?

Yes. It can be done. I can think of three different shops here in L.A. where they make it a point to hire more women and get women in technical roles.

What are the three shops?

One of them is Sony Pictures Imageworks, another is Ingenuity Studios, and then there's Luma Pictures, which is based in Australia and also here in Los Angeles. It can be done if there's a commitment to doing it.

Let's talk about labor organizing among VFX artists. Given what you've described, why haven't people formed a union?

I remember I used to think, "At least I'm going to get my name in the credits." But even so, VFX workers are treated differently. When you work on a film set and you're unionized, your name *has* to go in the credits. Not so for VFX. The reason why the visual effects credits come after the people who pick up the trash—no offense to them, they do a great job—but the reason we come all the way at the end is because we don't have a union. So guess what? If the producer says, "We ran out of roll and so we'll cut out the three hundred VFX credits," it's not like anybody cares. Who are you going to turn to because your name isn't on the credits?

People are finally talking and they're organizing. They're talking not only in Hollywood, but around the world. So the way to think about this is that a lot has changed over the past five years and it can get better, but people have to commit. VFX can be a wonderful industry to work in. We just need to change it.

24

Daniel Lay, VFX artist

Daniel Lay worked as a VFX artist for more than a decade, specializing in hair simulation on films like *Tron: Legacy* (2010) and *X-Men: First Class* (2011). Lay is best known for starting the blog VFX Soldier, where for years he anonymously discussed the problematic working conditions in the industry. Besides describing his work, Lay offers in-depth criticism of production subsidies and offers proposals for changing the ways the industry operates.

How did you get started in the VFX industry?

My first job was as a technical assistant with Sony Imageworks, which is one of the biggest shops in the VFX industry. I worked from four in the afternoon to two in the morning for about two years straight, watching renders from various artists. Eventually I got to know a lot of people and got to work on a little film called *I Am Legend* (2007), which became a huge success. That boosted my career to move on to places like DreamWorks Animation, where I worked on *Monsters vs. Aliens* (2009) and *Shrek Forever After* (2010), which my mother calls the second-worst *Shrek* she ever watched. And then I moved to Digital Domain, where I specialized in hair and cloth for a lot of characters. I was kind of the hair guru there. I was part of a team of software engineers working on proprietary tools. You can see some of that work on *Tron: Legacy* and *G.I. Joe: The Rise of Cobra* (2009). I had some pretty good jobs, but a lot of my friends got the short end of the stick, which is what compelled me to begin blogging about problems in the industry.

Walk us through a typical workday.

On a film like *Tron: Legacy*, for example, I would come in early in the morning at Digital Domain for dailies and team meet-ups. I would get a list of shots that they would want completed that week or even that day. My goal would be to pick which shots I thought I could finish as soon as possible and try to get director comments and also supervisor comments. There is usually a chain of supervisors, producers, and directors who are all going to have some input. And a lot of them I never met or even saw. I usually just got a list of notes and spent my day working through the list. There'd also be a bit of triage where I would be working between departments, so that could affect my schedule. There is a pipeline of people who put this work together, so I try to get those assets and finish them off so I can pass them on to the next department.

A typical day involves a lot of meetings and then the grind of trying to complete the work, which can be technically difficult. Things can change quickly, too. You might be thinking, oh, I'll be able to get out at around seven or eight in the evening, but then there's this last-minute note or this last-minute shot that they want you to complete. All of a sudden you're pulling an all-nighter. That happens quite often.

How many shots are artists responsible for at one time?

It depends on the complexity, but generally speaking, I can say I've had situations where I run from between five to ten shots in a given week. On *Tron*, where I was responsible for a lot of the hair animation for the characters, I might get a lot of shots that are, "Well, this character is way in the background and only needs a little bit of movement." That shot will run quickly, so I put it together and run it and try to get it rendered. While it's rendering, I'll work on another shot that I think will be technically difficult because it involves a lot of hand animation or a lot of changes in the room.

When does the workday typically start?

Typically, they like people to get in around nine in the morning, or half past. If you have a pretty good day, you're out by seven. But if it's going to be a crazy production, you can see yourself going until nine or ten.

You mentioned that you were lucky to work at fairly good shops throughout your career.

I had niche expertise, the hair expert, which is a unique skill set. That allowed me a bit of leverage to push back on some of the typical problems that a lot of artists run into, such as unpaid overtime or really late hours. The supervisors didn't want to burn me out. Whereas if you're a traditional compositor, you're just given shots to grind away on, and then after the production they let you go. So you might work for a few weeks and then you're trying to find your next job. I was usually a staff employee. While I write about labor problems in the industry, I am talking about the problems for the vast majority of visual effects workers.

Tell us briefly about your skill set. What made your work so distinctive and valued?

When I was at the University of California, San Diego, I was studying visual arts, but I saw that there was a technical aspect that was going to be needed in the future, so I started studying computer science and learned to work with code and solve some of the technical problems. I'm a bit of a software engineer and an artist. That was how I ended up doing hair.

When you're watching a shot, nobody notices hair. An animator or lighter manipulates the total look of what you see in the shot and is responsible for every element. I was involved in just this one little element, so it didn't have a lot of cachet, but it helped me find a lot of work, and that's what made me say that I was a lucky guy. When I first started at Sony Pictures Imageworks, there was a huge need for hair and cloth artists for films like *Beowulf* (2007) and *I Am Legend*, and they just couldn't find the people. So I was able to move up very quickly.

How do visual effects artists get associated with a specific technique like hair or cloth?

The biggest mistake anybody can make coming out of school is to say, "I am going to be an expert on just this one thing." Usually what you do is start off very broad. I tell a lot of young artists that they should work on commercials where you have to run the whole gauntlet. You have to do animation. You have to do lighting. You have to touch every little element. It's so fast. Once you gain that expertise and you move on to bigger and bigger projects, they are looking for people who specialize in things, and that's when you get your foot in the door. They can't find the expert, but they see that you've touched on this aspect before, and they'll give you a few shots to test you out. If you're okay, you get your first feature film credit and it goes on your demo reel and then you are considered an expert. It's not something that you go to school for.

Let's talk about the artistic dimension of your career. Of all the films you've worked on, do you have a favorite?

Some of the best work I've done was on *Tron: Legacy*. As you know, it starred Jeff Bridges, who was in his early sixties at the time, and they wanted a young version of him, called Clu, to be the villain. It was very important that we had a real, life-size actor, which meant that we replaced basically everything from the neck up with CG effects. Digital Domain did work on *The Curious Case of Benjamin Button* (2008), where they took Brad Pitt and made him look like a very old person. With *Tron* we had to make Jeff Bridges into a very young person. We actually developed our own set of tools with a huge software development team. We had a whole team of people working on just his head: software developers, shader writers [VFX artists who create shading and texture], and others, figuring out how to get the light working with the hair correctly. Some of the shots are just a few seconds long, but I would work a good month or two on them. Multiple iterations. A lot of craftsmanship. A lot of technical work that needs to be done by a lot of very talented people. If you don't notice our work, we did our job.

Some of these shots go through dozens and dozens of versions. Why? Who in their right mind would order so many changes?

It may sound expensive, but it's not. At least it's not for the studio, because they don't have to pay for the changes. It's a fixed bid. They don't have to worry about change orders. To make an analogy, when UC Santa Barbara needed to build the Pollock Theater, they probably went to a contractor and asked, how much is it going to cost for this building? The contractor made blueprints and they all agreed on the design, the textures, the wood, everything, before they got started. If any of the elements are changed during construction, there's a change order. Maybe you want to make it two stories instead of one. Well, that wasn't in the contract or the blueprint. We have to agree on how much it will cost to change the design and the contract.

In the visual effects industry, it's different. "Make me a tiger." Okay, well, is there a blueprint for what kind of tiger you want? What stripes does it have? How long is its hair? Its teeth? How does it move? Those are all moving and changing parts, and there is no blueprint.

With the fixed bidding system you have a studio saying, make me a tiger. Digital Domain says it can make it for $12 million. Rhythm & Hues says it will do it for $10 million. Oh, wait, there's a company in the UK, Double Negative, that says it can make the tiger for $12 million, but the bid comes with a 25 percent government rebate for the producers. That means the studio can get it for $9 million. So the studio says, let's do the work in London. You have a lot of these subsidies, which are a great deal for the studios, but the VFX shops are all working from a fixed bid that they make on a project with a very vague blueprint.

The studio is saying, make me a tiger for this amount of money. It's almost like you're jumping in a taxi and saying, take me down to the Santa Barbara airport, but along the way you get to change directions. Can we drive along the coast? Go down by the zoo? Will you wait here while I take a walk on the wharf? But you're not going to change the price at all. It's still going to be $10. That's a key reason why the visual effects industry has suffered, because of these fixed bids.

You mentioned subsidies, which brings us to the issue of globalization. Besides subsidies, what are some of the other issues raised by globalization?

Five or six years ago the *Huffington Post* did an article saying that VFX work is being sent to places like India because computers have made it so easy to ship this kind of work around the world. I checked around the industry and what I found was that the simple work, what we call rotoscoping and paint, was mostly being sent to India, but it gets very complicated once you move above that level to simulation effects like hair or character animation. A lot of that wasn't being sent to India. The reason why is because it's hard to produce high-quality elements in the low-cost labor regions. They've been trying and they've been improving, but it hasn't come through.

That's when I started the VFX Soldier blog, saying the work was actually going to very expensive places: the UK, Canada, Australia, and New Zealand. I was getting offers to go to New Zealand and I would say, why is the work going there, where it's more expensive? The reason why is because the government there was offering a huge kickback to the producers. So let's say I'm a producer with a project that would cost $10 million to do here in Los Angeles, but the government in British Columbia says it will give me a rebate of 60 percent on each person's salary. I will essentially get a $6 million rebate if I spend $10 million doing the work in Vancouver. And before you even get that check, you can use the rebate as collateral to go to a bank in Canada for financing on your film. That's liquid cash.

What made you decide to start VFX Soldier?

Even though things were comfortable for me, a long-term gig in this industry isn't actually so long. I had the luxury of working three years at Sony Pictures Imageworks, three years at DreamWorks Animation, and three years at Digital Domain, and I only got laid off once. Yet even in my situation, the future was always a question mark. And for a lot of compositors and a lot of animators it's much worse. They have to find new work every few months or so.

On top of that, the competition between VFX companies is so fierce that they keep going bankrupt and people lose their jobs. Why is it that these blockbuster films like *Avatar* (2009) are making so much money, yet the people who create the visual effects, which are considered to be the big stars of these films, are not only not getting their fair share, but actually being treated quite poorly relative to movie actors or directors or anybody else in the industry?

A lot of people started saying computerization was the culprit because now all the work can be done in India. I started my blog—as a soldier in the trenches—to say, that is not what's really happening. The big threat to the industry is not cheap labor in Asia, but actually subsidized labor that is creating a cycle of displacement. I predicted that, even if you were a really good artist, you wouldn't be able to escape the effects of government subsidies. When I look back at the predictions I made in 2010, most of them turned out to be true. You can see it in some of the hacked Sony documents that verify a lot of things I was saying about the industry.

Describe some of the smoking guns in the Sony documents that confirmed your suspicions and predictions.

When I was writing in 2010, I would point to documents from people in the financial industry that would say, "Look, there is going to be a 10 to 15 percent rise in labor rates in places like India and the quality isn't going to rise as fast." And I predicted that we would not be in India for very much longer.

The Sony hack documents revealed many of the executives talking about closing Sony Pictures Imageworks India, a division they opened in 2006. The Sony hacks were pointing out that there was a 10 to 15 percent rise in labor rates every year, so it wasn't cheap anymore to do work there. The quality of the work they could get in places like Canada was better and more cost effective because the government was paying 60 percent of the salaries for people working in the visual effects industry.

But there are a lot of other examples, too. For example, the documents show wage rates that make it possible for workers to know where they stand when they negotiate with an employer.

Are you saying that other than internal studio documents, there was no reliable information about wage rates?

That's correct. There's a company called Croner that does a lot of wage surveys. They go to companies individually and say, "Would you like to participate in our wage survey? We won't reveal the individual wages that each company pays, but we will give you this study that shows baseline wages and best-in-class wages." So, they collect information from the executive level all the way down to the low-level, beginning technical director level. It can be a very useful tool for human resources managers to figure out compensation packages for employees. But then the unions wanted to get involved and asked to buy that information too, so they could adequately negotiate rates for our workers. I believe that Croner said no. I think they were worried that if they got the unions involved, all of their other customers would not want to participate. It's not in their interest to share any of that information with workers. This is some of the information we found in the Sony documents.

Why was VFX Soldier anonymous?

It was actually much more innocent than it seemed. A lot of people thought it was anonymous because there was somebody nefarious behind the blog trying to go after certain companies or something like that. That wasn't the case. I wanted to give the idea that this was somebody in the trenches, and that this wasn't about me. I didn't want my position in the industry or how things were going for me to dictate what I was writing about on the blog. But my anonymity also was an effective tool. It caused certain companies to wonder, "Hm, is VFX Soldier working at my company? If so, I should be careful about what I'm doing and saying, because I don't want it to end up on this blog."

The blog provided a cover for me and others to blow the whistle. The comments section became a place to share information. It gave people a place to let others know what was happening in their shop. People in the industry would rather come to my blog than go to their supervisors or human resources director. That's kind of sad. People trusted somebody who was anonymous talking about the problems in the industry more than the people they worked with daily.

So partly it's an issue of trust, but it also seems like many people fear retribution. Is there a culture of fear in the VFX business?

Obviously when people talk about unionization, some people respond skeptically in part because artists tend to be individualistic and competitive. There is also concern that there might be some nefarious issue or event that could work against their personal interest. And there is a culture of intimidation in the industry. It is similar to football where there is this jock-like mentality: some people openly boast about how many hours they work or the fact that they are willing to move overseas or sacrifice anything for these projects. Anyone who doesn't think that way isn't considered part of the team. There's an attempt to marginalize people who think rationally about work in this industry.

So that's one kind of fear. Another has to do with subsidies. In places like Vancouver or New Zealand, people are threatened by any attempt to shed light on how subsidy programs work. They know they're not sustainable, but they know in the short term, they benefit. So they try to instill fear that getting rid of subsides will destroy their industry or that it will lead to all the work going back to California. There is a lot of fearmongering, and that has led to a huge amount of distrust in the industry, which makes it hard to solve the problems that would be relatively easy to manage if people came together.

You mentioned a football mentality. Do you think it's useful to compare what's going on with VFX to the controversy over concussions in the football industry? It took so long for the NFL to acknowledge the problem even though everybody knew about it. And now everybody acknowledges the problem, but they don't know what to do about it, because it's so bred into the institution itself.

Absolutely. I am a former football player. I remember wearing T-shirts that said "Pain is temporary, pride is forever," and that is true of visual effects. A lot of people are too proud of what they do, and it's treated as the gospel: You have to work on *Star Wars*. You should not doubt anything about the movie *Star Wars*. You're working on the visual effects, and it's a privilege to be here. You just have to accept things. You should be very proud to work in this industry.

When you make it seem like it's a privilege, any concern about pain or unpaid overtime or anything like that gets swept under the rug. In football it's very much the same. If you're an NFL player, it's a privilege. I know people who made it into the NFL, and the reality is that your average NFL football player only plays for three years, and you don't get the pension unless you're in there for five years. For those players who fall in that donut hole, which is many of them, they don't have very good careers, and many of them have lifelong debilitating injuries. Of course, the amount of money being paid in the NFL is much larger than in VFX. And it's not the same; I mean, obviously we're talking about physical injuries in the NFL. But in the visual effects industry, there are similar situations regarding the way workers are treated and the problems they go through.

So what are the possible solutions? What is ADAPT's approach to these issues? [ADAPT, or the Association of Digital Artists, Professionals, and Technicians, filed a lawsuit to levy a financial penalty against studios that benefit from production subsidies. Daniel Lay and Scott Ross dissolved the entity and dropped the case in January 2015 due to burdensome legal expenses.]

Subsidies are a huge problem, causing a lot of price distortion in the industry. That's the reason a lot of companies went out of business here in California. Do any of you have Nike shoes on right now? They're probably made in Vietnam, where the government offers big subsidies. New Balance, which is based in the United States, makes shoes here, and they are being injured by those subsidies. What did they do to alleviate that injury? They went to a federal court in New York that allows for countervailing duties to be placed on subsidized goods coming from overseas. They invoked anti-subsidy laws that effectively negate the effect of those government subsidies.

The visual effects industries could do something similar. If $10 million of visual effects work earns a $6 million subsidy in British Columbia, the US government could levy a $6 million duty on the imported work, essentially negating the subsidy. So it disciplines the system. There's a process to do that, but it has never been done before for electronic media like ours. I flew out to Washington, DC, about two years ago and met with a law firm. We formed ADAPT, and we're looking to challenge these international subsidies for visual effects in the court of international trade.

Let's say you are successful, and countervailing duties are applied on these subsidized productions. What's to stop North Carolina from coming up with its own subsidies?

Great question. I get that asked a lot. Our countervailing duty effort only affects international subsidies. So let's say that North Carolina says, well, we want to get those visual effects workers here, we're going to offer that same 60 percent rebate. Our proposed law wouldn't apply. But what have we seen with the state subsidies in Florida and New Mexico? They are incredibly volatile and they mostly focus on principal photography, which only lasts a couple of months. Even in states that have subsidies, there are still a lot of debates. *House of Cards* (2013–ongoing) was lured into shooting in Maryland because of huge rebates there, but now they are threatening to move somewhere else because the state government is putting a cap on the program or somebody else is offering more. A lot of states are questioning whether or not they should continue. It has become volatile for the producers. Their job is to manage risk. So it's great to go to a place like New Mexico or Louisiana for principal photography, but effects are different.

For the visual effects industry, projects usually last one to two years and you need to move a huge number of people around. So you need the backing of a national government in order to maintain the effectiveness of the subsidy, because otherwise it could get capped or removed while you're in the middle of a project. I should add, there is not much [feature film] visual effects work in US locations outside of California. Some, but not much—not as substantial as the UK, British Columbia, or New Zealand. And the reason why is because of this volatility. If you move your production there, you may get a subsidy one time, but then after that you're going to have to move again.

What about the flip side of the argument? Looking at it from the perspective of New Zealand or the UK, what's wrong with subsidizing work that will help to build their capacity in creative industries?

I think it's great for the short term. A lot of the international readers of VFX Soldier say, you know what, I love these subsidies. I get to live in the UK. I get to live in New Zealand. But what they soon find is that, oh, somebody else is offering more money. Even though producers may be getting subsidies in New Zealand, they'll say, either you increase them or we're going to make your workers move somewhere else. So effects workers are affected by what I call a cycle of displacement in the industry. Even if you play this game—let's say you move to British Columbia, you move your family there—and you think it's great, but then suddenly Montreal is matching the BC subsidy and on top of that they offer a 25 percent subsidy on nonlabor costs. Now they are actually losing a lot of work in Vancouver and the jobs are shifting to Montreal. And that's the key here: we're not against subsidies. If you have, let's say, a farm industry in your country and you want to subsidize your own farming industry, that's fine. It's the causing of injuries to other industries in other countries that is the issue.

The irony with VFX subsidies is, if you're in the UK and you think you're building your own industry there, you're not. You're actually just trying to get US studios to do the work there, and they will probably leave the minute those subsidies are gone. They leave the minute you offer one penny less. So you're not building a sustainable industry. Look at places that have built their industry. In India, for example, they are doing visual effects for their own films in India. And they haven't done it with subsidies. They've been able to do it with just the content that they create there.

You're saying that imported VFX shots are content, but the studios are saying that they are buying services that are conveyed electronically, not content. On the other hand, they want copyright protection for their films and television shows that are recorded and distributed electronically.

This is one of the big issues. Countervailing duties can only be placed on goods, not services. And the argument is, well, electronic signals coming through the Internet are not goods because they're not tangible. I can't drop one on your foot and send you to the hospital. A few weeks ago I got a phone call from the law firm saying, hey, guess what? There was an obscure patent infringement case concerning 3D models of dental braces that were being created in Pakistan and sent here via the Internet. The judge wanted to know, Are these data? Are they goods? And does this court have jurisdiction over that? If it is a good, they do. If not, they don't. Well, the judge asked for public consultation. Who shows up? The Motion Picture Association of America. And they argued that encoded data are goods. Why did they say that? Because they want to protect their line on piracy of digitally encoded versions of films and television shows. So, interestingly, we may be able to use the most powerful tool the MPAA has created, their antipiracy laws, to end their subsidies. It's ironic. It's sort of a storybook ending. We may be able to use Sauron's most powerful weapon against him.

Where do things currently stand with the subsidy issue?

It used to be that the vast majority of US states were offering huge film subsidies. They are starting to scale those back significantly. Louisiana offers huge subsidies for the film industry, and they are taking a look at it because of the amount of the debt their government is accumulating. Even in Canada, we've had two provinces—Quebec and Ontario—announce already this year that they are going to cut back their subsidies. There are smaller provinces that have virtually ended them. There is a big debate right now in Nova Scotia about ending the film subsidy there because it just costs too much. A while back, I think Saskatchewan ended their film subsidies when they realized that one side is making a commitment for long term—the government wants to have the studios there for life—but the studios are in it strictly for money, if they get a better deal elsewhere, they're gone. It's like a bad marriage.

Governments are rethinking this stuff. Nevada is a good example. They offered film subsidies for movies like *Paul Blart: Mall Cop 2* (2015). Then they started talking to Elon Musk of Tesla and realized, "We can offer the same amount of subsidies to Tesla and they will build a factory where they would have to stay." So they decided to cut the film subsidies and used some of that money for Tesla. On the other hand, the big boys—New Zealand, the UK, Vancouver, British Columbia—have been trying to increase their subsidies. It's going to get interesting as we go forward: as things start changing, as deficits get larger, at some point governments are going to have to say, "We can't keep cutting teacher pay and health care while giving $300 or $400 million to a film industry that doesn't make any commitment to us."

What happened to the countervailing duty suit?

The law firm we were going through was in Washington, DC, and they were doing great work. We talked to folks at the Department of Commerce, and they were receptive. This was going to be about a one- to two-year process. The next step was to get funding to pay the law firm to do the work. We tried approaching the California State Legislature for funding, because this past year they passed a $300 million subsidy bill to try to lure some of the industry back. I testified in numerous meetings, saying, "You can take a fraction of that amount and pay for our legal effort and you could end the game completely." They gave us verbal support but said they would not be able to give us financial support. Given how small the industry is, and given the amount of money that we needed, and the fact that a lot of people were unemployed, there simply wasn't the funding there. So we knew where we wanted to go, we had the vehicle to drive there, and we needed people to pitch in for gas money, but unfortunately, we just didn't get enough gas in the tank.

If you had won, it seems that the implications would have been enormous.

If you look at the Sony hack documents, there were emails between the head legal honcho at Sony, the MPAA, the Sony executives, and the executives at other studios. At the end of one of the emails an attorney says, frankly, the VFX guys did a good job turning this one around on us. They were concerned. They were in a real bind. I was already being invited by MPAA officials to Paramount studios to initiate some talks. They were concerned about what we were doing with the California subsidy bill AB 1839. They were concerned about us already getting wording in there that was supportive of our effort. They were afraid that if this were to snowball, we would have had a chance to negotiate something with them.

How much would it have taken to keep going forward?

At the end of the day, we were looking at something that was going to cost $1 million over two years. This is the first time I'm revealing this publicly. You're talking about a top-notch law firm working about two years to solve this problem, but unfortunately, we couldn't make it there.

Isn't there a deep-pocketed angry angel out there?

Fund-raising is very difficult. I have learned such incredible lessons about non-profit fund-raising. You have to be an expert to do it, and the amount of money that you get at the end of the day is often very little. You also have to remember that for me there were personal costs. I was doing this pro bono. I was flying to places like Washington, DC, New York, San Francisco, and Vancouver to lobby for this. Scott Ross and I talked about it, and we talked about it with the ADAPT team, and we said, look, the personal costs are going to be too high for us to get to the finish line. It's unfortunate. I wish we could have done it.

25

Steve Kaplan, union official

Steve Kaplan worked for years as a visual effects artist on feature films, TV shows, and commercials. He then became an organizer for the Animation Guild [IATSE Local 839] in charge of the animation and visual effects sectors. He recruits new members, leads organizing drives, and educates existing members on the value of unionization. In this conversation, Kaplan discusses the distinctive challenges of organizing VFX workers.

You work for Local 839 now, but you started your career in visual effects.

Yes, I was part of a five-person team working on the production of *The Sorcerer's Apprentice* (2010). We were answering directly to John Nelson, the visual effects supervisor for the production, heading up a small in-house team.

Around that time I got my first iPhone. I started listening to podcasts. One of the first podcasts I subscribed to was called *fxguide*. I heard a guy named Jeff Heusser interview Steve Hulett, who talked about a union for visual effects artists. And I found that intriguing. Back when I was working for the Unified Film Organization we had talked about working under a union, but we all kind of scoffed and laughed at the idea since we were bulletproof twentysomethings who did what we did. No one gave it much thought. But when I heard that interview, and now being in my late thirties, I started to think more seriously about it.

Why didn't we all have health care? Why didn't we all have some kind of representation? And then Lee Stranahan's open letter to James Cameron came out just before *Avatar* (2009) was released. We all felt it would get the Oscar for visual effects. Lee wrote this long open letter saying, "Look, if you are going get the award for visual effects, and visual effects essentially is the reason everybody goes and sees film these days, why don't you give us a nod? If the effects artists are not going to get good conditions, if they are going to work themselves to death, if they are not going to have health care, how about you give them a pat on the back?"

But the conversation kind of died right there—most of my friends and certainly the four other people in the little FEMA trailer that we were in at Jerry Bruckheimer's editorial facility didn't want to talk about unionization. About that time the job was winding down, so I started to look for my next gig. I found this place that was looking for an organizer. I thought, I could at least apply and say I tried. I didn't think I was going to get it. There were about sixty people applying. They whittled it down to ten, and called me back for a second round of interviews. Two weeks later I got the call. The job was with the Animation Guild, but they wanted to hire someone to organize VFX workers.

Tell us about your job.

In broad strokes, my job is to organize animation and visual effects workers at facilities of all sizes. If work is being done in and around the Southern California area, which is our geographic boundary, we feel it should be union represented. So we identify places where work is being done without a union contract and then figure out if we have support from those working there in order to get a union contract. Typically that takes the form of identifying people at nonunion studios who have worked in union shops before. If you work in animation, chances are you carry an 839 card or did at some point in time because you inevitably pass through one of the studios that we have a contract with.

Starburns Industries, which is down the road, just signed a union contract. When Starburns started to do animation work in addition to their typical stop-motion work, we found out about it because somebody sent me an email saying, "I'm at Starburns now and I would love to have my union health and pension plan again. What would it take?" My first response is to get a crew list. Then you reach out to people. You gauge the level of interest. If there is a high level of interest, then the steps are pretty well defined by the Wagner Act of 1935. We distribute cards and gather signatures. If we get enough support through the cards we then knock on the door and say, "Hello, we are the union. The majority of your shop supports us. Do you want to talk with us?" If they tell us to go kick rocks, then we go to the government [National Labor Relations Board, NRLB], which then directs the company to recognize our showing of support and allow a representation election. If we win the election then we put a committee together and we sit and negotiate a contract. And if the negotiating committee and the employer are able to come up with a contract, then we go back to the unit and get the contract ratified.

How long does that process take?

Nick CG took five years. Now, it is important to note that Nick CG is a computer graphics unit inside Nickelodeon, which is in fact a union studio. So how long would it take to organize visual effects? I get this question all the time. My flippant-sounding but actually quite accurate answer is that it will take as long as the visual effects artists want it to take. When Rhythm & Hues was in its death throes we had a ton of people send us cards. We easily had well over the percentage we needed to feel comfortable going to the company and starting the process, but by that time Rhythm was in bankruptcy.

What were we going to do with that? There was no way we could make a contract with a company that was about to fold. So that hurt us in the sense that we had to then tell these people, "You came to us a little late." But at the same time, it's a pretty unique story. John Hughes's company was so artist-centric, and people felt such an emotional tie to it, that even when John said, "If you guys want a union, bring them in and I will talk to them," they said, "No, John. We love you. We are not going to do it." You have to realize that the attitude toward unionization in and around the United States is very, very cold. Just take a look at the numbers. The percentage of union membership in the United States in the 1970s was approximately 27 percent. Now it is approximately 8 percent. We are seeing a massive decline in what people understand a union to be, and that's part of the reason for the decline.

Do you think it's different in the animation business? Do those workers have more experience with a union and therefore more confidence in union representation? Does that make them different from visual effects artists?

I don't think there's much of a difference between the two. Overall, being a member of a union doesn't mean much to people today. I think it's because they don't understand the benefits. When you ask somebody what the benefit is of unionization they will show you their health card. But nobody understands the power of the collective voice. Nobody understands the intangible benefit of having those protections. It is unfortunate, but now in order to instill these you have to give a history lesson. And that makes you seem like a schoolmarm, rapping people on the knuckles, trying to tell them, "Hey, this is good for you." The biggest challenge to unionization in the animation world, and doubly so in the visual effects world, is that you have to answer, "Why union?" And you have to do it in a way in which you are not berating or coming across like a used-car salesman.

You need to talk about the collective voice and the power to make change. But it is not like the union would have been able to stop Rhythm from dying. Rhythm died because John overextended himself in an industry that is asking people to overextend themselves. Rough Draft [another nonunion shop] survives because Claudia Katz [the firm's executive vice president] is a shrewd businessperson.

The artists at Rough Draft may not understand that being a part of a union means being able to keep these tangible benefits as you float around the industry, because plenty of people come and go from Rough Draft. What 839 wants to offer is a seamless cloak of benefits—that is, to make it possible for artists to move from studio to studio and maintain the same health and pension plans. Simply having a pension plan, an actual "defined benefit" pension plan—you don't see those anymore today.

The animation industry is in fact mostly union, or at least the places that most artists aspire to go: DreamWorks, Disney, Cartoon Network, Nickelodeon. But again, Rough Draft keeps a core staff of people and instills this culture of belonging within the studio and treats their people well. So because of that, you don't see a union at Rough Draft. Organizing small nonunion studios becomes difficult because people feel a sense of allegiance. Titmouse was very difficult to organize because Chris Prynoski is such a huge personality and he comes from Disney. He is a kid at heart, a big animated character himself. When you work for him you are like, "I love Chris Prynoski, he is so cool, and he makes these great films, so why would you want to attack Chris like that?" It's a disconnect. People think if they band together with their colleagues and form a union they're attacking their employer, and their city. People just don't understand the value of unionization.

You're making an argument for the union as a foundational package of benefits and protections. Yet in the visual effects business the workers you're trying to organize are deeply worried about the fortunes of the companies they work for.

It becomes very, very difficult to un-muddy the line. I think there is an extreme distinction between the visual effects artist working for major studios and the visual effects studios working for the producers. Scott Ross disagrees with me on this, but I don't feel that unionization means the death of the independent visual effects shop. Scott does, because Scott worked for Industrial Light & Magic (ILM) and then Digital Domain. He saw how much the health and pension contributions cost. Therefore, he says, that burden would crush the shop. I counter that by saying, "How can music videos, commercials, and low-budget features survive with union contracts?" As a union, we need to be willing to adjust the contract to the conditions of the company we're working with. The goal and purpose of the union is to protect the member, but not at the expense of running their company into the ground.

Back in the late 1960s all the union had to offer the employer was the Hollywood basic agreement. You simply signed that. But then the entertainment paradigm started to change. The basic contract was written in the 1940s and 1950s. Things changed and unions needed to adjust the agreement. Overall, it is better to be doing covered work than non-covered work. So let's figure out a way to make it work.

We have three tiers of budget that are considered before somebody signs the basic. And if those tiers aren't met, then you have production agreements. We have agreements for feature films, movies of the week, music videos, and commercials. All of these agreements now take different budget concerns into consideration and they make adjustments for what the workers want. Is there a pension contribution at all? Are you a part of our Cadillac health plan or are you part of this other health plan that still offers health coverage but at a lower cost and therefore might be a better fit for particular shops?

I think that model can easily translate into visual effects. If you take a look at how the IATSE National Benefits Funds are structured, it already is geared toward visual effects. It is geared for the "day player." It is geared for people who work outside the coasts and in the middle of the country where maybe costs are down but benefits are still needed. We can easily bring that into the visual effects world and make it work. So I reject Scott's notion that an $8 per hour, per employee contribution is going kill the visual effects shop. Sony Imageworks can afford the Motion Picture Industry Pension and Health plan. Could Joe VFX, down the street? No. Joe VFX is battling with Imageworks, or is trying to get episodic work, or is competing against subsidies in Canada. It may have a core team of six to ten people who render through an Amazon service so Joe doesn't have to buy his own render farm. He is making it work and we want him to succeed. That is where the flexibility of today's union comes in, and yet very few people are aware of that aspect.

Who are the key players in the VFX business right now?

Scott Ross says eight shops in the world are capable of doing what he calls A-level work: Imageworks, ILM, Motion Picture Company (MPC), Weta, Framestore, and a few others. For 839 to organize them is almost impossible at this point because none of them are here in Southern California. If you are a big player, you are in Vancouver or somewhere that's offering attractive subsidies.

So who is left in L.A.? Digital Domain went through bankruptcy. Rhythm & Hues went through bankruptcy.

But they're still around. They went through bankruptcy and then were sold. Rhythm & Hues is now owned by the holding company that owns Prana Studios.

They have approximately eighty people [down from more than five hundred] in the El Segundo office who are still bidding for work.

Digital Domain is alive. They have approximately three hundred to four hundred people in Vancouver who do feature work. Ed Ulbrich made the announcement that Digital Domain was never going to do feature work in Los Angeles again and they were going to vacate that facility come hell or high water. That decision was made because of subsidies. Originally their plan was to expand their Playa del Rey facility where commercials are done, and add feature work. But instead they moved most of that work to Vancouver, where it's subsidized. They did keep some feature workers here; I want to say 150 or 160 people have been shoehorned into the Playa del Rey facility. So Digital Domain is still around, it is still in Los Angeles, but it mostly does commercials here.

There are a range of smaller shops, like Zoic, that remain in L.A. but aren't doing feature work here. Most of their revenue in L.A. comes from commercials, maybe some episodic television, but even that has moved to their offices in Vancouver.

Lower-tiered mom-and-pop shops are opening up all the time in L.A. I think that what is left in Southern California are either houses with roots too deep or wills too strong to move. And what they are doing is finding a way to make it work. VFX is not just for feature films or TV. It's in Internet, mobile, and magazine art. In addition to media clients, it has industrial, military, medical, and education clients. Visual effects and visualization are being done in a lot of industries. I mean, we are not seeing the end of it here in Los Angeles. Plus, the technology itself is growing with 3D and virtual reality. The opportunities are still out there.

Can you tell us more about the mom-and-pop shops?

Sure. As I was pointing out, I know plenty of people who worked at Rhythm & Hues, Digital Domain, or Imageworks who are starting their own shops. They say, "We have enough contacts. We have enough money. We have enough skill to land small contracts or pieces of big ones." These people are working out of garages and back rooms like they did twenty years ago. They have gone back to that model and have tried to streamline it, and in addition to traditional content formats, all of a sudden now they are doing other things like web and mobile content. They diversify in medical and military.

Is anyone doing feature work in L.A.?

No. Well, I want to say no. But it's also true that Imageworks had three or four hundred people working on *The Smurfs 2* (2013) and *Cloudy with a Chance of Meatballs 2* (2013) here because they couldn't fit more people into Vancouver. Now it is becoming very difficult to send work to Vancouver. Vancouver is becoming very protective of its subsidies because over the course of three years it spent more than a billion dollars and they're not getting the returns they imagined. They now realize that the same tax coffers that pay for a provincial health system are being tapped for the Hollywood Big Six. And it is strictly in bags of cash, by which I mean it is simply a cash handout. These are not tax breaks. It is just, "You can have the money if you do the work here, but you must do the work here." That is what is written into a lot of production agreements.

We've been talking a lot about contracts, companies, unions, and benefits. What about the VFX artists who are still here in Los Angeles and working for, let's say, a medical device company?

A buddy of mine works as a supervisor in one of these alternative companies and longs for the day when he can go back to television or feature work. Yet he enjoys more security in his new position. In previous incarnations of his work he worked for big companies but not *inside* of a big company. He didn't work for an Imageworks or a Digital Domain. He worked for a smaller firm that subcontracted with Imageworks or Digital Domain. So because he worked for these smaller firms doing feature work, he essentially took it in the shorts. Smaller firms are more likely to be the ones that cut costs and pass that cut down to the artists in order to get the big feature work. They're looking for prestige, or at least looking to get their foot in the door. Creatively, my buddy would rather be doing feature work, but he's better off where he is now. If you are absolutely stuck on feature work or stuck on episodic work, then go buy a plane ticket.

And people are picking up and relocating.

Yes. A lot. Vancouver, London, Wellington. Five of my personal friends are working on projects in London right now.

Did the closing of Digital Domain and Rhythm & Hues mark the end of an era in Los Angeles?

Yes. You had Imageworks, Rhythm, and DD, which were the big houses working on features. If you go further back in time you had some of the smaller houses working on features. There are still plenty of artists in town working on games. Games are still here. But that's leaving for the subsidies as well.

What's your take on the subsidies issue?

You can't tell Vancouver what to do. You can't just say stop with the subsidies over there. Officials were elected lawfully by their constituencies and they decided to offer subsidies. Nothing the United States can do would change that, short of a trade war with sanctions and posturing. So our only recourse as VFX artists in Los Angeles is to go through the World Trade Organization because there is language in the WTO trade agreements that talks about the harm of subsidies. The challenge, however, is that the US trade representative has to pick up that charge. And that person has all sorts of political ties and commitments. It's difficult to use a politician to further your cause, so we're taking the legal route.

Countervailing duties have been used to change practices in lumber, shrimping, and other industries, but in those cases you were physically able to go to a dock and say this lumber came from Canada, or this shrimp came from Japan, or something else that you could physically touch. We need to understand digital files of visual effects in the same way. Digital files are just as valuable as that shrimp or that lumber. So the argument has to be made in a courtroom that this was the industry in the United States before subsidies and this is the industry after, and this is the effect it has had on workers. This local homegrown industry has been injured and subsidies are the reason.

What is it like to work in a VFX shop in Los Angeles these days?

Much of the work is doing commercials, which are six- to eight-week gigs. You are likely going to be misclassified as an independent contractor, which means the company will pay you a flat rate and most likely without any overtime, but you *will* work overtime: long, long hours. Eighteen hours per day is a norm. Independent contractors don't get benefits or unemployment insurance. If you report $120,000 a year as an independent contractor you have to have a business license and you have to worry about taxes, accounting, health care, and retirement. Most likely it's best for you to incorporate. And then you have to spend a good amount of time finding yourself some tax shelters. You learn to play "funny-money" games. All of this takes time and energy.

Conditions at these studios aren't terrible as far as actually sitting there and doing the work if you don't mind the long hours. These studios tend to be retro and cool. A lot of them buy food for employees or provide the means for storing and preparing food. They have refrigerators and microwaves. They will do a barbecue once a week, some things like that. They have ping-pong tables. If you are an artist you know the name of everyone at these houses and hopefully you are on good terms with every one of these houses. You have to be. It's long hours and tight quarters. It is not conducive to what I would consider a family lifestyle. I'm forty-two years old and all of my friends in the industry are around that age, and plenty of them have families and work in this environment. It is stressful, but so is my job.

How old are the employees in these small shops?

I would say they're dominated by people from their mid-twenties to early thirties. Most people in my age group are either managers or they work for a regular studio, or they've moved on to something else.

If someone is thirty-five and wants to get out of the game, where do they go?

I was speaking to a friend of mine this weekend who is writing a business plan for a paleo food truck. Another colleague has a Kickstarter campaign going for 3D-printable chocolate. He is going to try to start a business that prints novelty chocolates that are company logos. So it's all over the place.

What about the gender dynamics in these shops?

I think we are seeing more women in animation than ever before. But it is still a heavily male-dominated profession. Unfortunately, visual effects is like animation. There are far more men working in the industry than women.

We've read that wages have dropped anywhere between 20 and 40 percent.

Absolutely. I know people who used to make $75 an hour and now are making $55. I also know people who used to make $75, but are now making $35 or $40—that's a really tough drop. There are people who still earn a good living at, say, $65 an hour. If you're employed throughout the year, you're pulling down six figures, which is very, very nice. But most people are seeing their incomes decline. I have one friend, for example, who has done vast amounts of feature work. He is now working episodics in L.A. His feature rate was around $70 per hour. He is making $50 now. He is extremely good at what he does. He is in demand. But he still spends maybe three to four months a year unemployed.

Is that common?

Yep. Unless you work for DreamWorks or Disney. Disney hires and doesn't let go. Well, that is not entirely true. Disney lets some people go. Near the end of a film, Disney will put out a 911 call, the, "Oh, my god, we've made too many changes and the drop day is coming! We need tons of people!" So they will hire folks for a six-to-eight-month stretch and then let them go.

But if you are working in a union environment, like Disney, you can get long-term gigs. DreamWorks will keep people on. In fact, DreamWorks is now starting a television division. It's indicative of the changing entertainment paradigm. Amazon wants to take on Netflix. So Amazon approaches Viacom and says, "We need content. Would you sign an exclusivity deal? Hey, we love kids' material." So what does Netflix do in return? Their people go to Jeffrey Katzenberg at DreamWorks and say, "We need content." Jeffrey says, "Pay me." To which Netflix replies, "Sure, we will give you X amount over three years as long as you can deliver thousands of hours of content."

So what is DreamWorks doing? They rent two floors in a building on Central Avenue and they are starting DreamWorks Television. They are hiring folks who do television animation and they are going to put two hundred to three hundred people to work doing these thousands of hours of content. If you can get a gig like that you can plan for a year. You can plan for two. But for most people, it's not like that, so it's hard to be married and have kids and feel comfortable.

Are the animation and VFX shops at the major studios unionized?

Not necessarily. Disney owns Pixar. So we often hear, "Disney is union; does that mean Pixar is as well?" The answer is no. Our contracts are very specific in regards to scope. People also ask what will happen to ILM now that Disney bought LucasArts.

Disney owns visual effects studios, but they hate them. They don't fit their model. Why? Because Disney is very money-oriented. They will spend $4 billion on LucasArts or $7 billion on Pixar because they will make money on that deal, but not on visual effects. When you buy Pixar, you own Pixar. If you spend $7 billion on it you will make that back in two years because Pixar movies make money. Disney bought LucasArts because owning LucasArts means you own *Star Wars*. Acquiring ILM as part of that deal is another story. Visual effects companies simply don't make money. There is a lot of money that flows through them, but the companies themselves don't make money.

Do you think it would make sense at some point for the effects companies to form a trade association?

They absolutely should. If I'm going to advocate organization for the artists, the next step is to advocate for an organization for the VFX studios. Both groups need to do this so that we can go to the producers and say, "You need us." Organized artists couldn't go to the producers alone to demand change. Organized shops couldn't do it, either. Producers would simply exploit the situation by playing one group against the other. They would go to the artists and say, "Start your own companies." Or they would go to the companies and say, "Hire more nonunion artists." The producers will shuffle the cards.

But if you can combine those fronts, you can go to the producers and say, "You are going to sit with both groups and bargain. If you are going to do work with us you are going to guarantee certain things. Here is what change orders cost. Here is a proposal for realistic scheduling. You are going to agree to all of these terms if you want to work with us."

But you have to be able to do that on a global basis.

Sure, eventually. That's not to say it has to start globally or be enacted globally at the same time. That would be practically impossible, but eventually that's where you want to go. The axiom "A rising tide lifts all boats" would best describe my point of view. You are not going to get them all at once. Just like you are not going to get every visual effects house in Los Angeles to go union at once.

Is there a culture of fear in the VFX community right now?

Absolutely, but it's not just fear. You might say, "fear-greed." Getting owners and managers of the shops to sit down and talk to each other is difficult. Scott Ross did it. He brought the shops together around a table to discuss a trade association. Everyone at the table had a lawyer behind them, I kid you not. They spent two hours talking, but it was very difficult. Scott literally pulled the rest of his hair out. He was like, "What are you doing? I'm one of you. I have seen this. I ran ILM. I ran DD. I saw the independents. We need to do this together!" And they are all like, "You know what, we have six people [the major Hollywood studios] who pay us. There are six people who use our services. If two of them are mad at us, the rest of them get mad because they are all buddies."

So the ultimate irony in all of this is that the only people who are organized and use collective leverage are, in fact, the feature film producers working for the big Hollywood studios.

And the worst part is that the globalization of VFX work enhances their leverage.

Exactly, but I still believe this industry will eventually organize. The producers are so money driven that they don't care about the plight of the visual effects shop or the workers. They know they can just get it from somewhere else, either another shop locally that's hungry for work or from somewhere else on the other side of the world. They just follow the money. They didn't even engineer the subsidy game; Canada did. But producers have leveraged it. So now they've got people paying *them* to do work on their movies. At some point in time that is going to fail. You are going to see it in British Columbia first, an environment that has become a bubble economy, where you wonder if in the end it all adds up. Eventually something is going to fail. What happens then? I don't really know.

26

Dusty Kelly, union official

Dusty Kelly worked in the film industry for ten years as a scene painter for films like *Juno* (2007) before becoming a union organizer in 2007. She is now vice president for IATSE Local 891 in Vancouver. In this conversation, Kelly discusses the challenges of running a local union in a highly competitive, globalized industry. Although Canadian studios have been criticized for luring jobs away from Hollywood, she provides an alternative perspective.

Can you give us some background on Local 891?

Local 891 is the fourth-largest IATSE local union. We're the largest local in Canada, and we represent motion picture technicians, artists, and craftspeople who work in twenty-three departments in Vancouver and all over British Columbia. We were chartered in 1962, so we've been around for quite a long time.

When did Local 891 see its biggest period of growth?

Our growth came in waves. I think it was a very small local until the late 1980s, when membership spiked a bit. There was definitely a spike in membership from the early to mid-1990s. In 1992 we probably had about 1,900 members. From that point until now, we've grown to more than 5,000 members.

What do you think contributed to that growth?

There are a number of factors. The currency exchange rate in the 1990s was extremely favorable and continued to be favorable for quite some time. At its low point in 2002, the Canadian dollar was about 65 cents to the US dollar. Another factor that contributed to growth was the fact that we were the first jurisdiction outside of Los Angeles to negotiate collective agreements directly with the Alliance of Motion Picture and Television Producers. A majority of work done here is indeed studio work, so we created a relationship very early in the process, around 1995 or 1996, by forming a film council to negotiate directly with the studios. Then we created the master agreement, which created an air of certainty. And of course the tax credits have helped.

You said you have twenty-three departments in your jurisdiction. Is membership more heavily concentrated in certain departments?

The construction department—which includes carpenters, scenic carpenters, sculptors, and lighting—is significant. Following that would be grips, the paint department, and set decorators. Costume is a pretty big department as well.

Does that list illustrate the types of jobs that are most common in Vancouver?

Yes, we're known for big-build shows. The size of the soundstages at studios in Vancouver allows us to accommodate projects that require large indoor facilities, which has been a major part of our business. Right now, *Night at the Museum: Secret of the Tomb* (2014) occupies every square inch of Mammoth Studios, which is thousands of square feet. Even given the rising importance of visual effects, we are still known for big-build productions.

Most of the jobs you mentioned are craft or trade occupations. Are there job categories that haven't been unionized?

We're highly unionized here in British Columbia. Ninety-nine percent of all production is union. There's the Director's Guild of Canada, BC District Council, Union of BC Performers, Teamsters Union Local No. 155, the International Cinematographers Guild IATSE 669, and the Canadian ACFC West. So union labor covers most productions. Yes, there is stuff that flies under the radar, but anything of midrange significance or above is definitely covered.

When did you become interested in organizing VFX artists and workers, and why?

I came on as an organizer with the local union when nonunion production was occurring in town. This was around 2006 when *Battlestar Galactica* (2004–9) was being made. There was an in-house visual effects crew, and it started reaching out to the local about working under a union contract. The employees were working extraordinarily long hours and not being paid in the same manner as other crews working on the show, so we negotiated. According to the collective agreement, certification applies to all in-house visual effects crews. So when a production hires an in-house or on-set team, they should be part of the collective agreement: supervisors, data wranglers, compositors, animators, and so on.

Producers soon decided to subcontract that work, which was their right within the collective agreement. VFX companies from L.A. also started to open up satellite offices in Vancouver. This was the beginning of the big migration of visual effects companies. Artists, of course, started calling me and talking to me about the issues they were having, and I recognized that we needed to do something about this. I made a presentation to our executive board, and we decided to go ahead with organizing visual effects artists. We officially announced this in the fall of 2010 or the spring of 2011.

How many shops would you estimate there are?

There are more than thirty.

And how many workers would you estimate?

It fluctuates. If you're going to include the animation houses, a couple of those have about three hundred employees each. Overall, it might be as many as two thousand workers at any given time. It depends on the day. You look at Sony Pictures Imageworks, their animation has gone down to about eighty people right now from a high of three hundred. There's a finite group of workers, and they move around between companies. I think 1,500 is a fair estimate.

Are animation workers and VFX workers separate within Local 891, or do they fall into the same department?

We cover live action within our contract, so VFX is part of the live-action component. However, the status of animation houses that are completely focusing on CG animation is something that has yet to be determined. The animation and VFX workers have many skills in common that would facilitate one department, a VFX-CGI department. This would not limit their employment to one or the other.

What's happening with visual effects houses is that they are not hiring employees for long periods of time anymore. They are hiring people on a project-by-project basis, which is the same way we work in live-action productions. They are hired for the show, not for the company. When they are done they move on to another project. Each province in Canada has its own labor code, and there is no national labor relations board. We have to work within the confines of the BC code and only organize within a specific company. You can't do a broad-based organizing drive. So, in essence, you would be creating shop contracts. It has to be company by company, which is one of the obstacles to getting VFX artists organized.

Overall, what are the most significant issues in trying to organize VFX workers?

It's truly interesting. It runs the gamut. You can be speaking to people right out of school or who have just a couple of years in the industry. You also run into workers midway through their careers or workers with eight or ten years in the industry, or they could have been in the industry long term. Of course, based on where they're from and what work they're doing, they all look at unionizing differently. There's always a concern about being paid proper overtime. It's a big issue. Another issue is job security. People don't know when they're going to lose their jobs. There's so much insecurity.

Then there are the quality-of-life issues. People are not getting adequate time off on the weekends or between shifts. Respect is a big thing as well, especially for women. I've seen more and more women enter the field, and they experience bullying and harassment. These issues would bring anyone to the union.

We are especially interested in gender dynamics. Can you talk more about that?

We did a survey about three and a half years ago. At that point the majority of the workers were male, but that has changed. I have met a lot more women in the industry. I find that they relate to collectivization and strength-in-numbers arguments. I've had people concerned about discrimination as well. You could have two people side by side, same skills, but somehow one person gets that job over the other. Whether there's a basis for that or not, I don't know. I think it's beginning to change. The makeup in the schools is certainly mixed. The oldest senior members are predominantly male, but the younger group moving up includes a lot more women.

What other issues confront VFX workers?

They've told me about bullying and harassment. Not knowing when you're going to have a job or how long your job is going to last is also a problem. Specifically people will get extensions and be retained on a project for another couple of weeks or so, but there are no promises. When you put that kind of pressure on people, they feel like they don't have a voice. Employees want to have a voice in the workplace, and be able to talk about issues and know that everyone is interconnected. I find that there's a feeling of isolation with everybody assigned to their cubicles. Somebody told me the other day that he had to hold a meeting over Skype with a guy who was in a cubicle two feet away. There's a disconnect. You start to lose your identity within the whole project. Folks are not at all willing to speak up and question whether they are being paid properly for fear they will not have a job the next day. It seems ludicrous, but that's how it is. There are mechanisms in place to redress these issues, but the way our employment standards are set up, they are all complaint driven and worker initiated. And so there is an absolute reluctance to go against any of it. I've had people come meet me, and I make sure we have a safe place, but if they'd see their supervisor, they'd tremble in fear.

Can you give some examples of what you mean by bullying? What makes a worker tremble in fear?

There is fear to question your employer and fear about attendance at work. Even when someone has worked twenty-one days straight and they suddenly need to stay home to look after their sick kid, they worry about what will happen to them because they have to miss work to tend to their family. I've heard reports about sexual harassment, and these people have said there's nowhere to go to talk about it. They feel like they're being blamed for it. Conditions vary with the company. Some companies have bad managers. There is one company in particular where managers shout at the workers: "What's the matter with you? Aren't you a team player?" All kinds of things happen in VFX and animation shops. It's not the same as the studio-based system with distinct labor relations.

One company has a clock that measures each worker's productivity. For some reason the clock never seems to be in the green. The clock is always in the red no matter how good you are. When that clock goes into the red, you have to stay over on your own time. You are not being paid to get your clock back into the green. And that takes its toll on people psychologically. Folks have said that when they go out for lunch, they just see the clock looking them in the eye. They can't even rest and eat their lunch comfortably.

Do you think that represents a significant number of workplace environments?

No. That's one specific company. But when the animator gets out of there and goes to a better company, he thinks it's just fantastic. If that company is just a little bit better, it's perceived as *so* much better.

Can you talk more about the toll this takes on families?

I've met many artists who are starting young families or want to have a life, and they aren't able to do that with the way the work is being done. That's not dissimilar, in a sense, from the situation in motion picture production. It's a very difficult business. But in British Columbia's motion picture industry, weekend turnaround is worked into our contracts. That is a very real, desirable thing that folks want. They want a weekend. They don't want to work day in and day out. They don't want to be told at six o'clock, "I'm sorry, but you have to stay later because we have to get this done." They can't have a personal life or a family life or even contemplate having a family because they work all the time.

What about the issue of mobility?

That also ties into family issues. Folks are not going to want to hear this down in Los Angeles, but I hear from many artists, whether they are from L.A. or Toronto or Auckland or London, that they just want to be in one place and do their job. And they would be happy to stay in Vancouver and continue their work. The prospect of having to get up and move again to work somewhere else is worrisome. I knew one guy who worked in four different cities in one year. How can you have a life? How can you put down roots? That is disturbing for a lot of artists. When some folks get out of school, they're living the VFX dream, working at Weta Digital in New Zealand and it's all so great, but then they have to move on and on. After a while it wears them down. There is more to life than traveling the world for job after job, not knowing where your next job is going to be.

You mentioned that close to two thousand folks are working in the VFX sector in British Columbia. Do you have a rough estimate of how many of those workers are Canadian nationals and how many come from other countries?

We did a study about three years ago and the respondents in the study were about 45 percent Canadian, 55 percent from elsewhere. I don't know what that number is right now. I might have to do the survey again. I do know that a number of the artists I've signed up over the years are applying for their Canadian residency and would like to work here and stay here. Of course they're more likely to be employed if they're a Canadian resident because then the tax credit kicks in.

What is your general take on the tax credit itself? Do you think it's a devil's bargain?

I think some level of incentive has been instrumental in breeding a significant crew base for live-action motion picture production here in British Columbia.

Prior to the introduction of labor-based tax credits there were all kinds of tax shelter scams going on, and the federal government looked the other way. I've met producers in Los Angeles who said the labor-based tax credits are the most effective way of creating real, good-paying jobs. And it has done that. Incentives have now spread to other cities and countries, and the competition has escalated, and in some places, the return on investment isn't there. That hasn't been the case here in British Columbia, but it has been elsewhere.

Why have incentives worked well in British Columbia?

The government continues to support the labor-based tax credit and believes that there is a multiplier effect. When you add the Digital Audio Visual (DAV) tax credit, it's a pretty substantial package. I'm still not 100 percent clear about whether shows that are not shot in British Columbia also get the labor-based tax credit or if they're only eligible for the DAV tax credit. The actual DAV tax credit has also been instrumental in the growth of the visual effects and animation industry here.

If VFX workers from outside Canada are able to find multiple jobs and stay in the area, are they pressured to apply for residency so their salaries are subsidized, or is that up to them?

I have not heard of anything like that. I have heard of people who wish to stay here and have their visas extended. Their ability to negotiate higher wages doesn't seem to change. But I have not heard of anyone being pressured into citizenship. Citizenship is very, very specific. In fact, the Canadian government has introduced legislation [in April 2015] called the "four in and four out" rule. It says you can only work here for four years. After that, you have to wait another four years in your home country or as a non-working visitor in Canada before applying for a new work permit, unless you apply for permanent residency, which exempts you from the rule altogether. Right now, it's still too soon to tell how workers are responding to the change.

Do people in the VFX business now think that Vancouver is one of the premier centers for VFX work worldwide?

Yes, it is. I was at an L.A. event a couple years back where they said that Vancouver would surpass London as a destination where producers would want to do their visual effects.

Are there any places that directly compete with Vancouver for VFX work?

Montreal. But it's interesting because Montreal has a completely different makeup of companies. Some of the big studios like Industrial Light & Magic also have contracts with Montreal studios to do their work. You'd have to look at that. Even though some of the top visual effects producers may not have facilities in Montreal, they do engage Montreal companies for some aspects of their work.

I don't want to overlook the fact that Vancouver is now on track to become the third-largest production center in North America. The visual effects industry wouldn't even be seeing its notable growth if it wasn't for the motion picture industry we already had in place. The two are intertwined. We were a motion picture production center before we did visual effects. In the mid-1990s, MGM had a lot of productions here, like *The Outer Limits* (1995–2002) and *Poltergeist: The Legacy* (1996–99), and then there was *The Andromeda Strain* (2008) and *Stargate* (1994). Each of those had a heavy visual effects component. We were known for the science fiction stuff. This is where our local industry cut its teeth. The senior artists I'm talking to now, who have been in the industry fifteen or twenty years, they cut their teeth on the in-house visual effects that were necessary for the productions that came our way at that time. That's what I mean when I say we wouldn't have the visual effects without having the motion picture industry already here.

What gives Vancouver its competitive advantage? Why are producers saying it's going to surpass London?

People enjoy coming here, and it's close for many producers and in the same time zone. All of the things that make British Columbia a desirable place for live-action production are the same things that make it desirable for visual effects.

We've heard folks say the most pernicious aspect of the VFX industry is the fixed-bid contracting system that pits shops and localities in competition with each other. Do you see that as a significant issue?

It is cutthroat. VFX companies underbid each other all the time to get work. Certain bids are too low to even do the work. Hollywood studios want to pay the least possible amount of money. They love to work with nonunion labor. The studios are completely complicit in what's going on, with the labor practices that are going on in India and wherever else. I mean, it's crazy. All in all, the companies here are abiding by the laws of the land, but that's not the case overseas. If these companies aren't being challenged about their practices, then it's going to be business as usual. They want to get the next show, and they can't afford to not keep projects in their pipeline. So, sometimes they're robbing Peter to pay Paul.

Given that situation, what's the path forward? What is the best way to address these issues?

I am going to go back to Rhythm & Hues, a company that was the gold standard in terms of a pension plan, a 401k, medical, and good pay. It would have been impossible to organize Rhythm & Hues. But when the company failed, the studios didn't let their feature film projects dry up. The movies were going to get made, it just depends on who would make them. No matter who you're working for, the work still has to be done. The question is, by whom and under what conditions?

Intellectual property security is another one of Vancouver's strengths. When you start sending stuff to China, you're not sure about the safety of your project or your work materials. You're not going to send the most critical scenes overseas. Artists have been concerned that if we unionize, the jobs are going to go to other countries or they won't be able to afford to have a union. Those are two things that get mentioned a lot. I refer to live-action production in those cases. We've been threatened many times that work will be sent elsewhere, and sure enough, work does get sent elsewhere. But at some point you can't lower your standards. A producer can say, "I'm going to shoot my project in Bulgaria so I only have to pay $10 a day." Well, great, but we can't live on $10 a day in Vancouver. I guess maybe they should go to Bulgaria and do their project. We'll just close up and not be here when we're needed. You can't let yourself be taken to the very bottom.

The other part is that we're not in the business of putting companies out of business. That's why, even within our live-action contracts, there are tiers. You negotiate based on what is reasonable. When I talk to workers about organizing, I tell them we're not in the business of shutting down their facility. What would be the point of that? The point is to be able to bring in nonmonetary items that can be translated into monetary terms. But everything comes down to the money. In many cases there are advantages to being part of a bigger group. For instance, a facility not being able to afford a benefits plan, but if its employees were part of a larger group, it may be able to realize much better cost savings. There's a benefit there. There is only so much apple, but you can make all kinds of things out of the apple.

Do you think there is a possibility of organizing labor organizations across international lines?

IATSE already has a relationship with the United Kingdom's Broadcasting, Entertainment, Cinematograph and Theatre Union. But no matter what, the laws of the land prevail, so that's a challenge. But in terms of organizing an international union, the benefit of it is that the employers are the same everywhere. We're currently working toward improving information sharing, communication, and working together on shared concerns to raise the bar for all workers. There's loads of international union organizations that have affiliates all over the world who get together and work on the same issues. Corporations are global. Unions have to collaborate as well.

We've also talked to Scott Ross, who comes at the issue from the perspective of a manager. He says that even before we get to the question of whether unions can cooperate, there must be some cooperation among the VFX shops themselves. He advocates a trade association. Do you have any thoughts about that?

Scott Ross tried to get that happening, and he didn't get too far. In Ontario, they have the Computer Animation Studios of Ontario (CASO). So they have a trade organization, but I can tell you right now that you can form all the trade organizations you want, but unless the workers collectivize and create their own union, nothing is going to happen.

And why is that?

It's really nice when you have company owners who are respectful and good with their employees. Every year they give them a raise, and they have a pension plan for them and a welfare plan for them, but those types of owners are few and far between. The shops are competitors. Their bottom line is getting the next job. And the big Hollywood studios are part of multinational global companies. It's the same with some of the big VFX companies. I mean, MPC is part of Technicolor; Method is Deluxe. These are global companies on stock exchanges. They've got their marching orders, their managers, their human resources people. It's about the dollar and the bottom line. In order to deal with that, you have to organize the workers.

Have you been able to organize any of the stand-alone VFX facilities in British Columbia?

We haven't gotten one yet. I'll be honest, it's a very long, protracted process due to rapid growth and the fact that people are coming from all over the world. And that's specifically in Vancouver. It's fascinating. I'll meet people from all over the world. Some of them will say, "What's wrong with the union, why are people so weird about having a union?" They tend to come from fairly socially oriented societies like Italy or France. They come here and there are so many people from so many places, so many cultures, so many age groups, and folks become isolated, especially when they're on three-month contracts. Once again, I have to refer back to the labor code. Our labor code is not constructed in a way that makes it easy to organize. If you sign one of the cards, the card is only good for ninety days and then you have to go and get the card signed again. By that time, the person may already be working at another facility.

So, because of the large number of workers and all this mobility, my goal is just to continue the conversation and help workers organize themselves. I've spoken with sectors of people who have been in a union before or whose parents have been in a union, and I've even spoken with those who have no experience with a union. Many people are isolated from the live-action motion picture piece, where everyone is in a union. It's a completely different world. Many of the VFX and animation workers have no experience with that.

Has 891 pulled back on its efforts to organize VFX workers?

It comes in cycles, waves. There was the wave during the Digital Domain bankruptcy. Then there was the wave during the Rhythm & Hues bankruptcy. There is a production cycle with visual effects as well. There will be a lot of ramping up, a lot of work going on, and then there will be a lot of layoffs. People will be off for a few months, and then it begins to ramp up again. Legally we can't organize a shop when there are only eight people in it because those eight people do not represent a substantial volume of work. The first people who show up are the people who are digging the hole, so to speak. There are not a lot of people digging the hole or putting up the crane, if you're talking about a construction project. Eventually there are hundreds of people working on that building, so you have to be able to get all of those people. It's the ramp-up model.

Somewhere at the top is the real number. That's who you have to go after, but it's incredibly difficult to find out who's working in those facilities, especially because they are all so isolated. Those employees work in cubicles. They do not talk to each other. It's not a regular workplace. That context means it takes longer. When I started doing this about four years ago, none of these workers knew anything about unions, or they had negative attitudes about them. That has really, really changed, especially after the *Life of Pi* (2012) stuff. But it's still difficult. They work in a virtual world, and you can't be virtually organized. You have to actually come together. You have to sign a physical piece of paper. You have to have a meeting. So, it's not easy, but it's not impossible.

What do you think about L.A.-based VFX workers who criticize subsidies and are advocating that countervailing duties be imposed by the WTO?

I was at ground zero for a moment last year and took fire from both sides after I talked with artists who were opposed to tax credits. It was assumed that I was also opposed. I look at that as divisive. It doesn't matter what tax credits are in place; workers can be exploited. For me, it's about making sure workers are paid, looked after, have a retirement plan, have a decent living, and are valued for what they do. It doesn't matter whether you have subsidies or not, abuses still happen. You can have subsidies and still have worker exploitation, so I focus on that piece and not the subsidy piece. I'm very aware of all that stuff, and many of the artists I speak to couldn't care less. They just want to work. Some of those artists are American as well.

I think I summed it up a little bit when I wrote a letter to VFX Soldier after the Pi Day demonstration. I was kind of upset with him. He jumped onto this whole subsidy thing, making it seem as though this was the answer to everything. But what about the fact that people are getting exploited regardless of where the work is taking place? That has nothing to do with the subsidies, and that's what we need to address.

APPENDIX

Interview Schedule

Mara Brock Akil, Los Angeles, August 2015
Tom Schulman, Santa Barbara, November 2012
Allison Anders, Santa Barbara, July 2015
Lauren Polizzi, Los Angeles, August 2014
Mary Jane Fort, Los Angeles, March 2015
Anonymous makeup artist, Los Angeles, August 2014
Stephen Lighthill, Los Angeles, February 2014
Calvin Starnes, Los Angeles, March 2015
Steve Nelson, Santa Barbara, August 2014
Rob Matsuda, Los Angeles, March 2015
Anonymous studio production executive, Los Angeles, June 2013
David Minkowski, Prague, June 2013
Adam Goodman, Budapest, July 2013
Stephen Burt, Dublin, March 2015
Belle Doyle, Glasgow, March 2015
Wesley Hagan, Los Angeles, March 2015
Scott Ross, Venice, February 2014
Dave Rand, Marina del Rey, February 2014
Mariana Acuña-Acosta, Santa Barbara, April 2014
Daniel Lay, Santa Barbara, April 2014
Steve Kaplan, Burbank, October 2013
Dusty Kelly, Vancouver, February 2014

www.ingramcontent.com/pod-product-compliance
Lightning Source LLC
Chambersburg PA
CBHW030530230426
43665CB00010B/838